The poetry of
Louis MacNeice

D. B. MOORE

The poetry of
Louis MacNeice

With an introduction by G. S. FRASER

Leicester University Press
1972

000 25854

First published in 1972 by Leicester University Press
Distributed in North America by Humanities Press Inc., New York

Copyright © Leicester University Press 1972

Designed by Arthur Lockwood

Set in Monotype Perpetua
Printed in Great Britain by Western Printing Services Ltd, Bristol

ISBN 0 7185 1105 0

To my wife

Contents

Introduction

If asked who were the most exciting new English poets of the 1930s, many readers would have said then, and would say now, "Auden, Dylan Thomas, Louis MacNeice . . .", but would hesitate or disagree in adding a fourth or a fifth or a sixth name. Yet there must be a dozen critical books or monographs about Auden and about Dylan Thomas. MacNeice died in 1963, in his early fifties, at a time when, after a period of middle-aged sag, his poetic powers were displaying themselves with a new concentration. He had been famous as a poet since his youth, he was a public figure (as a B.B.C. dramatist and feature writer, not only as a poet), and he was all his life near the centre of the London literary world. His individual volumes of verse, of which there were many, were always respectfully, often enthusiastically, sometimes intelligently reviewed. Yet there are very few really comprehensive and interesting general articles on his poetry, and this book-length study of his work appears nine years after his death. Mr D. B. Moore, its author, is moreover not a professional scholar or critic. He is a businessman who met MacNeice, when the poet was teaching Greek at Birmingham in the 1930s, liked him, and thereafter followed his work closely. He produced this excellent pioneer study in the spare hours of a very active working life.

Mr Moore himself discusses some of the possible reasons for this comparative critical neglect of such a versatile, prolific, and piercingly intelligent poet. Some of the reasons are, I think, to MacNeice's credit. Many of the books that have been written about Auden and Dylan Thomas are concerned, so to say, less with placing a poet than with cracking a code. There is no code to crack in MacNeice. He had his eye on the outer world, he observed things that we all observe, but more sharply and more vividly. His tone is conversational. His rhythms and stanza forms are often popular ones, owing something to jazz or nursery rhymes or folk poetry; he even owed a great deal, Mr Moore reminds us, to a poet of swinging rhythms and gaudy images whom he enjoyed in his childhood, and whom a fastidious critic could hardly mention today without wincing, Alfred Noyes. His poems lend themselves excellently, as Mr Moore points out in some very good pages here on 'Bagpipe Music', to performance, to what the Victorians called 'recitation'. He is very much the poet as an urban man, speaking to urban men.

Yet clearly, all the same, he is not a mere entertainer. He was acutely, sometimes delightedly, sometimes painfully, aware of the contradictoriness of life. He saw the outer world clearly but had to grope for his own deepest inner motives and responses, which always remained ultimately mysterious to him. He looked all his life for a unifying vision, but was too honest to persuade himself that he had ever quite found one. It was difficult to find a formula for him: I once described him as "the poet as liberal humanist". Mr Moore has no difficulty in showing that this label is totally inadequate for a poet who was certainly liberal and certainly humane but was consumed also by a restless impatience with human mediocrity and compromise, whose view of the state of our culture was a melancholy and ominous one. If one describes MacNeice, again, as a hedonist, the poet of phrases like "the moment cradled like a brandy glass", one is faced by the fact that there was a kind of iron harshness in him, something puritan, coming out of an Irish Protestant ancestry; he liked pleasure, but had an almost Calvinist sense that pleasure has to be paid for. It is difficult to find an over-all pattern. When I had to write a long essay on MacNeice in 1957, I found that the easiest way to do this was to stitch a number of short reviews of individual volumes together with a few threads of very tentative generalization. Some personal acquaintance with MacNeice did not greatly help. He was a very sociable and talkative man; but each time I met him I felt I understood him less well, not better, than the last time. I called the essay, I remember, 'Evasive Honesty'.

Perhaps the best fairly early account of the kind of puzzles that MacNeice creates even for a sympathetic and intelligent critic is to be found in a review written in *The New Republic* of June 1941, by the American poet, Conrad Aiken. Marianne Moore and I.A. Richards both agree that Aiken, a close friend of T. S. Eliot's at Harvard, is the most perceptive reviewer of new poetry in the English language that our century has produced. He is generous and eloquent about MacNeice's gifts, but wonders just how seriously they are being used:

For sheer readability, for speed, lightness, and easy intellectual range, Mr MacNeice's verse is in a class by itself. Open it anywhere, whether in narrative, eclogue, or lyric, and at once you are swept away by the tireless and effortless enumerative pace, the rush of nominal images, the gay prodigality of the scene, the so easily caught tune and mood. Yes, this is the world we know all right, and this too is a fellow we can like. Here are pubs and football games, and Freud and the dreary economic muddle and the confused political ideologies through which we try to think, or feel, our way, and the sad glad conquests and vapours of love too, the whole great blooming buzzing confusion (to quote William James) – it's all here, bright and quick as a river to swim in. And so, in we go; and out we come; and it is only then that we find how little of all this has stuck to us. Not a thing – practically not a thing. For the trouble is, it is *too* topical, *too* transitory, *too* reportorial – it has that sort of merit and vividness which is good in the presence of the object, and by virtue of the object it has a kind of quick and momentary magic; but it has, one fears, very little *residual* magic, very little of that quality of intricate and teasing wroughtness which sends one back to a poem not for the meaning but to see how the meaning was said.

MacNeice in 1941 might have appreciated the sharpness of this as much as its generosity. His first volume was called *Blind Fireworks*. There is an element, in his earlier work, of aiming at a scatter of hits on several targets rather than a bull on one. He was himself stringently self-critical; an honest quality of self-dissatisfaction is one of the most engaging qualities of the *tone* of his poetry (it is a wry, ironical self-dissatisfaction, never self-pitying or mock-humble). One might say in answer to Aiken, however, that the topicality of a poem like MacNeice's *Autumn Journal* of 1938 is still topical; it is no longer a matter of Hitler or Munich, the names of the characters and places have changed, but the plot of the human play is still very much the same. One might say that the sense of the transitory can express, as in Keats's *Ode to a Nightingale*, a thwarted lust for permanence:

> Let all these so ephemeral things
> Be somehow permanent like the swallow's tangent wings.

One might say that the reportorial side, as in a poem like 'Sunday Morning', the householder washing his car and the schoolgirl practising her scales, reports a reasonably permanent quality of suburban life. And finally one might say that poetry of apparently off-the-cuff improvisation, *Autumn Journal* again or Byron's *Don Juan*, can attract us back "not for the meaning but to see how the meaning was said" just as much as poetry of "intricate and teasing wroughtness". Just *how* is the apparently casual turned into art? Only a handful of poets in our language, Skelton, Byron, Clough, MacNeice, to name the most obvious four, have managed it.

Yet for all that, MacNeice would have recognized some justice in Aiken's strictures. Writing around 1948, about the time a new collected volume of his poems had come out, MacNeice explained that he was tired of 'journalism', tired of 'tourism', tired of the poem as a mere footnote to experience; he now wanted all the parts of a poem to fit together properly, even if that meant the sacrifice of the brilliant inorganic image and the witty irrelevant sally. He instanced as lines that he was proud of in his most recent book a description of the aftermath of war in England:

> The joker that could have been at any moment death
> Has been withdrawn, the cards are what they say
> And none is wild

and a line about a prostitute:

> Mascara scrawls a gloss on a torn leaf.

In such games as poker, a card that can by convention become any other card is called 'wild': the joker, not really a member of the pack, is often used in this way; and in wartime (MacNeice's war was – he was working at the B.B.C. – the London civilian war of the bombing raids) any card we draw can suddenly become the joker. The other line, I think, owes something to the example of MacNeice's friend Empson. Mascara scrawls either a sheen on a torn piece of foliage (the prostitute's sad eyelid, shaped like a leaf, perhaps someone has punched it or bruised it) or it scrawls a commentary on a torn page (from a diary, say, a record of illicit self-indulgence). And the prostitute herself is like a leaf torn from the living tree of life.

Commenting on this piece of self-criticism by MacNeice, I thought this might be an example of what he meant by 'tourism' in his early work:

> impending thunder
> With an indigo sky and the garden hushed except for
> The treetops moving,

and that this might be an example of what he meant by 'journalism':

> that a monologue
> Is the death of language and that a single lion
> Is less himself, or alive, than a dog and another dog.

I said, writing about MacNeice in 1957, that the two passages he quoted had obviously demanded harder work than the earlier passages I quoted. But I am not now sure that the harder work produced a better result. The passage about the impending thunder seems to me now to have more sap, the passage about the single lion and the two dogs to have more bite than the two passages which MacNeice especially admired. He was always a man of very great physical and mental energy but I think that in his forties he felt rather desperately the loss of a youthful spontaneity, and used skill, craft, determination to take its place.

Mr Moore feels this, also, very strongly about *Autumn Sequel*, which is a complete contrast to the earlier *Autumn Journal* in that MacNeice is obviously, having set himself the hurdle of a metre very difficult in English, *terza rima*, forcing himself along: he called it a "rhetorical poem", and in a good and bad sense it is, where *Autumn Journal* has the carelessness, the intimacy, the lack of rhetoric, of an actual intimate diary. But MacNeice, always acutely self-critical, himself felt that the period of early middle age is a very difficult period for a poet. Skill and will have to take the place of the sense of the writing of poetry as what James Reeves calls a "natural need". The poet is aware that he is perhaps merely forcing himself towards self-dilution, self-repetition, expanding his production while perhaps deflating its total value. One day begins to seem tediously like another, yet there are fewer days ahead of him:

> This middle stretch
> Of life is bad for poets: a sombre view
> Where neither works nor days look innocent
> And both seem now too many, now too few.

Yet a melancholy like that which these lines express underlies the gaiety of MacNeice's earlier poems, too, and it had complex causes. It is a melancholy typical of Irish writers; Thackeray in his *Irish Sketch Book* noted that the humour for which the Irish are famous is a humour springing from a deep sense of the sadness of things; and this is as true of MacNeice as it was of Goldsmith or Lever. It was partly a matter of personal temperament. The natural expression of MacNeice's very handsome face, when he was not being sardonically gay, when one saw it sometimes in repose, was a jaunty but bleak one. It was partly, of course, a reaction against the violence and wickedness of our age: but MacNeice, with his fine historical scholarship, knew that most ages are violent and wicked. The Saturnian age exists in a legendary past and the Republic of Candour and Friendship in an ever receding future. (This realism, of course, never made MacNeice passive about or indifferent to the immediate evils, which he could combat, of the age he lived in.)

More deeply perhaps the roots of the melancholy lay in a need for faith, certitude, commitment. A staunch anti-Fascist, MacNeice was the only poet of the Auden group who was never in the least attracted by Communism; in his later poetry, and indeed in some fine early poems, like 'An Eclogue for Christmas', he quite frequently uses Christian imagery, but as a metaphor for some deep and thwarted need for renewal, rebirth, not as a mode of doctrinal assertion. Part of him was an excited and delighted pluralist, exulting in the sheer multifariousness of things; another part of him was a man on a quest (he loved medieval quest literature, romance and allegory). But the deepest roots of the melancholy were, I think, philosophical.

One binding thread in MacNeice's poetry from beginning to end is a preoccupation with the problem of the One and the Many. It was a preoccupation he shared with T. S. Eliot, who felt a greater personal affinity with MacNeice than with any of the other young poets whom Eliot helped in the 1930s. As a young man Eliot had studied deeply, and indeed completed a doctoral thesis on, the philosophy of F. H. Bradley: MacNeice in his Oxford years had been briefly fascinated by the philosophies of Croce and Gentile, who are, very broadly, of the same philosophical family as Bradley. Bradley had said that both our thoughts and our personalities are secondary, or comparatively unreal, they are part of a world that each man creates out of the raw immediacy of experience. But we each create different worlds, and between our worlds there is what MacNeice, in a fine poem, called an "incommunicableness". My world reflects yours, yours mine, but our worlds are not directly in touch with each other. We are each enclosed as in a glass bubble, as in Dante's "horrible tower".

Bradley also believed that there is an Absolute, an Ultimate Reality, in which these isolated and contradictory centres of experience are somehow fused and made one with each other in a higher immediacy. The young Eliot could not believe this, being unable to believe it made him melancholy, and at length led to his conversion to orthodox Christianity. More robust than Eliot, MacNeice could find more real zest in the plural dance of things than the young Eliot, and to the last he was too restless and independent a spirit to submit his judgment to any institution. Yet his poetic journey is, starting 30 years later, oddly parallel to Eliot's. The last two volumes, suggesting a wonderful renewal of his talent, *Solstices* (1961) and *The Burning Perch*, posthumously published in 1963, are utterly unlike *Four Quartets* in form and content, but like that great poem, or set of poems, in the sense they convey of ruthless self-examination and spiritual exploration. They have a certain thrillingness and chillingness which is not un-Eliotesque either.

Eliot felt this affinity, and in his generous obituary tribute to MacNeice in *The Times* – Eliot was very generous in practical help to younger poets, but chary of generosity in published praise – he described MacNeice as a great poet and said how much he had valued MacNeice's friendship. Auden has noted that, though Eliot obviously must have had a pervasive influence on younger poets, it is extraordinarily difficult to trace that influence down in detail. It is perhaps more easy to trace it in MacNeice's work than in that of any poet of comparable stature, in the generation that followed Eliot's. In a tribute to Eliot, published on the older poet's sixtieth birthday, MacNeice noted how Eliot had taught the poets of his generation to play Hamlet behind the gasworks. He shared Eliot's vivid and detailed knowledge and gift for evocation of the London scene, seeing it as wholly real – "Euston, the smell of soot and fish and petrol" – but also as a phantasmagoria, an allegory.

16

Both poets had a formidable, hawk-like handsomeness and an extreme elegance of dress and bearing. MacNeice was a great social mixer, Eliot was not; MacNeice was volubly witty, Eliot sparsely and enigmatically urbane; but if Eliot's remoteness was more on the surface, MacNeice was, under his social gaiety, perhaps even more remote. The tip of the iceberg showed; at some pub or club near the B.B.C. he would keep his listeners laughing; but the deep self, the deep preoccupations were miles and miles away.

It is one of the many merits of Mr Moore's book to attempt to chart, for the first time, with tentative precision, just where that deep self, those deep preoccupations, may have been. I think MacNeice, who had great academic gifts but not an academic temperament, would have been glad that this considerable study of his poetry should have been written by a practical and successful man of affairs (as a B.B.C. producer and dramatist, MacNeice was very much that himself). Mr Moore is more or less MacNeice's contemporary. Never having enjoyed bridge or golf, the usual hobbies of the successful businessman, he has taken up in his late fifties the more interesting one of working part-time for higher university degrees. This book, in its original form, was an M.A. dissertation submitted to the University of Birmingham. Richard Hoggart, as internal examiner, thought it worthy of publication, and I, as external assessor, agreed; this opinion was confirmed when the Leicester University Press consulted William Empson, one of MacNeice's closest friends.

The problems about MacNeice's achievement, intentions, and reputation which I have sketched out broadly here are dealt with by Mr Moore sensitively, in scrupulous detail, and with a close examination of individual poems. But he uses his close detailed criticism to work towards a more general sense of MacNeice the poet, and perhaps MacNeice the man. Mr Moore is now working for Leicester University on a Ph.D. thesis on a poet superficially very different, James Thomson of *The City of Dreadful Night*. No two poets could at first sight seem more different than the lower-class Scottish alcoholic, who seemed born to frustration and

failure, and the jaunty and formidable radical ascendancy Ulster-
man who seemed, and indeed was, born to success; but poets
judge their success or failure in their hearts. There is a deep
melancholy in both MacNeice and Thomson; both are obsessed
like Eliot also (a linking case) in *The Waste Land*, by the haunting
image of the labyrinthine and enigmatic modern city, in whose
endless streets we seem to spend not only our waking and working hours but the puzzling and monitory quests, and failures to
find, of our dreams.

G. S. FRASER

CHAPTER ONE

From early influences to 'Bagpipe Music'

I

Although MacNeice, Auden, Spender and Day-Lewis have been called the "Poets of the Thirties", there was no 'school' of poetry, no formal relationship, no manifesto. Day-Lewis in his auto-biography said "We did not know we were a Movement until the critics told us we were." But they knew each other reasonably well. MacNeice and Auden met at Oxford. MacNeice and Spender edited *Oxford Poetry* together in 1929, as Day-Lewis and Auden had done in 1927. They had roots in common and each responded to important common influences. Their background was upper-middle-class: their fathers were parsons, doctors and politicians. They went to Sherborne, Marlborough, Gresham's, and to Oxford. Poetically they were the heirs of Ezra Pound and Eliot. (They were the heirs, but not necessarily the direct descendants: poets in a more English tradition, with whom some of them felt a deeper affinity, included Hopkins, Hardy and Wilfred Owen.) They took their imagery from the urban world around them, as Eliot had done. They seized on the freedom they had been given for their prosody, though on the whole they tended more to regular stanza forms than Eliot or Pound. They respected each other's work and personalities. Auden and MacNeice became lifelong friends. Above all equipped – some might think inappositely equipped – with the traditional training of the great Public Schools, they faced a world in which

> when we go out into Piccadilly Circus
>   They are selling and buying the late
> Special editions snatched and read abruptly
>   Beneath the electric signs as crude as Fate.
> And the individual, powerless, has to exert the
>   Powers of will and choice
> And choose between enormous evils, either
>   Of which depends on somebody else's voice.

A similar background, a shared poetic heritage, and a common awareness of a world in a state of crisis gives the work of these four poets a common atmosphere, at least during the decade when they became known. So Spender introduces pylons into his poetry, MacNeice is eternally fascinated with means of transport, Day-Lewis bases two of his poems on railway symbolism and has much to say about the urban industrial world as a source of images in his Clark Lectures; and Auden rides upon the Night Mail and walks down Bristol Street. These are superficial likenesses, important only because each encourages the other to find both inspiration and illustration from the world as they knew it. The differences are more profound and important. Richard Hoggart, in his pamphlet on Auden, has rightly said:

Auden's poems tend to be remembered not so much for their sensuous effects (apart from a few striking exceptions) as for the articulation of their phrasing and the pattern of their moral insights. His poems have little colour, smell or touch . . . Similarly, his epithets usually have a conceptual rather than a sensuous relationship to the nouns they qualify; they comment rather than describe . . . a lover's head on his arm is caught, beautifully, as a moral pattern rather than a visual:

> Lay your sleeping head, my love,
> Human on my faithless arm;

Spender, whom MacNeice described as a "towering angel not

quite sure if he was fallen", had in his poetry a high seriousness, so that when he writes "Oh young men oh young comrades" or "I think continually of those who were truly great", whatever may be the opinion of his work as poetry, it is impossible either to doubt its sincerity, or to doubt that belief is hardly won. Day-Lewis, husband, schoolmaster, socialist, possessed the skill to work out "a tough, intellectual proposition" in his search for "the single mind". Auden, Spender, Day-Lewis, each in his own way achieved some sort of faith – religious, political, or metaphysical. MacNeice could never do this. He was receptive to the world about him and in his poetry he recorded his impression of it. In sharp distinction from Auden, its effect upon his five senses is a predominant source of inspiration and of imagery. In spite of these differences, MacNeice and Auden, Spender and Day-Lewis were inextricably trapped in that sense of being set apart and among the chosen, that was the "ambiguous gift" of the Public Schools to the upper middle classes of their time. Even though by temperament all four were rebels, they came from a class that had been trained to rule. From this they took their special flavour, their sense of being self-sufficient, whether, like MacNeice, they were, though vividly aware of the external world, introspective and self-absorbed; like Spender, earnestly seeking to share the outlook of the proletariat; or like Day-Lewis, a late developer, experimenting with Communism and romantic love, relentlessly high-minded. However worthily they wished it otherwise, they were, and are, distanced by their class. Perhaps it was left to Auden to tell the truth in *About the House*:

> Some thirty inches from my nose
> The frontier of my Person goes,
> And all the untilled air between
> Is private *pagus* or demesne.
> Stranger, unless with bedroom eyes
> I beckon you to fraternize,
> Beware of rudely crossing it:
> I have no gun, but I can spit.

He speaks for them all.

In the three central 'Case-Book' chapters of MacNeice's book, *Modern Poetry*, dealing respectively with 'Childhood', 'Public School' and 'Oxford', MacNeice himself attempts a summary of the major forces that shaped his verse. Many of his comments are illuminating and of interest, but as so often in self-examination, there is a certain lack of perspective. He is not wrong in his identification of the dominant prosodical influences, but he does not carry his analysis to its conclusion. First among them was the Christian Church. "From a very early age" he says "I was fascinated by the cadences and imagery of the Bible." He also mentions hymns as his "first melancholy poetry" and a number of his poems (like 'Prayer in Mid-Passage') owe a direct metrical debt to well-known hymns. He forgets to mention the Prayer Book and yet it had its influence on his language and on his form, as in 'Prayer Before Birth'. The rituals, celebrations and festivals of the Christian Church were sources of imagery and inspiration. The Easter story and Christmas celebrations found a place in his poetry and the Old Testament also served as a source of imagery and illustration, till near the end it is pressed into use for the biting disillusion of 'New Jerusalem'.

The second strong influence on MacNeice was the literature of Greece and Rome and yet, apart from brief references to Virgil, Homer and Horace, the influence of the Classics on his work is ignored in *Modern Poetry* and little spoken of elsewhere. He was educated in the classic tradition at preparatory school, at Marlborough and at Oxford, and became a lecturer in Classics. Classical subjects recur in his poetry, classical allusions abound, classical philosophies are examined. The loving care for the sound of Greek and Latin verse, and for the craftsmanship that shapes it, must be accepted as a dominant influence perhaps second only to that of Christian literature. In the series of poems he calls *Visitations* he achieves a synthesis of sources of inspiration and it is significant that he commences in the golden age of Hellas, and after a survey of metaphysical, allegorical, romantic, religious and mystical verse, he closes on a sequence in which recollections of the Jehovah of the Old Testament mingle with references to the vision of Plato's *Republic*.

Nobody can be an English poet unless he knows, loves and understands the work of the best English poets who have come before him. It is not appropriate here to inquire why some men respond so early to poetry and feel the need to read yet more and to write poetry, and others do not. In the chapter in *Modern Poetry* on 'The Personal Factor' MacNeice holds with Freud that most poets are neurotic above the average; and he notes that "the great majority of poets comes from the middle classes". Moreover he comments "I doubt if I should have written poetry myself if I had not been the son of a clergyman . . . most clergymen have plenty of books in their houses." Perhaps the crucial point here, emphasized in Louis MacNeice's case by the comparative (but not total) loneliness consequent on his mother's death, lies in the last sentence. When we read the three 'Case-Book' chapters of *Modern Poetry*, we must be struck by two factors in his reading. First by the almost natural progression of his study of English poetry, and secondly by the good fortune that brought him from Blake and 'Sir Patrick Spens' through the whole gamut to Eliot and Yeats. Spenser attracted him early and held him long, both for the subtlety of versification, the extension of imagery, and the development of parable and allegory. It is perhaps as well that this was so, for another boyhood idol was Alfred Noyes. Noyes was a versifier of genius; he had an infinite capacity for complications of rhythm and rhyme, and no restraint on his loquacity. His thought is simple and indeed meretricious, and his philosophizing of the most obvious kind; but it would be unfair and unkind to deny the fascination of his ballads, and his influence on the adolescent mind. There can be little doubt that reading Noyes provided MacNeice with a wide range of metre (very obvious in his early poems) which he might otherwise have neglected, while his reading of Spenser combined with his classical knowledge ultimately (but not entirely) rescued him from Noyes's sentimentality. So although the *terza rima* of *Autumn Sequel* may owe its origin to

23

more established models, he had certainly met it early in the poetry of Noyes. The metre of 'Birmingham'

> Smoke from the train-gulf hid by hoardings blunders upward, the brakes of cars
> Pipe as the policeman pivoting round raises his flat hand, bars
> With his figure of a monolith Pharaoh the queue of fidgety machines
> (Chromium dogs on the bonnet, faces behind the triplex screens).

may well owe a debt to 'Orpheus and Eurydice':

> Only now when the purple vintage bubbles and winks in the autumn glory.

A sentimentality over animals was common to them both. In these four lines of 'The Bird Shop':

> There, the dull bleared eyes of a drunkard, blindly
> Stare at the dew-bright eyes of the pining captives;
> Here, an anaemic clerk, snub-nose to the window,
> Reads the price on a cage to the girl beside him

Noyes reminds us that his reader later wrote 'Pet Shop' and the opening of 'Trilogy for X':

> When clerks and navvies fondle
>   Beside canals their wenches,
> In rapture or in coma
>   The haunches that they handle,

His influence, or a natural sympathy, stretched beyond the limits of prosody to the border of class consciousness and anthropomorphism.

To balance what might have been an unfortunate influence MacNeice had an instinctive feeling for the work of T. S. Eliot. Nearly 40 years later, when writing of his schooldays in an essay he calls 'Eliot and the Adolescent', he says "while (again like most adolescents?) we were at heart romantics . . . What we wanted was 'realism' but – so the paradox goes on – we wanted it for romantic reasons. We wanted to play Hamlet in the shadow of the gas-works. And this was the opening we found – or thought we found – in Eliot." Then he adds, and it is a perceptive comment, "What we should have found in the *Four Quartets*, had it been published then, is a puzzler; youth finds it easier to face the end of the world than its beginning." We may perhaps ignore the final generalization. But the statement serves to remind us that Eliot was the new poet of MacNeice's schooldays, and still the Grand Old Man of Poetry who contributed *ex cathedra* a funeral oration when the younger man died. The earlier work of Eliot certainly influenced the thinking and practice of the younger poet; but there was no parallel in their later development. The *Four Quartets* were written about the same time as 'Plurality' and 'The Stygian Banks', but MacNeice's poetry has neither the late Eliot's depth of understanding nor his prosodic control, as we shall see.

In another generalization MacNeice says, "The adolescent is peculiarly sensible of his physical surroundings." As a generalization it might be hard to justify, but it was true of MacNeice, not only in adolescence, but throughout his life. He goes on:

I had only occasionally visited great cities – London, Belfast, Liverpool, Birmingham – but the fact of these cities was mysterious, compelling, frightening; it was one of the great inescapables of my world which a poet, I thought, must recognize. But, until I met these poems of Eliot, I had not seen it recognized duly. In *Preludes* I found not only that 'smell' of a modern city which your first visit establishes as part of your mentality but also the human element below the surface, something which even the young and innocent can guess at –

'The conscience of a blackened street
Impatient to assume the world.'

However sheltered our young lives, however rural our normal surroundings, however pre-Industrial Revolution our education, we knew in our bones, if not explicitly, that this which Eliot expressed so succinctly and vividly, this was what we were up against.

In this same essay MacNeice goes on to a brief analysis of the effect upon himself and his contemporaries of *The Waste Land*. He is honest enough not to claim that they had in their schooldays complete understanding of the poem, but he rightly insists that it is great because its meaning remains 'qualitatively' the same in their maturity as it was in the late 'twenties. This, he says, is the feat of a great poet. What was yet more important to the nature and development of his own poetry was Eliot's cinematic technique:

The cinema technique of quick cutting, of surprise juxtapositions, of spotting the everyday detail and making it significant, this would naturally intrigue the novelty-mad adolescent and should, like even the most experimental films, soon become easy to grasp.

It was MacNeice's singular contribution to English poetry that, encouraged by Eliot's example, he developed the inspiration of the City to the point where in 'Charon' death itself is presented in cinematic technique and in modern imagery that is yet universal. From the same source he was encouraged to develop this technique to convey his delight in "things being various", a delight that makes high poetry of 'Snow'. Finally from the secure knowledge that images of the City could be as important to modern poetry as rural images were to Wordsworth, he developed the capacity for "brilliant quotidian reportage" that Philip Larkin was to find in *Autumn Journal*.

The world of man-made things always meant a great deal to MacNeice. When he says "The dwellers in Xanadu never saw a van going down the street and piled with petrol tins in beautiful reds and yellows and greens" he meant precisely that this described a true, if contemporary, aesthetic experience. He felt the need to express in words the impact of 'things' upon his senses, and he did this unusually well. While still at school he had written that "Romantic poetry is the stuff of personal dreams made sufficiently impersonal to be palatable to others than oneself." In a sense both the strength of his poetry and some of its weaknesses are made clear by the contrasting implications of these two statements. He was always affected by the impact of the modern world upon his senses. This is sharply recognizable throughout his poetry, and it is frequently in piquant contrast to the stuff of his personal dreams, regressive for the most part, nostalgic, often enervating; and from the contrast comes one element of his appeal. His enjoyment of the outer world as it impacted upon his senses is balanced by the sadness verging on self-pity with which he contemplated his inner life. He comes perilously close to self-pity in *Modern Poetry* when he says, with some perception:

Speaking for myself I should say the following things, among others, had conditioned my poetry – having been brought up in the North of Ireland, having a father who was a clergyman; the fact that my mother died when I was little; repression from the age of 6 to 9; inferiority complex on grounds of physique and class-consciousness; lack of social life until I was grown up; late puberty; ignorance of music (which could have been a substitute for poetry); inability to ride horses or practice successfully most of the sports which satisfy a sense of rhythm; an adolescent liking for the role of *enfant terrible*; shyness in the company of young women until I was 20; a liking (now dead) for metaphysics; marriage and divorce; Birmingham; an indolent pleasure in gardens and wild landscapes

Fortunately he does not leave it here but develops his theories of poetry in later work. In *The Poetry of W. B. Yeats* he says:

Every poet does two things, though he may be more conscious of one than of the other and though his success may be due more to one than to the other. He reacts emotionally (though emotion may be strong or weak, conscious or unconscious) to his subject matter and he selects and arranges that subject matter – consciously or unconsciously – in order to square it with some intellectual system of his own. But even this distinction is too crude, for these two moments of the poetic activity are inseparable like the positive and negative elements in electricity. Even before the artist has started his art-work proper he is not only reacting emotionally to his subject but he is also automatically systematizing it.

He adds: "I think that human activity begins at a stage below thought with an urge which I can only describe as mystical." Later he elaborates: "This intimate connection between a poem, its author's life and the wider life beyond the author (a life which expands in concentric circles through both time and space) establishes certain conditions for the truth, and therefore for the value, of poetry." Though in the same book he disclaims any thought of "subscribing to a Wordsworthian doctrine of poetry" as he had been half tempted to do 30 years earlier when he wrote: "Wordsworth's *Preface* to the *Lyrical Ballads* is very sympathetic to a modern writer", his descriptions of his relationship to his own poetry are sufficiently precise to establish him as a poet whose work can be expected to follow in the Romantic tradition.

Although there may be no generally accepted definition of the word 'Romantic' in connection with literature, we must find some criterion against which to judge MacNeice's work. In so far as it proved adequate to the study of Baudelaire we can do worse than turn to Marcel Raymond's description of the Romantic poet:

le poète romantique renonçant à une connaissance qui ne serait pas en même temps un sentiment et une jouissance de soi — et un sentiment de l'univers éprouvé comme une présence — charge son imagination de composer le portrait métaphorique, symbolique, de lui même, en ses métamorphoses.

This was well translated by J. Hillis Miller in the *Critical Quarterly* as:

The Romantic poet, renouncing any form of knowledge which was not at the same time a feeling and an enjoyment of himself – and a feeling of the universe, experienced as a presence – charged his imagination with the task of composing a metaphoric or symbolic portrait of himself in his metamorphoses.

When MacNeice refers in *Modern Poetry* to the *Preface* to the *Lyrical Ballads*, he is speaking for himself, not, as he seems to claim, for other modern writers. He was a Romantic poet at a time when his contemporaries would have questioned that title. While Auden wrote in the light of his "admiration for the objective world . . . founded on that cosmic pride which lies at the base of Christianity" (a perceptive criticism by MacNeice in 1938); while Day-Lewis sought valiantly for the Higher Dreams, and Eliot suffered in increasingly rarefied intellectual heavens, Louis MacNeice, with occasional conscience-smitten scurries down political or religious paths suggested to him by his contemporaries, for the most part wrote from the evidence of his five senses. He used a fine though never fully developed intellectual capacity, a high degree of craftsmanship, a mature sense of prosody, a free-ranging vocabulary and understanding of imagery, in the service of a sensuously and subjectively apprehended approach to the problems of self, of society and of the universe. These three themes will be traced through his poetry as it develops from his Juvenilia to his final volume. The chapters that follow are divided so that poetry dealing with self, with society and with philosophizing, are dealt with in that order, except in the section on Juvenilia which follows, and also in that dealing with *Autumn Sequel*, where it is more convenient to reverse the sequence.

This study will concern itself only with the non-dramatic poetry of Louis MacNeice, and will not include the verse plays and radio presentations. It will refer to MacNeice's biographical and critical prose only where that helps in the better understanding of his poetry. Nearly all the poetry referred to is contained in *The Collected Poems of Louis MacNeice*, edited by Professor E. R. Dodds, and published by Faber & Faber in 1966.

II

Blind Fireworks was the laboratory notebook of the sorcerer's apprentice. In 1949, in an article he called 'Experiences with Images' MacNeice himself says "my first book *Blind Fireworks* (published 1929) . . . is the most artificial or literary. This is usually so with juvenile verse."

In those of his youthful poems which he has chosen to preserve, the predominant element is experiment in versification. We should perhaps be grateful for his schoolboy enthusiasm for

Alfred Noyes. There are in his first volume, as in the verse of
Noyes, trochaic hexameters, iambic heptameters and hecta-
meters, as well as poems in the more usual metres. In 'The
Creditor' (notable as the one poem by MacNeice which definitely
admits the existence of God) there is imitation Hopkins:

> In quiet in diet in riot in dreams,
> In dopes in drams in drums in dreams,

There is pastiche 'Façade':

> Descending out of the grey
> Clouds elephant trunk
> Twitches away
> Hat;
> THAT
> Was *not* what I expected,
> A
> Misdirected
> Joke it seemed to me;

in 'Elephant Trunk', to say nothing of 'The Lugubrious, Salub-
rious Seaside'. There is lack of discipline, as in 'Evening Indoors'
with its use of 'the', 'and', and of 'like' at the beginning of lines.
(There was no attempt here at Auden's control.) There is
'Mahavveray' which holds out only the faintest hint of 'Bagpipe
Music'. But there is also much promise. We are told that the

> old maid, the sea,
> Rehangs her white lace curtains ceaselessly.

– a packed metaphor recalling both the breaking of the surf and
the seaside boarding-house windows, yet still full of restless, useless movement. There is modern imagery, not sudden and startling like Spender's pylons, but apposite and easy, as in 'Breaking
Webs':

> Over asphalt, tar, and gravel
> My racing model happily purrs,
> Each charted road I yet unravel
> Out of my mind's six cylinders.

Shutters of light, green and red,
Slide up and down. Like mingled cries,
Wind and sunlight clip and wed
Behind the canopy of my eyes.

– and in 'Happy Families':

Dutifully sitting on chair, lying on sofa,
Standing on hearth-rug, here we are again,
John caught the bus, Joshua caught the train,
And I took a taxi, so we all got somewhere;
No one deserted, no one was a loafer,
Nobody disgraced us, luckily for us
No one put his foot in it or missed the bus.

An examination of the first volume of the poetry soon discloses
that MacNeice showed good judgment in the choice of those
early poems he included in his collected edition. It is no service
to him to resurrect the others for critical comment. It is enough
to recollect that these poems contain, among absurdities such as
in 'A Conventional Serenade':

Ululate and ululate and ululate
Your amorous runes are desperate.

an occasional felicitous line or striking image. From the few
felicities one might mention from 'The Sunset Conceived as a
Peal of Bells':

The dárk empúrpled cánvas béats
Over the slúmbering drúnken shíp.

This, with its long 'u' sounds and four slow major beats has a
strong emotional appeal not supported either by the two introductory, or the two final lines of the stanza. Again, in 'Inaugural
Rant', MacNeice speaks of "culling wild starlight". In 'A Conventional Serenade', already stigmatized, he exclaims:

See how the trees with vegetable desire
Stretch themselves upon the yielding sky

31

lines which remind one simultaneously of Marvell and of Eliot; but in 'Adam's Legacy' he can so overstretch an image as to say that we are

> tost on the whalespouts of the firmaments
> As waterbalancing balls one shoots at a fair.

The image here may owe something to Eliot, as does the line from 'Bound in Stupidity and Unbound' – "Still dallied with my spoon in pools of tea", which parodies "I have measured out my life with coffee spoons".

There are elements in MacNeice's early poetry which informed his work for the rest of his life. He wrote always what he described as "impure poetry . . . conditioned by the poet's life and the world around him". In these very early verses we find from among them fascination with his own experiences and the capacity to illustrate these experiences by means of images drawn, or recollected from the world which the Industrial Revolution had ushered in. Of a poem in which these two elements of self and experience are combined, 'Trains in the Distance' (written in 1926) he says in 'Experiences with Images':

the noise of trains – and this goes for the foghorns and the factory hooters also – had a significance apart from what caused that noise; impinging on me before I knew what they meant, i.e., where they came from, these noises had as it were a purely physical meaning which I would find it hard to analyse. It is partly this meaning which I am concerned with in an early autobiographical poem (1926):

> 'Trains came threading quietly through my dozing childhood,
> Gentle murmurs nosing through a summer quietude,
> Drawing in and out, in and out, their smoky ribbons . . .'

Clearly these trains were not primarily intended for transportation, they are homey things, familiars:

> 'And so we hardly noticed when that metal murmur came.
> But it brought us assurance and comfort all the same,
> And in the early night they soothed us to sleep,
> And the chain of the rolling wheels bound us in deep'

And here comes the other image I have just mentioned:

> 'Till all was broken by that menace from the sea,
> The steel-bosomed siren calling bitterly.'

These things sound trivial, but they form an early stratum of experiences which persists in one's work just as it persists in one's dreams.

D. S. Savage, writing on 'The Poet's Perspectives', was aware of "an acute elegiac sensibility" in *Blind Fireworks* and of "flamboyant imagery informed by a humorous or melancholy defeatism." "One receives" he says "the impression of a solitary, sensitive individual amusing himself."

Perhaps Geoffrey Grigson said the last word in the introduction to his anthology *Poetry of the Present 1948–9*:

After these poems one should have had no more doubts. Indeed, it is curious and profitable to read them all again, and discover in those immaturities the seedlings of his maturity, the mixture of the tea-yellow of Poussin and the plushiness of Renoir, the picture and the garden, the formal shape and the wilderness of colour

and an earlier comment "and there in these juvenilia were stretched to tautness criss-crossing wires of form with this spangled acrobat performing on them".

III

In his next two volumes, *Poems* published in 1935 and *The Earth Compels* in 1938, we step over the ill-defined border that separates juvenilia from early poetry and we can begin our consideration of MacNeice's poetry under our three major headings of self, society and philosophy. Although D. S. Savage feels that during this interval of six years "MacNeice's growth towards maturity took the form of a greater awareness of society, of the claims of the outer world", in these works much of his inspiration still derives from his personal life. 'Intimations of Mortality' is one of those poems devoted entirely to reminiscences of childhood which we shall find throughout his work, including his final volume, *The Burning Perch* (1963). The subject of 'Intimations' recurs in 'Autobiography' five years later, and again in 'The Blasphemies' more than 20 years later. Each time, as we shall see, it is explored in greater depth. The early poem is not among his best; the language is either trite, as in "His parents snore in conjugal bliss", or forced – "The murderous grin of toothy flowers". But the effect of dark and shadow on a sensitive child which he emphasizes in 'Experiences with Images', "Our house was lit by oil lamps (not enough of them) and so was full of shadows" – the longing for light, and the lack of understanding by the adult world, are well caught. The childhood tendency to mythologize – "The night watchman with crossed thumbs" that grows into an idol, is a common but terrifying experience, and the final words – "The Kingdom comes . . ." – with its reference to the Lord's Prayer and its sense of an unknown doom, catches the effect which the unexplained use of a familiar rune can have on the infant imagination. 'Carrickfergus', published in 1937, also an autobiographical poem, does not soar. It is a plain statement and should, together with *The Strings are False*, effectively destroy the lingering myth of the rural Irishman who becomes a townsman *malgré lui*. The place of his birth, Belfast, with its "hooting of lost sirens and the clang of trams", and "Smoky Carrick", were reasonably adequate preparation for Birmingham. 'Carrickfergus' is a descriptive poem and pitched in a minor key but concluding on a note of effective summary and contrast:

> I went to school in Dorset, the world of parents
> > Contracted into a puppet world of sons
> Far from the mill girls, the smell of porter, the salt-mines
> > And the soldiers with their guns.

As we read this we remember 'Valediction' in which he had the perception to see that, however much he wished, he could not cut himself off entirely from his Irish heritage:

This is what you have given me
Indifference and sentimentality
A metallic giggle, a fumbling hand,
A heart that leaps to a fife band:
Set these against your water-shafted air
Of amethyst and moonstone, the horses' feet like bells of hair
Shambling beneath the orange cart, the beer-brown spring
Guzzling between the heather, the green gush of Irish spring.
Cursèd be he that curses his mother. I cannot be
Anyone else than what this land engendered me

In the same poem he shows that even at this early stage he is aware of excessive preoccupation with self:

I will exorcise my blood
And not to have my baby-clothes my shroud
I will acquire an attitude not yours
And become as one of your holiday visitors,
And however often I may come
Farewell, my country, and in perpetuum;
Whatever desire I catch when your wind scours my face
I will take home and put in a glass case
And merely look on
At each new fantasy of badge and gun.

When we turn to 'The Jingles of the Morning', a poem from that unsatisfactory dramatic gallimaufry, *Out of the Picture*, we enter a new element of autobiographical poetry, which by its nature and its sensitive implications foreshadows, however faintly, 'Prayer Before Birth':

Shall we remember the jingles of the morning,
The pipers the pedlars and the brass farthings,
The buds of music, the imagined darlings?
    No, we shall *not* remember.

Again he is looking back on these "so ephemeral things", and now despairing even of their memory. He passes from earlier to later childhood; to the games of 'this year, next year, some time, never', as we blow away the dandelion seeds (an image which

occurs again in 'Bluebells' nearly ten years later). He speaks of
"Searching for the lost handle to the silent fountain", a striking
line which recreates all those childhood hours of vain attempt to
unlock the secret of the past. "Hiding in the shrubbery, shutting
our eyes and counting" was a ritual of hide-and-seek. MacNeice
had vivid memories of one such occasion which he described in
detail in *The Strings are False*. He asks if we shall remember the
flowers and scents and sounds of the garden, and the sensuous
pleasure, the fun "of dragging a stick along the paling". So he
moves on to schooldays and youth's "early adult pleasure" – "The
dive in love's lagoons of brilliant azure" (*The Blue Lagoon* of de
Vere Stacpoole, perhaps?), "the gay martyrdom" suffered by
"Love's Martyr" (Donne's 'The Funeral') and "the excellent
phantasy, brave notions" (Jonson) compressed in "brave fantasia".
Then come more adult experiences, "the kick of inspired
religion", "The visions in drink" (later so well expounded in 'The
Drunkard') and the extraordinary feeling of the rightness of time
and place when we are like "the homing pigeon/Drawn by a
magnet to an intuited region". 'Intuited' here, by association
with the animal world, is used to do service both for unexpected
insight, and for instinctive response. Shall we remember these
moments of our past lives, he asks, and then on a universal plane:
"Shall we remember the noise of the moving nations"? This was
in 1936 when Germany was expanding, the Spanish civil war
beginning, when the mutterings that led to the Second World
War could be heard as nations moved into place. But finally he
asks:

> shall we remember the gusty sun's creations,
> The night and the never-to-be-climbed constellations?
> No, we shall *not* remember.

He foresees nothing but forgetfulness; after life, nothing. This is
the scepticism from which he never really moved, and which
brings him, so often, when he compares so bleak a prospect with
so full and perceptive a present life, to a position of nostalgic
despair.

'Eclogue between the Motherless', criticized by Geoffrey Walton in *Scrutiny* as being "in Mr. Auden's cheapest and nastiest manner", is strongly personal in inspiration and the mother-oriented title is significant. 'A' and 'B' in the dialogue are the two sides of MacNeice's *persona*. On the one side is the mother-fixated man, doomed always to search for a wife who will be a mother-substitute, but who finds

> They are all distorted now the beautiful sirens
> Mutilated and mute in dream's dissection,
> Hanged from pegs in the Bluebeard's closet of the brain,
> Never again nonchalantly to open
> The doors of disillusion.

The reason is not far to seek:

> I thought 'Can I find a love beyond the family
> And feed her to the bed my mother died in
> Between the tallboys and the vase of honesty
> On which I was born and groped my way from the cave
> With a half-eaten fruit in my hand, a passport meaning
> Enforced return for periods to that country?
> Or will one's wife also belong to that country
> And can one never find the perfect stranger?'

The other party to the dialogue, 'B', speaks of his unsuccessful marriage:

> Never you marry, my boy. One marries only
> Because one thinks one is lonely – and so one was
> But wait till the lonely are two and no better

As he does later in *Autumn Journal*, he describes vividly the attraction he found in 'Mariette':

> The first half year
> Is heaven come back from the nursery – swansdown kisses –
> But after that one misses something

(again that seeking for the mother image) and:

> My wife was warmth, a picture and a dance,
> Her body electric – silk used to crackle and her gloves
> Move where she left them.

but:

> My complaint was that she stayed a stranger.
> I remember her mostly in the car, stopping by the white
> Moons of the petrol pumps, in a camelhair rug
> Comfortable, scented and alien.

If these are two typical MacNeice pictures which make Mr Walton's criticism seem less than fair, he is perhaps justified by the macabre conclusion of the poem which has the same apparent lack of humour and compassion as Auden's 'Miss Gee'.

This loneliness, which marriage did not cure, and which was still there after divorce, is the main theme of 'Postscript to Iceland', a poem written in 1936 and published as 'Epilogue' in *Letters from Iceland*, the high-spirited potboiler that he and Auden produced between them. He opens with

> Now the winter nights begin
> Lonely comfort walls me in;
> So before the memory slip
> I review our Iceland trip —

The poem from then on is a lyric in a metre familiar in many hymns and ballads, contrapuntal in construction and swinging between reminiscence of a shared holiday and consideration of his present lonely (if comfortable) estate. The holiday is seen in the wider perspective of the time:

> Down in Europe Seville fell,
> Nations germinating hell,
> The Olympic games were run —
> Spots upon the Aryan sun.

Here the references are to the Spanish civil war, and the Berlin Olympic Games which were made the subject of controversy and propaganda by an elastic system of scoring apparently devised to bolster the Nazi theories of the superiority of the Aryan races. He sketches the aesthetic arguments he and Auden enjoyed during their travels, and points them with stark pictures of the Frozen North while they watched

> Ravens from their walls of shale
> Cruise around the rotting whale,
>
> Watched the sulphur basins boil,
> Loops of steam uncoil and coil,
> While the valley fades away
> To a sketch of Judgment Day.

There were no miracles, no visions, no conversions on that journey, but he is content because

> Holidays should be like this,
> Free from over-emphasis,

He is back now to the academic world where

> Rows of books around me stand,
> Fence me round on either hand;

but "Through that forest of dead words" he longs for the "living birds":

> Great black birds that fly alone
> Slowly through a land of stone,

The nostalgia of *fin des vacances* combines here with the loneliness of one who can only

>   wait
> For the 'phone to ring or for
> Unknown angels at the door;

Remembered from this "desert in disguise" the "northern skies" – where there was "Time for soul to stretch and spit" – have attraction. Then in a highly subjective verse he says

> For the litany of doubt
> From these walls comes breathing out
> Till the room becomes a pit
> Humming with the fear of it

Frequently when MacNeice wishes to analyse his feelings he uses words which his early association with the Church made familiar.

39

'Litany' is a word of worship and associated therefore with faith and with the repetitive chanted assertion of faith. From the walls of his lonely room, from the rows of books standing around him, only doubt can pulse, a familiar experience to the scholar and intellectual. MacNeice takes it a stage further, and makes it more subjective still. He says the "doubt" breathes from his rows of books "Till the room becomes a pit" – a black pit, a bottomless pit, "Humming with the fear of it", as pits tend to hum with insects, with echoes, with one's own heartbeats. This is not all that MacNeice finds in his room, now become a pit. There is also "fear of loneliness" and this we can understand. He has lost his wife; fear of loneliness is doubly sharp. Even so it is hard to forgive, as a line of poetry: "And úncommúnicáblenéss". It is perhaps adequate to say that the poem itself is so compelling that one can overlook this massive *bétise*. Returning to the subject of his dedication, he says:

> I write these lines for you
> Who have felt the death-wish too,

Then finally he returns to his ever-present fear of death and annihilation:

> Our prerogatives as men
> Will be cancelled who knows when;
> Still I drink your health before
> The gun-butt raps upon the door.

This is fundamentally a simple poem and it has the kind of dignity which simplicity gives. As R. L. Cooke points out (in his 'Appreciation of Louis MacNeice' in *The Poetry Review* of 1947), in it he "approaches more closely to the style of Auden than any-where else". A lonely man remembers his holiday with a friend and comments on his loneliness and the hopelessness of the future. It is in the idiom of his time. He is in Hampstead, waiting for the 'phone to ring. He is deserted because "the wires are cut", and finally his vision of the end is that of the gun-butt which "raps upon the door", a vision so soon to become reality to his generation and which in this context brings inevitably to mind Auden's 'Let History Be My Judge' and the 'Ode' from *The Orators*.

IV

It was as an urban man writing from an urban setting that MacNeice wrote this postscript to an excursion away from modern civilization. He was always sensitive to the colour, sound and complexity of city life in the twentieth century and, as a civilized intellectual, took much pleasure in it. It was mainly from the secure base of his prolonged love affair with the City, or with his memories of many cities, that he developed his social and political comment. He says himself in 'Subject in Modern Poetry', contributed to *Essays and Studies* in 1937:

The Modern poet is very conscious that he is writing in and of an industrial epoch and that what expresses itself visibly in pylons and gasometers is the same force that causes the discontent and discomfort of the modern individual, the class warfare of modern society, wars between nations in the modern world.

In a review published in the *London Magazine* 20 years later and called 'Lost Generations', he notes that the poems of the "social and or political category remain to my mind, highly personal . . . and often even 'romantic' in the tradition of that earlier social political poet, Shelley."

In 'Belfast' for example, an early poem in *Poems* (1935), the third verse:

> And in the marble stores rubber gloves like polyps
> Cluster; celluloid, painted ware, glaring
> Metal patents, parchment lampshades, harsh
> Attempts at buyable beauty.

paints a vivid and all too familiar suburban picture, with the social comment implicit in the last line; but the rest of the poem is overwrought ("Glares from behind the mica of his eyes") and gives the impression that he had no sympathetic feeling for that town. In the next poem, 'Birmingham', we find much greater sympathy; a love-hate relationship with the great city in which he and his wife made their first home.

This poem, since we are analysing it in detail, is worth quoting in full:

Smoke from the train-gulf hid by hoardings blunders upward,
    the brakes of cars
Pipe as the policeman pivoting round raises his flat hand, bars
With his figure of a monolith Pharaoh the queue of fidgety
    machines
(Chromium dogs on the bonnet, faces behind the triplex
    screens).
Behind him the streets run away between the proud glass of
    shops,
Cubical scent-bottles artificial legs arctic foxes and electric
    mops,
But beyond this centre the slumward vista thins like a diagram:
There, unvisited, are Vulcan's forges who doesn't care a
    tinker's damn.

Splayed outwards through the suburbs houses, houses for rest
Seducingly rigged by the builder, half-timbered houses with
    lips pressed
So tightly and eyes staring at the traffic through bleary haws
And only a six-inch grip of the racing earth in their concrete
    claws;
In these houses men as in a dream pursue the Platonic Forms
With wireless and cairn terriers and gadgets approximating to
    the fickle norms
And endeavour to find God and score one over the neighbour
By climbing tentatively upward on jerry-built beauty and
    sweated labour.

The lunch hour: the shops empty, shopgirls' faces relax
Diaphanous as green glass, empty as old almanacs
As incoherent with ticketed gewgaws tiered behind their
    heads

From early influences to 'Bagpipe Music'

As the Burne-Jones windows in St. Philip's broken by
    crawling leads;
Insipid colour, patches of emotion, Saturday thrills
(This theatre is sprayed with 'June') – the gutter takes our
    old playbills,
Next week-end it is likely in the heart's funfair we shall pull
Strong enough on the handle to get back our money; or at any
    rate it is possible.

On shining lines the trams like vast sarcophagi move
Into the sky, plum after sunset, merging to duck's egg, barred
    with mauve
Zeppelin clouds, and Pentecost-like the cars' headlights bud
Out from the sideroads and the traffic signals, crême-de-
    menthe or bull's blood,
Tell one to stop, the engine gently breathing, or to go on
To where like black pipes of organs in the frayed and
    fading zone
Of the West the factory chimneys on sullen sentry will all
    night wait
To call, in the harsh morning, sleep-stupid faces through the
    daily gate.

The first six lines are straightforward and powerful descriptive verse. The images are strong. The hoardings hide a "train-gulf" and the smoke "blunders upward". The brakes of cars "pipe". The policeman looks like a "monolith Pharaoh", a thought which doubtless owes much to his helmet, so reminiscent of the 'pschent', the pharaoh's head-dress reproduced on many papyri. The machines with their "Chromium dogs" (described in the same breath with the "faces behind the triplex screens" and conveying the same sense of affluent fatuity) are "fidgety", an excellent description of the waiting line of cars, shuddering then perhaps more than they do now. The next line – "Behind him the streets run away between the proud glass of shops" – recreates the endless perspectives of the city, and of the shop fronts with the gewgaws which are their contents – "cubical scent-bottles" (with its implication of commercialized Cubism), "artificial legs" (crude purposeful medical technology), "arctic foxes" (unnecessary luxury) and "electric mops" (the new leisure). Beyond this perspective the "slumward vista" (what a good word "slumward"!) "thins like a diagram". Here the sense of sprawled, scrawled streets and houses is economically conveyed. "Unvisited" (by whom? by the poets of this world?) are the factories "as foul as Vulcan's stithy". Vulcan, we remember, was the God of Fire, now domesticated by association with the modern process of vulcanizing. By a further extension, we are reminded of 'Brummagem ware', for Vulcan "doesn't care a tinker's damn" (a good Midland phrase). "Splayed outwards", no longer thinned "like a diagram", we come to the suburbs where the houses are seducingly "rigged", a word that can mean either 'fitted out' (as in a ship) or fraudulently prepared (as in jerry-building). The half-timbered houses he describes, the so-called 'stock-broker Tudor', were typical of the 'twenties and 'thirties, often built with diamond-paned windows, and with heavy studded oak doors that looked like "lips pressed tightly", secretive and disdainful, staring at the traffic through dusty hedges, the "bleary haws". Their foundations were notoriously shallow, so that their "concrete claws" had only a precarious grip on "the racing earth". MacNeice was often aware of the spinning globe; in 'Perseus' he says "And one feels the earth going round and round the globe of the blackening mantle, a mad moth." Here he sees the suburban houses but weakly attached to their slight place in the universe. The occupants of these houses are, he finds, as pretentious as their surroundings. They "pursue the Platonic Forms" (an ironic but apt reference to Book X of Plato's *Republic*) with all the superficial trappings of modern life, "wireless and cairn terriers and gadgets". Finding God and scoring "one over the neighbour" are equated. In these houses men climb upward "on jerry-built beauty and sweated labour".

The note of social criticism is not sustained; it gives way again to ironic description. Somewhat abruptly, perhaps too abruptly, we move to "The lunch hour", to the shopgirls' faces "diaphanous as green glass" (perhaps "a sea of glass like unto crystal" remembered from his permitted readings from *Revelations* during church services). They are "empty as old almanacs", a phrase no less expressive for the fact that Isaac Walton thought of it first – "as useful as an almanac out of date". Standing in their shops, before their labelled goods, "gewgaws", they make a picture as "incoherent", as rambling as the stained-glass windows by the pre-Raphaelite Old Edwardian, Burne-Jones, that do so little for the Pro-Cathedral.

The second half of this verse has a melancholy understanding of the life of momentary feeling, "Saturday thrills" that pass away, and yet are sought again in eternal optimism, in the hope that next time the fruit machine will pay up:

> Next week-end it is likely in the heart's funfair we shall pull
> Strong enough on the handle to get back our money; or at any
>   rate it is possible.

MacNeice was a poet of the contemporary scene and in the opening of the next verse painted a picture which has now almost disappeared. The electric trams were once a notable and magnificent feature of city life; grand and ponderous they combined all the mystique of trains running on rails and of the double-decker buses dominating traffic. They were long, and narrow, and distinctly coffin-shaped:

> On shining lines the trams like vast sarcophagi move
> Into the sky,

It was the industrial sky against which he saw them, plum coloured, "merging to duck's egg, barred with mauve/Zeppelin clouds". With the next picture we are more familiar. The headlights of cars "bud/Out from sideroads" "Pentecost-like", that is as we recall from the *Acts* "with tongues parting asunder as fire". The traffic signals are the colours of drinks, "crême-de-menthe or bull's blood", and allow us to go on to where factory chimneys are "black pipes of organs".

Ezra Pound and Eliot had, by widening the choice of poetic subject, made it possible for MacNeice to write his love poetry

45

to the great city. He was a townsman by birth and by inclination and he saw in the town colour and romance where Eliot saw the "newspapers from the vacant lots". Eliot had given a new dimension to poetry by taking the world about him into its structure as an integral part of his thought and feeling, by turning his back firmly and finally upon ruralized romanticism. He and Pound sought "something for the modern stage". Spender could write of "the silent crowd/Who stand behind dull cigarettes" or "squat buildings/With their strange air behind trees, like women's faces/Shattered by grief". Or Auden: "Beams from your car may cross a bedroom wall/They wake no sleeper". The poetry of Day-Lewis is loaded with imagery that mirrors the technical world:

> I thought, since love can harness
> Pole with contrary pole,
> It must be earthed in darkness
> Deeper than mine or mole.
> Now that I have loved
> A while and not gone blind,
> I think love's terminals
> Are fixed in fire and wind.

It is left to MacNeice to paint with a sympathy that is occasionally ironic the life of the modern town. In 'Sunday Morning', for example, he captures the atmosphere of the middle-class suburb as it was in his day and as it is still:

> Down the road someone is practising scales,
> The notes like little fishes vanish with a wink of tails,
> Man's heart expands to tinker with his car
> For this is Sunday morning, Fate's great bazaar;
> Regard these means as ends, concentrate on this Now,
> And you may grow to music or drive beyond Hindhead anyhow,
> Take corners on two wheels until you go so fast
> That you can clutch a fringe or two of the windy past,
> That you can abstract this day and make it to the week of time
> A small eternity, a sonnet self-contained in rhyme.

The imagery of modern life, of machines, of gadgets, of 'gew-gaws', was available to all his contemporaries, but it was Mac-Neice who gloried in the colour and movement and inspiration of it. From this power of apprehending the magnificence of things come the fine lines of 'An Eclogue for Christmas':

> On all the traffic-islands stand white globes like moons,
> The city's haze is clouded amber that purrs and croons,
> And tilting by the noble curve bus after tall bus comes
> With an osculation of yellow light, with a glory like
>   chrysanthemums.

Here both the versification and the vocabulary are cunningly employed to convey the picture of the double-deckers "tilting by the noble curve", the 'nobility' of the curve (the lists) echoing the noble sport of tilting, so appropriate for these armoured mastodons. The street lamps are reflected in their shining sides – "With an osculation of yellow light", a resounding kiss which suits these monsters, which remind him in their colourful size of the full-blown "chrysanthemums". The movement of their stately procession is caught in the rhythm of the first line – "And tílting by the nóble cúrve bús after táll bús cómes", with three strong slow stresses to end the line and prepare for the magnificent description in the next one. If one is reminded of Drinkwater's "tramway down the hill" which "Across the cobbles moans and rings", one also remembers that Drinkwater's pleasure in that poem was not in the trams for their own sakes, or the town for its own sake, but because

> There is about my window-sill
> The tumult of a thousand wings

a nostalgic longing for the romantic rural scene. MacNeice's lines shine out from a poem which holds out little hope for civilization, as though the sheer sensuous joy in colour and movement caught him off guard and made him, in spite of foreboding, take joy in the kaleidoscope of the great city.

R. L. Cooke sees in 'An Eclogue for Christmas' a debate

between rural and urban attractions by a poet equally, or almost
equally, divided between them. In spite of the odd line of sensual
rural feeling: "Let the balls of my feet bounce on the turf, my
face burn in the wind", the scales are loaded against the countryside. There are few lines in the poem on the rustic side of the
argument, to compare with those we have been considering. Two
characters comment on their time from contrasting viewpoints
of the countryman and the townsman, each with the ironic relish
in his environment which is so typical of MacNeice; so we have
the contrast of "The commercial traveller joking in the urinal"
with "The jutlipped farmer gazing over the humpbacked wall".
Hoggart in his *Auden: An Introductory Essay* finds this "effective".
But the description of the countryside does not rise much above

> in the heavy shires
> Greyness is on the fields and sunset like a line of pyres
> Of barbarous heroes smoulders

which lacks the relish which is in this picture of the city:

> Our street is up, red lights sullenly mark
> The long trench of pipes, iron guts in the dark,
> And not till the Goths again come swarming down the hill
> Will cease the clangour of the pneumatic drill.
> But yet there is beauty narcotic and deciduous
> In this vast organism grown out of us:

A *Times Literary Supplement* reviewer found MacNeice in this poem
obsessed with the impending doom of capitalist civilization:

> The jaded calendar revolves,
> Its nuts need oil, carbon chokes the valves,
> The excess sugar of a diabetic culture
> Rotting the nerve of life and literature;

This is followed by a description of the years of ballroom dancing
which never escaped fully from the memory of 1914:

> Jazz-weary of years of drums and Hawaiian guitar,
> Pivoting on the parquet I seem to have moved far
> From bombs and mud and gas, have stuttered on my feet

> Clinched to the streamlined and butter-smooth trulls of the
> élite,
> The lights irritating and gyrating and rotating in gauze –
> Pomade-dazzle, a slick beauty of gewgaws –

We then have a brilliant analysis of the deeper, in fact hidden, feelings of the uneasy 'twenties by means of a metaphorical analysis of its art. Graphic art, a tactile art, is frequently closer to the atmosphere of a period than other forms of artistic expression. In terms of graphic art, MacNeice expresses the malaise of the first third of the twentieth century. He reminds us that his early years coincided with the romantic 'blue period' of Picasso's art:

> I who was Harlequin in the childhood of the century,
> Posed by Picasso beside an endless opaque sea,
> Have seen myself sifted and splintered in broken facets,
> Tentative pencillings, endless liabilities, no assets
> Abstractions scalpelled with a palette-knife
> Without reference to this particular life.

By the beginning of the First World War, Picasso had already extended his freedom of plastic association to the point where he painted 'The Card Player' or 'Woman with Guitar', both dated 1915. From that time onwards Picasso, Braque, Mondrian, Klee, Miró, Kandinsky produced pictures in which humanity became "Abstractions scalpelled with a palette knife/Without reference to this particular life". Of this MacNeice complains

> And so it has gone on; I have not been allowed to be
> Myself in flesh or face, but abstracting and dissecting me
> They have made of me pure form, a symbol or a pastiche,
> Stylised profile, anything but soul and flesh;

Here we have one of his perpetual philosophical grouses: again and again he objects to the idea of 'pure forms', an objection he repeats in six years' time in 'Plurality' and against which he is still making a positive assertion in 'Apple Blossom' a quarter of a century later. Here, in 'An Eclogue for Christmas', is the justification of the generation of the 'twenties that made its desperate small self-defeating endeavour to retain its 'particular' life in the face of the great depersonalized political systems against which abstract art was the unappreciated warning. He has not been allowed to be "soul and flesh":

> And that is why I turn this jaded music on
> To forswear thought and become an automaton.

Perhaps the most disturbing thing about this poem and the most human one is its despair. Though Day-Lewis in 'Transitional Poem' sought "the single mind" and struggled to possess the "Himalayas of the mind", though Auden flirted with Fascism in 'The Orators' and though Spender "thought continually of those who were truly great", MacNeice in contrast finds that man is the victim of "Mechanical Reason, capricious Identity" and feels that it would be better to be

> The tin toys of the hawker [which] move on the pavement
>   inch by inch
> Not knowing that they are wound up; it is better to be so
> Than to be, like us, wound up and while running down
>   to know –

There is only the "pretence of individuality" and there is no prospect either for the town "with its clangour of the pneumatic drill" or for "the country gentry" whom he criticizes as scathingly here as he does later in the opening to *Autumn Journal*. To the question "What will happen when the sniggering machine-guns in the hands of the young men/Are trained on every flat and club and beauty parlour and Father's den?", he can only answer that "the whore and the buffoon/Will come off best". So he retreats to the simplest physical sensations of the countryside, to the civilized satisfactions such as "the perfection of a grilled steak" but, above all, to "the cult of every technical excellence", ending with the prayer:

> Let all these so ephemeral things
> Be somehow permanent like the swallow's tangent wings:

G. S. Fraser writing on 'The Poet as Humanist' quotes these two lines as an example of MacNeice's defence of common sense "By the use of subtle dialectic and the frank acceptance of paradox", on which his consistency is based. "Thus" he adds "one of his favourite figures is oxymoron, the noun and the epithet appear to contradict each other."

It is too much to say of 'An Eclogue for Christmas', as the *Times Literary Supplement* critic did, that "this cliché symbolism of the decadence of society and the wrath to come is too smart and too easy to communicate an experience of any permanent significance." Day-Lewis in *A Hope for Poetry* found the poem "a little desperate" and this is nearer the truth. MacNeice himself said "I wrote with a kind of cold blooded passion." Today it breathes a kind of desperate frustrated honesty; as G. S. Fraser goes on to say, MacNeice is an "intolerant liberal or a large hearted nagger." Certainly the "permanent significance" is there for those who have similar feelings in the face of modern events. In many ways the strength and weakness of MacNeice's thought is first shown in this poem. The intellectual hedonist rushes up to the eternal problems, shudders before them − "That I could be able to face this domination, nor flinch" − and turns back with faint but persistent hope to "The drunkenness of things being various", to the hopeless wish that what is ephemeral could be, somehow, permanent. Nevertheless, as John Press in his pamphlet on MacNeice points out, " 'An Eclogue for Christmas' sums up what was to be a life-long relationship between flux and permanence, the allure of transient phenomena, the possibility of a permanent, divine order."

In 'Turf-Stacks' MacNeice develops the contrast between the price paid, in human terms, for rural 'peace' and the fate of those who have deserted it for more sophisticated pleasure. He takes as his theme the turf-stacks, the piles of peat that punctuate the rainy boglands of some Irish landscapes. He starts with the idea that these symbolize a primitive escape from the industrialized world:

> Among these turf-stacks graze no iron horses
> Such as stalk, such as champ in towns and the soul of crowds

The "iron horses" are both the trains that stalk and champ (like
Arnold's "wild white horses") and the iron-bound emotions that
bite into the soul of victims of the "mass-production of neat
thoughts". But if the rural scene itself, if the "tawny mountain,
the unregarded buttress" are "the peasant's conspirators" against
the "canvas shrouds for the mind", the peasant himself is not an
attractive figure "on his boots like hooves". If he does not want "to
run in grooves" like a train or a tram, or like those with "neat
thoughts", it is because he "shambles" along "without thinking at
all". Perhaps we should envy him, for the rest of us will feel the
need of some other kind of help or "fortress" (a frequent image of
the Christian church, in which MacNeice was reared, and which
he is now using ironically) against

> ideas and against the
> Shuddering insidious shock of the theory-vendors,
> The little sardine men crammed in a monster toy
> Who tilt their aggregate beast against our crumbling Troy.

This was written during a period when Spender was singing
Communism, and Auden, little as he may have realized it at the
time, a kind of benevolent Fascism, and Day-Lewis an intel-
lectualized and somewhat arid Socialism. MacNeice was aware of
the political divisions of his day, and of their dangerous poten-
tialities. He must have come under pressure to align himself in
his work on one side or the other. This he never found it possible
to do, in spite of several good-natured, if impatient, attempts. By
nature he resented and indeed rejected the idea that in politics
one must "take one's stand". Both the rejection and the resentment are stated clearly in the last stanza of the poem:

> For we are obsolete who like the lesser things
> Who play in corners with looking-glasses and beads;

Here again is the romantic longing after "those so ephemeral
things", the desire to escape into the Grantchester world of
"tunnels of green gloom" or into Asia (like the Apostles). Then,
in a typical burst of impatience, he presents us with the other
alternative to submissive conformity. We can "turn blind wantons

like the gulls who scream". We notice the pronoun "who" which humanizes the gulls and reduces those who "rip the edge off any ideal and dream" to the grey level of the "little sardine men" and the "theory-vendors". Politically this was MacNeice's difficulty. The attempt to cram political ideology down the throats of his generation drove him to a reaction of blind anger which he was at the same time sufficiently detached to recognize as unconstructive.

His detachment from political emotion is clearly shown in the two poems 'To a Communist' and 'The Individualist Speaks'. He compares dialectical materialism to the snow that turns the "gawky" earth into the all-embracing earth mother. But the image gives him the ironical rejoinder he needs. The communist theory, he says, will melt as does the snow and

> before you proclaim the millennium, my dear,
> Consult the barometer –

The poem to some readers may appear only a squib, throwing more light on MacNeice's inability to accept any 'system' than on his ability to dissect systems. Other readers might find in its anti-Utopianism a tough common sense.

While Spender was calling enthusiastically to his comrades to "step beautifully from the solid wall/advance to rebuild and sleep with friend on hill/advance to rebel" and Auden writing a sardonic appreciation of the Fascist attitude:

> For never serious misgiving
> Occurred to anyone,
> Since there could be no question of living
> If we did not win.

(a theme developed in *The Orators*), MacNeice was expressing his wish to evade political involvement in 'The Individualist Speaks':

> We with our Fair pitched among the feathery clover
> Are always cowardly and never sober,
> Drunk with steam-organs, thigh-rub and cream-soda
> – We cannot remember enemies in this valley.

As chestnut candles turn to conkers, so we
Knock our brains together extravagantly
Instead of planting them to make more trees
– Who have not as yet sampled God's malice.

Just as the horse-chestnuts are used for games and not for propagation, so rather than use his brain to "make more trees", he and his kind "knock them together extravagantly". They enjoy intellectual exercise and discourse, as small boys enjoy competing with conkers. This is an image of that modern intelligentsia which he describes in 'Experiences with Images' as "rhetorical, or cerebral". They do this, he implies, because they are innocent; they "do not remember enemies in this valley" and they "have not as yet sampled God's malice". Then suddenly he changes the image: we are "urchins playing with paint and filth" to whom the prophet utters the "old warning of the old sin/ – Avenging youth threatening an old war". Perhaps this was an echo of German resurgence already audible in 1933. MacNeice seems often to have an ambivalent attitude to the interest that his friends had in literature and art, and the feeling that it was somehow sinful is perhaps a puritan relic of the vicarage in which he was born. The "urchins" who play with "paint and filth" is a Nazi image for much in modern art, of which, as he made obvious in 'An Eclogue for Christmas', he felt the disintegrating influences. So he foresaw the Nazi hordes "crawling down like lava or termites". His reaction is consistent with his personality: "I will escape, with my dog, on the far side of the Fair". And this he did. As Press says, "MacNeice was, in politics as in religion a sceptic who mistrusted lofty idealism and self-righteousness in no matter what disguise they draped themselves. Nor did he trust any creed which exalted a bureaucratic hierarchy, whether of priests or politicians, at the expense of the individual."

It is too easy to look back and see in the writings of the past, especially a past with which one is familiar, warning and foresight of that future which inevitably engulfed it. 'Les Neiges d'Antan' was first published in *Out of the Picture* (1937). For MacNeice 'Les Neiges d'Antan' are the romantic security, the wealthy affluence which Lytton Strachey was taking so clinically apart and which has gone like the carriage horses that "once dunged the streets of London". He asks "What's become of the squadron of butlers, valets, grooms and second housemaids?" The rest of the poem is strangely prophetic; passing over the image of the blind leading the blind and leading each other in the Lord Mayor's Show (symbol of the established order), we come to a forecast of the years 1939–45 as obvious then to the troubled intellectual as is the inevitable outcome of the atomic arms race today:

> Fire will consume the lot, the game resume,
> And feathers of the birds of prey will singe as they tear the
> prey,
> And the corpses roast where they fell
> And the small blue flames will play
> Like kittens with a ball of wool . . .
> FIRE FIRE FIRE FIRE . . .
> Fire in Troy, fire in Babylon, fire in Nineveh, fire in London,
> FIRE FIRE FIRE FIRE
> The buckets are empty of water, the hoses are punctured,
> The city main is cut off, the holy well is dry,
> There is no succour in the dusty ground, the metallic sky,
> No rock will spout with water at the prophet's rod,
> Nor fate repeat the legendary flood,
> There is nothing to stem the mechanical march of fire,
> Nothing to assuage the malice of the drunken fire.
> FIRE FIRE FIRE FIRE

This poem might well be used to illustrate the way in which the poet's mind, sensitive to the 'winds of change', becomes prophetic and sees more surely than does the mind of the politician the shape of things to come.

V

Even in a prophetic and incantatory poem such as 'Les Neiges d'Antan' MacNeice's physical pictures are sharply defined and

colourful, as in "The long breakers topped with silver of expanding power and profits". So when he treated in his poetry, as he
did throughout his life, such themes as life and death, he did so
in relation to his acute sensory perceptions. His reactions to a
visual stimulus inevitably have a strong Bergsonian flavour, since
Bergson's views depend upon the predominance of the sense of
sight. Contrasting our sense of lived time, of *durée*, with the
point-instants of the physicist's time, Bergson uses the metaphor
of a cinema film, a set of 'frames' which, run through a projector,
fuse into each other and give a sense of visual flow and continuity.
MacNeice develops Bergson's theme further in 'August'. Life as
we see it, he says, is like the projection of a film, "The shutter of
time darkening ceaselessly"; just as the shutter whirls round
between the 'frames' of a film as it passes through a projector, so
is also the passing of time through night and day. But the mind
has too much capacity for selection and for system:

> the mind, by nature stagey, welds its frame
> Tomb-like around each little world of a day;

Here MacNeice seems to equate the mind, as does Bergson, with
brain; and it is a function of the brain to limit our mental life to
what is practically useful. So the "living curve" eludes us. While
the lawn mower spurts "its little fountain of vivid green"

> I, like Poussin, make a still-bound fête of us
> Suspending every noise, of insect or machine.

All this, he says, is "a dilettante's lie". Time is not turned to
stone (an image to which he often in one form or another returns),
it is our mind, itself dead, that

> wishes to have time die
> For we, being ghosts, cannot catch hold of things.

The argument seems to be that while we can only apprehend the
world by turning it into still life, this, in itself, since it divorces
us from reality, makes us ghosts unable to come into contact with
"things", the ultimate truth. Although Bergsonian philosophy,

with its strong reliance on sensual perception, and itself an imaginative and poetic view of the world, must have been particularly attractive to one of MacNeice's temperament, he could not follow Bergson into the second stage of his thinking about the nature of 'intuition'. This is MacNeice's perpetual dilemma. His perceptions were so sharp, he so enjoyed the diversity of the world, that he could not, and never did, arrive at any general philosophical conclusion. In 'The Glacier' he uses again the image of the buses that so held his fancy. This time "bus encumbers upon bus", a line that reflects in words the pictures of the clumsy traffic. This, he says, is the picture of our life, "who have always been haunted by the fear of becoming stone". In saying this MacNeice exposes his dissatisfaction with Bergsonian thought. He cannot bear to see the material world melt back into a single flux. Nor can he, any more than Bergson, find a moment of contemplative insight. So he is forced back to "seemingly slower things/And rejoice there to have found the speed of fins and wings".

The same sense of unavoidable doom informs 'Hidden Ice', a poem which with considerable perception contrasts the 'normal' and apparent life which most men lead with the truth behind the appearance:

> There are few songs for domesticity
> For routine work, money-making or scholarship
> Though these are apt for eulogy or for tragedy.
>
> And I would praise our adaptability
> Who can spend years and years in offices and beds
> Every morning twirling the napkin ring,
> A twitter of inconsequent vitality.
>
> And I would praise our inconceivable stamina
> Who work to the clock and calendar and maintain
> The equilibrium of nerves and notions,
> Our mild bravado in the face of time.

Then in an astonishing verse, he describes the utter suffocation

that can descend upon the suburban life and stand in the way of
escape by sheer determination not to recognize the danger:

> Those who ignore disarm. The domestic ambush
> The pleated lampshade the defeatist clock
> May never be consummated and we may never
> Strike on the rock beneath the calm upholstering.

The last two verses, as MacNeice himself explains in *Modern
Poetry*, are concerned with

the people who strike hidden ice, members of the routine world who
fall away from their allegiance. They are persons who become unable
to keep their aesthetic sense or their outside interests or their erotic
emotions pigeon-holed off into the hours when they are not on duty.
They become obsessed by something which, on their system, should
not be allowed to introduce into their eight-hour day. They kiss
flowers and like Judas because the act is treacherous to their whole
system (it is also implied that these 'flowers', as Christ to Judas, are
themselves potentially destructive of the system. Witness the routine
worker who becomes a Communist). And some of these people become
fatally addicted to what belongs, on their premisses, to their pet hours
only. Such people in everyday life may end in suicide or the asylum.
Such a man is like Saint Sebastian because his collapse is brought about
through the things he loved – the arrow in his body feathered from the
birds which he himself reared. ('Hobby' is an ironic understatement; for
a man who is a mere cog in industry or business, any love or any ideal
must be a hobby.) As for sitting 'between the clock and the sun', this
denotes sitting between the two great symbols of routine, one human
and the other natural. Further, both a clock ticking and a shaft of sun
entering a room (the dust-motes dancing in it corresponding to the
inevitable ticking of the clock) seem to me, at moments, sinister,
hypnotic. And – a minor point – the sun enters the room at the time
when the malingerer ought to be at his work. Further, I am not merely
using clock and sun as symbols, for I have a clear picture of a particular
man with suicidal thoughts sitting in a room with a clock on the
mantelpiece behind him and the sun creeping towards him over the
floor from a window in front.

The imagery that MacNeice has used in this poem overlays a fair
description of the ordinary man's "mild bravado in the face of

time" but informing the whole poem is his endless fear of the passing of life measured so remorselessly both by clock and sun.

Contrasting with this shrinking away from time's inevitability is MacNeice's sharp appreciation of the physical world. 'Aubade' is a strongly physical poem, where each sense lends its intensity to another. Life has the savour of "a sharp apple" or responds like a fish on a line. We have "felt with fingers that the sky is blue", we have "been happy"; but after that there awaits us "not the twilight of the gods" but only what is mundane: "a precise dawn/ Of sallow and grey bricks, and newsboys crying war." Once again the love of those "so ephemeral things" beats uselessly against the facts of life.

The quite short lyric, 'Snow', since it has been discussed in more exhaustive – and perhaps exhausting – detail than any other poem of MacNeice's (and possibly than any other modern poem of the same length) should be quoted here in full. It is an admirably condensed expression of one pole of MacNeice's philosophy:

> The room was suddenly rich and the great bay-window was
> Spawning snow and pink roses against it
> Soundlessly collateral and incompatible:
> World is suddener than we fancy it.
>
> World is crazier and more of it than we think,
> Incorrigibly plural. I peel and portion
> A tangerine and spit the pips and feel
> The drunkenness of things being various.
>
> And the fire flames with a bubbling sound for world
> Is more spiteful and gay than one supposes –
> On the tongue on the eyes on the ears in the palms of one's
>   hands –
> There is more than glass between the snow and the huge roses.

'Snow' is a lyric of sensual pleasure, and is an especially important one in the MacNeice canon. Here is a delight in externals, a surprised pleasure as the world of light, colour and contrast affects his senses. "The room was *suddenly* rich" reminds him that "world is suddener than we fancy it". It is "incorrigibly plural". It is endlessly diverse. MacNeice illustrates this by describing the peeling of a tangerine; he sees the bright fruit, he feels the skin and pith, he tastes it, he spits the pips into the fire and hears the "bubbling sound" of the flames; he feels "The drunkenness of things being various" and that the "world/Is more spiteful and gay than one supposes/On the tongue on the eyes on the ears in the palms of one's hands". He concludes with a line which eludes analysis (though it has received it) but which strikes that deep chord of feeling which sounds when a poet, having carefully built up his word-picture of an experience and having shared the experience with the reader through the sure technique of his art, arrives at a conclusion which both recognize as valid or even inevitable. So when MacNeice says "There is more than glass between the snow and the huge roses", we know that he is speaking of the whole range of sensory impressions, of the natural forces which alone can produce the two phenomena to be so strangely and suddenly juxtaposed, and is hinting at those meta-physical thoughts that deal with the subjective and objective nature of the world in which we live.

In Volume 8 of *Essays in Criticism* Marie Barroff has a long explication of this poem. She says that "in the last line of the poem the speaker harks back explicitly to the starting-point of his train of thought" and in this starting-point she finds that "An assertion like 'World is crazier and more of it than we think,/ Incorrigibly plural' has a direct, out-of-context interest and appeal in both the meaning and expression. It invokes a range of ideas fascinating to mankind since the days of Heraclitus and Parmenides, ideas which have been re-formulated and re-elaborated from century to century, and which include in their ramifications such problems as the Many and the One, nominalism and realism, mechanism and vitalism, everyday phenomena and the periodic table."

'Snow' must be one of the most remarkable short poems in the English language, if not in its own right, then by virtue of the

critical comment, mainly in *Essays in Criticism*, that it has elicited.
From 1953 to 1958, from Cragg to Barroff, each line, each word
almost, has been pondered over and fondled. Cragg sets out to
discover whether MacNeice is, in this poem, playing the
philosopher "for the sake of the imagery", but he concludes, and
it is a generous judgment, "*Snow* is a difficult poem. Its substance
is the whole of cosmology, its glossary the history of philosophy.
Not the least of its merits is its straight-forwardness; it speaks
openly and unashamed, avoiding the facileness of symbolical
meaning, and it moves without confusion, distortion or strain.
Snow – to borrow a phrase of Dr. Johnson's – has a sound bottom:
it rides on its own philosophy." In reply to this, M. A. M. Roberts
says "There is no need for philosophy here. Our day-to-day
experience of 'world' is lifeless, killed by the dead weight of our
abstract 'knowledge about' it. But there was a time, and there
still are times, of experiencing that world as a living thing, not
abstractedly but 'face to face'. This seems to me the 'substance'
of the poem". But in Cragg's reply we get a little nearer to true
human comprehension, to the understanding that monism should
have so got on the nerves of a man that he set out to prove that
"World is crazier than we think". To D. J. Enright this was
"perverse and childish mystery-mongering" or even "Criticism
for Criticism's Sake", and 'Snow' an "amusing little poem". When
dispute becomes so shrill the truth may be relatively simple.
Perhaps MacNeice himself puts it better, or at least with more
clarity, when he says (in 'Experiences with Images') "*Snow* has
often puzzled people though it means exactly what it says; the
images here are not voices off, they are bang centre stage, for this
is the direct record of a direct experience. The realisation of a
very obvious fact that one thing is different from another – a fact
which everyone knows but few people perhaps have had it brought
home to them in this particular way, i.e. through the sudden
violent perception of snow and roses juxtaposed."

In a poem of 12 lines of cunningly contrived syntax MacNeice
has recreated the details of an experience so that it becomes
universal, and he does so with such skill that each re-reading

enriches the experience. The same natural enjoyment in this apprehension of the sensuous world merges into despair in 'The Sunlight on the Garden'. He opens with a chilling verse which depicts the sunbeams shining through the branches of the garden and yet, in the same stroke, kills the warmth and colour:

> The sunlight on the garden
> Hardens and grows cold,
> We cannot cage the minute
> Within its nets of gold,
> When all is told
> We cannot beg for pardon.
>
> Our freedom as free lances
> Advances towards its end

As men able to choose about what we write, as knight errants choosing the targets against which we will tilt, as mercenaries choosing where we will serve, we are to lose our freedom. "The earth compels": it is an irresistible force which we cannot escape; our song, our sonnets fall back upon it as do the birds:

> And soon, my friend,
> We shall have no time for dances.

The end of relaxed living is in sight.

The next verse has a prophetic flavour. When in 1939/40 there was fear in the country of airborne attack, it was decided that one form of alarm would be the ringing of the church bells. Did anyone, learning this, quote

> The sky was good for flying
> Defying the church bells
> And every evil iron
> Siren and what it tells:
> The earth compels,
> We are dying, Egypt, dying . . . ?

A reviewer in the *Times Literary Supplement* feels that "Even so simple a stoic meditation on the coming doom is marred by its melodramatic quotation from 'Antony and Cleopatra' ". One is forced to wonder whether the critic has either read the poem, or read it with understanding. Egypt was a sphere of British influence. In many ways it stood, by association, for a civilization that had itself passed through all the phases of nationhood and empire, to serfdom. The end of another empire is in sight. The quotation from the mouth of the lover of a queen of Egypt emphasizes the universality of the poem. The passing of pleasure in the sunlight on the garden, the chill of fear as it "hardens and grows cold", is a universal experience common to all nations, all periods of history, and all estates of man. In this context the quotation is justified.

Then MacNeice turns to consider where we find the credit side of the account. It is little enough: because we cannot beg for pardon, we cannot therefore expect it:

> And not expecting pardon,
> Hardened in heart anew,
> But glad to have sat under
> Thunder and rain with you,
> And grateful too
> For sunlight on the garden.

We may well question the identity of "you" and may indeed find it in 'Mariette'; but the word contributes to the universality of the poem, since to each one of us, if we are lucky, there is someone with whom we are glad to have shared discomfort and fear, just as we are "grateful too/For sunlight on the garden."

This is a lyric which embeds in amber the sense of bitter foreboding that enters into each golden moment. It does so with great prosodic skill, economy of words and delicacy of feeling. The cunning use of both initial and terminal rhyme, together with extreme simplicity of language, make a poem whose craftsmanship enshrines the simple tragedy of "eheu fugaces" as a real but not unusual pearl is held in a fragile and beautifully designed setting.

'Bagpipe Music', which we shall deal with next, is the most 'popular' poem MacNeice ever wrote – it works, it goes over, as a serio-comic recitation, with every kind of audience. It is in Irish broadsheet ballad metre, quatrains made up of couplets, deliberately imperfect rhymes ("rickshaw", "peepshow", "bison", "python") which are literate imitations of the 'Come-All-Ye' Irish street song tradition. It has an Irish mixture of ferocious gaiety and jaunty despair. The earlier quatrains have, after every two of them, a couplet which acts as an ironic commentary or mocking refrain. The last two stanzas, the first more openly, less farcically bitter, the second profoundly and lyrically sad, close the poem with an astonishing transition of tone. We shall quote here the earlier stanzas and the last two stanzas at the end of our analysis:

> It's no go the merrygoround, it's no go the rickshaw,
> All we want is a limousine and a ticket for the peepshow.
> Their knickers are made of crepe-de-chine, their shoes are
>   made of python,
> Their halls are lined with tiger rugs and their walls with heads
>   of bison.
>
> John MacDonald found a corpse, put it under the sofa,
> Waited till it came to life and hit it with a poker,
> Sold its eyes for souvenirs, sold its blood for whisky,
> Kept its bones for dumb-bells to use when he was fifty.
>
> It's no go the Yogi-Man, it's no go Blavatsky,
> All we want is a bank-balance and a bit of skirt in a taxi.
>
> Annie MacDougall went to milk, caught her foot in the
>   heather,
> Woke to hear a dance record playing of Old Vienna.
> It's no go your maidenheads, it's no go your culture,
> All we want is a Dunlop tyre and the devil mend the puncture.
>
> The Laird o' Phelps spent Hogmanay declaring he was sober,
> Counted his feet to prove the fact and found he had one foot
>   over.
> Mrs. Carmichael had her fifth, looked at the job with
>   repulsion,
> Said to the midwife 'Take it away: I'm through with over-
>   production'.

It's no go the gossip column, it's no go the ceilidh,
All we want is a mother's help and a sugar-stick for the baby.

Willie Murray cut his thumb, couldn't count the damage,
Took the hide of an Ayrshire cow and used it for a bandage.
His brother caught three hundred cran when the seas were
    lavish,
Threw the bleeders back in the sea and went upon the parish.

It's no go the Herring Board, it's no go the Bible,
All we want is a packet of fags when our hands are idle.

'Bagpipe Music' written in 1937 was a *tour de force* of versification which has attracted much attention and to a great extent has
been accepted uncritically because of its lilting measure. Writing
in *The Review* in 1964, Stephen Wall says:

Perhaps, after all, 'Bagpipe Music' was MacNeice's best poem; few
of them, at any rate, are as memorable. Much of the pleasure of reading
him (usually in a state of slightly baffled good will) comes really from
recognition; like Betjeman, like Larkin, his material is quotidian and
familiar, and this is consoling, like reading adverts of a product you
have already invested in. But in this poem he doesn't merely connect,
but also fixes. It is rare for him to achieve such a degree of verbal
authority; the superbly assured rhythmic snap, the brilliant drone-like
use of dissonance, the valid relation with vernacular: these use the
random material far more powerfully than conscientiously collated
documentary detail about depressed Scotland, such as one finds in a
poem like 'The Hebrides'. The various disasters of 'Bagpipe Music' –
"John MacDonald found a corpse, put it under the sofa", "Mrs. Car-
michael had her fifth, looked at the job with repulsion" – are greeted
with elation, and the vitality of the "It's no go" riff effectively negates
what it appears to state.

This is only part of the story. If we remember the times when it
was written and ask ourselves what the poem says, then we are
not surprised at the angry humour it embodies; the mocking
despair that came so readily from the background of unemployment and lack of faith in the future.

The rhythm is that of the Irish Jig. The background is of
bawdy song and broadsheet ballad. "It's no go", a Midland phrase,

is used as a refrain (a device of which his boyhood favourite, Alfred Noyes, was over-fond). It is used to brush aside the palliative offered to the poor, "the merrygoround" (they can no longer become drunk with steam-organs), and the simple modes of life. "All we want is a limousine", and to be made free of the world of wealth and make-believe. To hide the seriousness of our envy even from ourselves we sing a sadistic popular song. When that is over we consider the philosophies offered to us by the "Yogi-Man", who recalls the 'bogey-man' who can no longer frighten us. Nor have we any wish, to quote Eliot, that "Madame Blavatsky will instruct me/In the Seven Sacred Trances". We want immediate satisfactions that we can't afford, "a bank balance and a bit of skirt in a taxi". This being denied, we make bawdy fun; but still want the rewards of this world, "a Dunlop tyre and the devil mend the puncture". Then back to the popular song, with side-swipes at "over-production" and over-population, and the refusal to accept circuses and sedatives and expedients, such as the gossip column, the ceilidh and the Bible, the Herring Board, the picture palace, stadium, government grants, or even elections. So in the last two verses is added to ironic contempt for the present, a derisive despair of the future:

> It's no go the picture palace, it's no go the stadium,
> It's no go the country cot with a pot of pink geraniums,
> It's no go the Government grants, it's no go the elections,
> Sit on your arse for fifty years and hang your hat on a pension.

> It's no go my honey love, it's no go my poppet;
> Work your hands from day to day, the winds will blow the profit.
> The glass is falling hour by hour, the glass will fall for ever,
> But if you break the bloody glass you won't hold up the weather.

The extraordinary change of tone in that last stanza (without any obvious change of rhythm, though the movement of the voice somehow has to become slower, and its pitch deeper and sadder) from the mocking to the mournful is one of the triumphs of the poem.

CHAPTER TWO

Autumn Journal

Autumn Journal was written between the dates that Eliot assigned to *Burnt Norton* and to *East Coker*. It was a time of extreme doubt and concern for sensitive and thinking men. The most fruitless war in history was looming to satisfy, or restrain, a madman. Intelligent people could see it coming; no one could, or would, act to stop it. For Eliot the time coincided with his development towards the "higher dream"; for MacNeice with the experience of losing his wife to another man. Both men chose to resolve the *mélange* of personal, social and universal conflict in contemplative poems of some length. Eliot's poems are intellectual, bleak, soul-searching, abstracted from life and all but the most etiolated hope; MacNeice's poem is sensuous, observant, fallible, controlled but not formal, despairing and infinitely human. Eliot in *Four Quartets* demands and obtains the admiration reserved for those works which extend us beyond our small capacity; MacNeice gains our confidence by drawing upon a range of experience common to all and making it universal, important, though inconclusive.

Autumn Journal is an intimate, personal record. It is not as near to the confessional as a diary, but contains such intimacies as a third party can in decency overhear. This is not a mode of expression for the reticent, but eminently suited to the Romantic concerned with the "portrait of himself in his metamorphoses". The poem is indeed a series of self-portraits, each coloured by the moods induced by recollections of recent events and reflections on the current situation. There is little with which to compare this poetic journal in our literature. Perhaps it is in the same *genre* as *The Prelude* and *The Excursion* and falls somewhere between them. It is not uplifted like the first by a sense of mystery and exaltation; nor is it controlled like the second by an earnest conviction of mission.

MacNeice describes *Autumn Journal* as a "long occasional poem". It *is* long. It is devoted to personal observation, introspection, recollection and reflection. The thought and feeling does not develop steadily, but ebbs and flows as it does in life. Though the cantos bear no easily discernible formal relationship one to another, ideas, sentiments, moods and cunning repetition link them into something which is, as he himself says "halfway be-tween a lyric and a didactic poem". The three themes that emerged from his early poetry remain the intertwining threads from which the structure depends. In *Autumn Journal* he is intro-spective, socially critical and struggling to resolve the antinomies of the universe, but he does not attempt to offer "a final verdict or a balanced judgment". His presentation fits the mood and purpose of the poem. The cantos of irregular length are appropriate to his varied subjects. The prosody, lines of anything from two to five stressed syllables and rhyming alternately, is simple but sufficient to provide some disciplined control.

II

Although the 'Autumnal' aspect of the poem is fairly obvious, it has its clearest justification in the fourth canto, which also touches the rawest nerve of his feeling at that time. September, he says, is *"hers"*, and he is speaking of 'Mariette' (to use the name he gives her in *The Strings are False*) who was his wife, the mother of his son, and who left him. He pays her in Canto IV one of the most moving tributes to a fascinating woman:

> Frivolous, always in a hurry, forgetting the address,
>> Frowning too often, taking enormous notice
> Of hats and backchat – how could I assess
>> The thing that makes you different?
> You whom I remember glad or tired,
>> Smiling in drink or scintillating anger,
> Inopportunely desired
>> On boats, on trains, on roads when walking.
> Sometimes untidy, often elegant,
>> So easily hurt, so readily responsive,
> To whom a trifle could be an irritant
>> Or could be balm and manna.
> Whose words would tumble over each other and pelt
>> From pure excitement,
> Whose fingers curl and melt
>> When you were friendly.

This is the kind of pleasure that Herrick took in his description of his Julia; here the description is that of a very lovely, maddening person. Perhaps not as she really was, for MacNeice says: "I thought of her as some kind of changeling, a creature crept out of a wood and making believe to be human." Time inevitably ripped the edge off his dream and the poignancy of this fine passage in *Autumn Journal* is underlined by comparison with the sad, inevitable disillusion of the first of the 'Novelettes'. That was still some way ahead. He had yet to come to terms with his sense of deprivation and find some way of living with the memory of their life together. Among the urban description and social and political comment of Canto VIII, he retails their life together in lines of regretful irony:

> But Life was comfortable, life was fine
>> With two in a bed and patchwork cushions

And checks and tassels on the washing-line,
    A gramophone, a cat, and the smell of jasmine.
The steaks were tender, the films were fun,
    The walls were striped like a Russian ballet,
There were lots of things undone

In Canto XI he catches with great accuracy that form of self-deception when the mind knows that the past cannot be recovered, but the emotions refuse to accept this inevitability. The nostalgic longing for a lost love has seldom been better displayed or better analysed – "my common sense denies she is returning" while "my pride, in the name of reason, tells me to cut my losses" and in spite of common sense and pride "doubt still finds a loophole". Sadly "I try to feel her in fancy". His memories of Mariette swing him now between love and hate; at one moment she is the sleeping princess, at the next he hates her and those about her. So we have another long description of her; this time not so starry-eyed and a little minatory, but still conveying the picture of a mercurial and beautiful woman. Whereas before he tried to "assess/The thing that makes you different", now

      if only for my own distraction,
        I have to try to assess
    Your beauty of body, your paradoxes of spirit,
        Even your taste in dress.
    Whose emotions are an intricate dialectic,
        Whose eagerness to live
    A many-sided life might be deplored as fickle,
        Unpractical, or merely inquisitive.

The words that would "tumble over each other and pelt/ From pure excitement" are now often spoken with "a bitter tongue". She is given to overstatement and is "at times malicious". But he is not free of her yet – "even when you deceive your deceits are merely/Technical and of no significance" – and he can still say "I see the future glinting with your presence/Like moon on a slate roof" – a cold and lovely simile. One is still reminded of his first conclusion in Canto IV:

> And it is on the strength of knowing you
>> I reckon generous feeling more important
> Than the mere deliberating what to do

But freedom is in sight. We had sentimental recollection in IV;
nostalgia and criticism in XI. In Canto XIX comes the beginning
of release:

> And I feel that my mind once again is open,
>> The lady is gone who stood in the way so long,
> The hypnosis is over and no one
>> Calls encore to the song.
> When we are out of love, how were we ever in it?
> . . .
>> Now I could see her come
> Around the corner without the pulse responding,
>> The flowery orator in the heart is dumb,

But "freedom is not so exciting" and this "history is almost/Ripe
for the mind's museum". His farewell is to say

>> thank you for the party –
> A good party though at the end my thirst
>> Was worse than at the beginning
> But never to have drunk no doubt would be the worst;

Loneliness is still there – "For where there is the luxury of
leisure/There should also be the luxury of women". At the end
he achieves a civilized and balanced acceptance. In the valediction
of Canto XXIV he can say

> And you with whom I shared an idyll
>> Five years long,
> Sleep beyond the Atlantic
> And wake to a glitter of dew and to bird-song.

Professor Dodds, in a commemorative broadcast in 1966,
described the married life of MacNeice and his young wife:
"They played" he said "an endless, innocent game of keeping
house, just like a pair of grown-up children." They lived in a
converted stable and "his wife saw this stable as an enchanted
island where the two of them would live happy ever after." It was

indeed an idyll; and like many idylls it ended unhappily, but it left an unforgettable lyric description of the lost woman. Strangely enough the break-up of his marriage is not reflected in a maturing of his emotions to extend the mastery of his technical resources. The introspective nature of his inspiration and the tendency to revert to the experiences of childhood remain and are perhaps intensified.

MacNeice looked out on the world of Munich with surprise that it should be the world into which he had grown. His pre-occupation with himself frequently takes the form in *Autumn Journal* of a survey of those factors in his education (and in his experience) which conditioned his approach to the social problems of his day. So in Canto X, the beginning of term at the University of Birmingham sets him thinking of "the beginning of other terms". He recalls "The alarm and exhilaration of arrival" at his preparatory school. Typically it is those items that impinged upon the senses that he remembers most vividly. He saw that the wooden boxes were "white"; he smelt the Lifebuoy soap in the changing-rooms; he heard the "impending" bell ring "with a tongue of frost", and he and his companions "sat on the hot pipes by the wall, aware/Of the cold in our bones". The desks were "escutcheoned" by the initials carved into them. He recalls that this was the time of the First World War – "maize and margarine/ And lessons on the map of Flanders", but he remembers vividly how little this impinged on the toys, games and preoccupations of childhood, with "Everything to expect and nothing to deplore". This was the little world of the preparatory school.

Then came Marlborough, where

> we jettisoned all
>   Our childish fantasies and anarchism;
> The weak must go to the wall
>   But strength implies the system;
> You must lose your soul to be strong, you cannot stand
>   Alone on your own legs or your own ideas;
> The order of the day is complete conformity and
>   An automatic complacence.

The Strings are False tells us that MacNeice was happy at school and fortunate in his fellows and mentors. To his highly critical mind this happiness was not enough and he could not deceive himself into the uncritical acceptance of superiority implicit in the public school ethic, or intellectually believe (Canto III)

> That freedom means the power to order, and that in order
>   To preserve the values dear to the élite
> The élite must remain a few. It is so hard to imagine
>   A world where the many would have their chance without
> A fall in the standard of intellectual living
>   And nothing left that the highbrow cared about.

Following on this, it is in a mood of irony verging on sarcasm that he describes his time in the Sixth and at Oxford (Canto XIII) where he had

> The privilege of learning a language
>   That is incontrovertibly dead,
> And of carting a toy-box of hall-marked marmoreal phrases
>   Around in his head.

It was here that a lesson was inculcated that we are paying for, and painfully expiating, today:

> That the boy on the Modern Side is merely a parasite
> But the classical student is bred to the purple, his training in
>   syntax
>   Is also a training in thought

Oxford, and the atmosphere of philosophic intellectual play, was "fun while it lasted", but afterwards he found that the "comparatively rare" occasions when "persons of intelligence and culture" "Are gathered together in talk" are spoiled by the dour necessity of life and by other people, because "There is always a wife or a boss or a dun or a client/Disturbing the air".

III

Oxford is made to provide the link between Canto XIII and Canto XIV, for he drove there the "next day", "by night". Canto XIV contains among other material of interest, an insufficiently appreciated aspect of MacNeice's poetry. The introductory lines are one of the most perceptive poetic descriptions of the sensuous aspect of driving a car that has been written. Here is a daily experience which to many men is of deep emotional and highly charged psychological import. In our poetry, which should seek the universal in the temporal, this is one of the rare occasions on which it is mentioned. He drives by night "Among red and amber and green", the signs of danger, warning, safety, among the "spears and candles" which are the dazzling lights upon the windscreen, and among the "Corkscrews and slivers of reflected light/In the mirror of the rainy asphalt". What driver accustomed to this battering upon the eyes could fail to respond to the feeling that here is a poet capable of recreating the very emotion of coping with "all perils and dangers of this night"? —

> And coming over the Chilterns the dead leaves leap
> Charging the windscreen like a barrage of angry
> Birds as I take the steep
> Plunge to Henley or Hades.
> And at the curves of the road the telephone wires
> Shine like strands of silk and the hedge solicits
> My irresponsible tyres
> To an accident, to a bed in the wet grasses.
> And in quiet crooked streets only the village pub
> Spills a golden puddle
> Over the pavement and trees bend down and rub
> Unopened dormer windows with their knuckles.

His purpose is to take a small part in an election campaign; one of those sudden attempts to oblige and assist his friends by subscribing to a cause. But he is doing it "Mainly for fun, partly for a half-believed-in/Principle". The occasion was the by-election for

Oxford City on 27 October 1938. Quintin Hogg, a contemporary of MacNeice, was returned against A. D. Lindsay, Vice Chancellor from 1935–8. Less than 50 per cent of the electorate voted, so that MacNeice was justified in commenting

> There are only too many who say 'What difference does it
>   make
>   One way or the other?
> To turn the stream of history will take
>   More than a by-election.'
> So Thursday came and Oxford went to the polls
>   And made its coward vote

When his party, or the party he half believed in, had lost the by-election, it is once again the sheer sensuous remembrance of the journey back that concerns him with "the trees/Standing out in the headlights cut from cardboard" and though he pays a final lip-service to the necessity for all to "align against the beast", he concludes by noting that

> The plane-tree leaves come sliding down
>   (Catch my guineas, catch my guineas)
> And the sun caresses Camden Town,
>   The barrows of oranges and apples.

The 1930s were overshadowed by the near certainty of disaster. Government, of whichever party, suffered from a paralysis of will. Hunger marches, the Peace Pledge, university resolutions, were ineffective in a country entrusted either to a docker of limited outlook and failing powers, or to a pipe-smoking gentleman-farmer. Socialism, if not Communism, became to the worker the only possible hope of prevailing against entrenched capitalism. To the intellectual, Socialism had, as a political creed, the apparent attraction of possessing a body of coherent thought and an ethic. To the bourgeois rebel, in revolt against his birth, education and conditioning, it had a sympathetic appeal, made sharper if conscience appreciated the suffering, hunger, deprivation and unemployment which were confined in fact to the working-class. Julian Symons speaks of many of the "young left-wing writers whose art was partly a form of mental therapy and partly produced in the service of an imaginary classless future."

In those years it was not easy for a young man to turn his back upon a middle-class home, the training of an established school and of a traditional university and genuinely embrace the cause of the proletariat. Robin Skelton in his introduction to the *Poetry of the Thirties* notes how the poets of the time were "products of public schools" and that "all their images of communal experience can be so easily translated into terms of the undergraduates' reading . . . party." Auden declares "It's farewell to the drawing room's civilised cry/The professor's sensible where to and why" ('Song for the New Year'), while MacNeice reassures himself "There is no reason for thinking/That, if you give a chance to people to think or live,/The arts of thought or life will suffer and become rougher" (Canto III).

The development of Italian Fascism and German Nazism on the one hand, and Russian Communism on the other, made the ultimate conflict between the two types of authoritarian government inevitable and then, intellectuals tended to think, socialist idealism would prove itself. The only questions were when and how the conflict would begin, and on which side would British democracy be committed by its rulers to fight. It was to many almost a relief to see the battle first pitched in the limited area of Spain, to Auden "that fragment . . . soldered so crudely to inventive Europe". On this convenient stage the forces of the Left, which were also the forces of Government, were challenged by the forces of reaction. It was so much more practical to have the fight out in the open than continue with the "flat ephemeral pamphlet and the boring meeting". Young men, sickened by the dilatory policies of non-intervention, turned from action no more positive than contributing to left-wing literary magazines and did battle for their ideals. Some went to Spain and fought in the International Brigade, among them a few souls who could say with John Cornford that Communism was their "waking time" and who in spite of the "fear of pain whose pain survives" died "for Communism" and, as they believed, "for liberty".

To those with less capacity for martyrdom, the issue was not simple. It soon became clear that the Spanish conflict was to be made, with thinly disguised cynicism, a laboratory of war, especially by the Fascist powers. Adequate organization, backed by German and Italian arms, faced an idealism rendered suicidal by the too close analysis of doctrinal differences and by the endless enjoyment of their discussion. In Catalonia the many shades of socialist doctrine, translated almost farcically into terms of warfare by groups such as the Anarchists, made defeat almost certain. British intellectuals observed with some distaste the inability to 'pull together' of those whom their puritanical consciences urged them to support. At the same time they railed against politicians whose policies of non-intervention were derived from a training in compromise similar to their own. Grigson describes the non-intervenors as "the handsome Minister with the second and a half chin and his heart-shaped mind . . ." and "the Minister, with gout, who shaves low on his holly-stem neck".

Shortly after his wife left him, MacNeice went to see his friend, Anthony Blunt, at his Cambridge college and got drunk because "Mariette was not with me". On the way back to Birmingham he gave John Cornford a lift and in *The Strings are False* he describes him as "the first inspiring Communist I had met". At Easter 1936 MacNeice visited Spain with Blunt, partly as his guest, and it is this visit which forms the basis of Canto VI of *Autumn Journal*. The trip was intended to be, he says in *The Strings are False*, "a gala holiday", but neither in the fragments included in his posthumously published autobiography, nor in *Autumn Journal*, does any sense of 'gala' enjoyment come through. They spent their time "walking and gaping" and for a tripper the rain "Was worse than the surly or the worried or the haunted faces". MacNeice was determined to be, if he could on this occasion, a sightseer. With his eye for detail, his capacity to catch with words the quick picture, he was ideal in the rôle. He noticed the "writings on the walls" and the "ranks of dominoes/Deployed on café tables the whole of Sunday". He described in one line the tourist cabarets "Of thighs and eyes and nipples". He sees the "peeling posters", the

> vulture hung in air
> Below the cliffs of Ronda and below him
> His hook-winged shadow wavered like despair

Impression crowds on impression, until in his mood as a disappointed tourist whose holiday was in jeopardy because of national preoccupations, he connects his lines by commencing them with a series of 'ands', so that each line is like a tripper's postcard. The journey ticks itself off. He visited the Prado, Aranjuez, Toledo, Avila (which was cold), Segovia (picturesque and smelly), Seville and so on, till they "caught heavy colds in Cordova". So back via Algeciras, where they saw "the mob in flower", to Gibraltar. "All that the tripper wants is the *status quo*."

The interest of Canto VI lies in a dichotomy of feeling. MacNeice was torn between his desire to be a tourist recording a tourist's impressions and his inability as a keen observer to ignore the signs of disorder to come. The dichotomy found petulant expression in the description of the Cambridge don who said " 'There's going to be trouble shortly in this country' ". He was "pudgy and debonair". He was "Glad to show off his mastery of the language". (In *The Strings are False* he "made this prophecy with sly pride as if he were doing a card-trick".)

What was MacNeice's own attitude to the warning signs? He says he remembers Spain (in a simile that does not bear too close examination) "ripe as an egg for revolt and ruin". He sees the hammer and sickle scrawled on the walls. He notes the "shadows of the poor" as he is also noting the "fretted stone . . . chiselled for effects of sun and shadow". He sees the "slovenly soldiers" and justifies Robin Skelton's comment on the influence of the public schools by comparing them to the "new boys in the Marlborough O.T.C., puny, bored little creatures". He admits he talked "glibly" of "how the Spaniards lack all sense of business" and, fresh from the bull-fight where the clumsy bull "died of boredom", he noted "the standard of living was low/But that, we thought to ourselves, was not our business". Nevertheless, he felt that "Careless of visitors the people's mind/Was tunnelling like a mole to day and danger." The holiday over, they

> took the boat
> For home, forgetting Spain, not realising
> That Spain would soon denote
> Our grief, our aspirations;
> Not knowing that our blunt
> Ideals would find their whetstone, that our spirit
> Would find its frontier on the Spanish front,
> Its body in a rag-tag army.

Here is no real foresight of socialism's testing time, but instead a recognition of "not realising". Here is a scarcely concealed wish not to know, and annoyance with the more prescient. Here is an almost peevish desire to be left alone with the "*status quo*/Cut and dried for trippers". Here were two young men who "thought the papers a lark". Here are the picture postcards from a foreign holiday. Here is a final pious, almost perfunctory, avowal that in Spain our "blunt/Ideals would find their whetstone". Yet the Canto is impressive and stays in the mind. Why?

Is it because we recognize a common experience not frequently so clearly expressed nor set down with so much emotional, as well as intellectual, honesty? There are few Cornfords and Julian Bells. Though their convictions and their sacrifices may be admirable, it is not possible for most of us even to want to share their experience. These are greater heights than we are likely to achieve, and we are held back by a variety of reasons, among the more respectable being the liberal scepticism shared by MacNeice. He is aware that in noting that the "Women who dyed their hair should have it dyed more often" in the same breath as he dismisses the papers "With their party politics and blank invective", he is mentally avoiding commitment. This is what most of us do most of the time.

The other 'Spanish' Canto (XXIII) is both one of the least

committed poems about the Spanish conflict and one of the most apparently sincere. In this canto MacNeice is much affected by what he sees of the behaviour of people under stress, new and strange to him then, but later very familiar to all who lived through the 'forties. His attention is drawn to the number of "people in circulation" in the dark street who "still . . . manage to laugh". He notes with surprise that life, it seems, is more "than merely the bare/Permission to keep alive and receive orders", and that the tension admits "An interest in philately or pelota/Or private jokes". He describes the external details and effects of war. "The slender searchlights climb" (and remind him that "Our sins will find us out"). The "eye-/Sockets of the houses are empty". He feels the sky "pregnant with ill-will". He notes the "Guy Fawkes show" of an air raid

> And in the pauses of destruction
> The cocks in the centre of the town crow.
> The cocks crow in Barcelona
> Where clocks are few to strike the hour;
> Is it the heart's reveille or the sour
> Reproach of Simon Peter?

The two streams of observation, of things and of people, reflect the puzzled discontent of an intelligent man who goes into a world where "here and now the new valkyries ride".

He is puzzled and is obliged to attempt a revaluation. The first element of this is particularly interesting. We have come, he says "to a place in space where shortly/All of us may be forced to camp in time", a space-time relationship which echoes the thought in the first part of Cornford's poem 'Before the Storming of Huesca': "And time was inches . . . Crashes in lights and minutes". The same echo is heard when later in the canto MacNeice, taking himself to task, says he must "No longer think of time as a waterfall/Abstracted from a river". Cornford in a similar imagery splits time into three, and to him the past is a "glacier". "Time future, has no image in space" but "Time present is a cataract". MacNeice's self-analysis contrasts with Cornford's dedication.

It is the thought of the New Year, "Time for resolutions, for stock-taking", that causes MacNeice to reconsider his attitude to life, inspired by the new and strange atmosphere around him. He asks God, "if there is one", to help resolve "the antinomies in which we live", where the option is to be either negative and safe or "free on the edge of a razor". He admits that "for myself I cannot straiten/My broken rambling track", but he remembers his roots in Ireland, roots composed of revolution and civil war. In a strong passage he finds that all his heredity and upbringing have brought him

> only to the Present's arms –
> The arms not of a mistress but of a wrestler,
> Of a God who straddles over the night sky;

He finds himself in the grip of the intellectual's dilemma, "academic sophistry – /The original sin". He has, he says, taken life as it comes. Now he must try to "correlate event with instinct". He accuses himself of laziness, of being negative. Soon or late, he says, "the delights of self-pity must pall" (a passage which recalls Canto III where he says the final cure is "in a future of action, the will and fist/Of those who abjure the luxury of self-pity"). The "cynical admission of frustration" must pall also. The "stubborn heirs of freedom" who nightly brave the air-raids "shame/Our niggling equivocations". But at the end he describes the "cock crowing in Barcelona" not only as a challenge but as an 'aubade', a word which must surely have recalled to his mind that earlier poem of the name (dated November 1934) which embodies the same 'antinomies':

> Having bitten on life like a sharp apple
> Or, playing it like a fish, been happy,
>
> Having felt with fingers that the sky is blue,
> What have we after that to look forward to?
>
> Not the twilight of the gods but a precise dawn
> Of sallow and grey bricks, and newsboys crying war.

If MacNeice makes no statement in this canto which breaks through into commitment, the finely wrought poetry is a measure of his emotional response. The rhyme scheme takes a form found only in one other canto (XXI) where he is also, though on a more personal plane, emotionally engaged. The music underlines the feeling. "And the sirens cry in the dark morning", with its long, almost wailing vowel sounds followed by the briefer, more definite "And the lights go out and the town is still", are sharply evocative lines. He uses again the device of the list to emphasize monotony and allies it to a deliberate breaking of the stress: "Though they have no eggs, no milk, no fish, no fruit, no tobacco, no butter" is, of itself, no line of poetry, but in context it effectively conveys a sense of shock.

Some clue to his ability to refine on the expression of his observations can be found in the occasional comparison of his prose version in *The Strings are False* with the canto. In prose he speaks of "bone-white leafless plane trees". This becomes sharper, has wider associations and sets the opening tone as "The white plane-trees were bone-naked/And the issues plain" (a daring pun, which I think in this instance is effective). His description of the working-class district is compressed in the poem to "The shops are empty and in Barceloneta the eye-/Sockets of the houses are empty". *The Strings are False* says "The houses were like skulls without eyes, without jaws, there was no more flesh in the world", a description which probably takes the imagery too far.

MacNeice had paid his second visit to Spain at a time when he could expect that there his "blunt/Ideals would find their whetstone". The experience provoked a reassessment of his outlook and this was wrought into poetry; but the quality most lacking in his revaluation is enthusiasm. He sees that "human values remain". He appreciates that in war-time Barcelona "the soul has found its voice" but he qualifies this discovery by "here at least", implying that the voice, when found, fails to stir him. His prayer is for "greater vision", for making "half-truth true". He can only be glad "for any measure so far given" (which conveys no overpowering joy). He cannot deny the heroism and devotion of the people of Barcelona and their disregard for safety, but the most he can say of them was (and he was doubtless aware of the doctrinal differences which divided them almost as sharply from each other as from their enemies): "these people contain truth, whatever/Their nominal façade".

MacNeice has been compared to a "post-Prufrock" Hamlet, "as irresolute as Shakespeare's prince". Certainly he takes up no clear political position. The domestic struggles of the 'thirties were seen, at the time, as a 'class' struggle, and MacNeice's indecisive political attitude is reflected in, and may indeed spring from, his ambivalent attitude towards class. From the guilt induced by their public school superiority his contemporaries sought expiation; Auden in verses like 'A Communist to Others', Spender in agony over 'An Elementary School Class Room in a Slum', and Day-Lewis by railing at "Scavenger Barons" and their "jackal vassals" in *The Magnetic Mountain*. Somehow all three contrived to appear like over-dressed visitors to a working-class Sunday School Treat; an air of condescension pervades their verses. MacNeice observed the world with irony; if he felt that, on the basis of every intellectual analysis, he should support the socialist cause, he could not pretend to a fire in his belly which was not there in truth. As Scarfe says "His intellectual honesty . . . kept this poet apart from the impetuous stream of Left poets."

Autumn Journal opens, strangely enough, with an ironic and, in so far as it is overdrawn, a sarcastic description of the 'County'. Although he is describing the 'county' of Hampshire, one is reminded, by the querulous tone, of his dislike for "the gentry" to which he gives vent in a typically personal digression in his commissioned pot-boiler, *The Zoo*: "As for the gentry" he says there, "I did not like them. They were patronising and snobbish and, it seemed to me, hostile." He had already described their probable fate in 'An Eclogue for Christmas', written five years earlier and published in 1935:

> The country gentry cannot change, they will die in their shoes
> From angry circumstance and moral self-abuse,

In 1938 they were still there (as they are today) and *Autumn Journal* opens with the intellectual's quick impatience with the ritual of their lives:

> And roses on a rustic trellis and mulberry trees
> And bacon and eggs in a silver dish for breakfast
> And all the inherited assets of bodily ease
> And all the inherited worries, rheumatism and taxes,
> And whether Stella will marry and what to do with Dick

At the same time there is more than a little nostalgic love for the home that

> is still a sanctum under the pelmets,
> All quiet on the Family Front,

When MacNeice considers the working class (we are using the terminology still permissible in the late 'thirties) he finds an ironical attitude equally appropriate. There is compassion in his realization that each holiday, "the annual spree", calls for stamina to get through to the next one. He can appreciate clearly enough how

> the till and the typewriter call the fingers,
> The workman gathers his tools
> For the eight-hour day

and he appreciates the solace that may be found in films, football pools, gossip and cuddle. He knew from personal experience those moments of self-indulgence that put "blinkers on the eyes of doubt". He sees most men as "accepters, born and bred to harness", and then tries to persuade himself that the present system is "utterly lost and daft" *because* it gives

> a few at fancy prices
> Their fancy lives
> While ninety-nine in the hundred who never attend the
> banquet
> Must wash the grease of ages off the knives.

Then in a passage which can be accepted either as devastating

honesty, or cowardly refusal to accept responsibility, according
to the critic's habit of mind and political outlook, MacNeice
stands, as Ian Hamilton puts it, in a "confessional stance" and
admits that

> It is so hard to imagine
> A world where the many would have their chance without
> A fall in the standard of intellectual living

His codicil

> There is no reason for thinking
> That, if you give a chance to people to think or live,
> The arts of thought or life will suffer and become rougher
> And not return more than you could ever give.

is left with the bare statement, is not developed and is unconvincing. Ian Hamilton finds this "limp" and half-hearted, and
the affirmation of social responsibility in Canto II he feels is
"frigid". We are reminded that in *The Strings are False* MacNeice
tells us how at this time he was friendly with Reggie Smith, "the
son of a working man", (later, as a producer of plays and features,
a close friend and colleague of MacNeice's at the B.B.C.), who
"thought that nothing was so funny as the Oxford and Cambridge
'proletarianisers'."

The main political background mood to *Autumn Journal* is the
threat of war. Not war in Vietnam, not in a "far away country of
which we know little" (as Chamberlain said of Czechoslovakia in
1938) but "in England, now!" So "posters flapping on the railings
tell the fluttered/World that Hitler speaks, that Hitler speaks"
(Canto V). The repetition of the phrase recreates the unbeliev-
ingly mesmeric effect of those broadcast tirades. They left us
dazed; it was so mad, why should it be meaningful? "And we
cannot take it in and we go to our daily/Jobs to the dull refrain of
the caption 'War' ". He catches the atmosphere of unbelieving
fear, "And we laugh it off and go round town in the evening",
where we try to think that life is normal, that we care that "the
Australians have lost their last by ten/Wickets". More immediate

and weightier worries force their way into our minds and we think of "Hodza, Henlein, Hitler/The Maginot Line", the foreign men and places with which our lives become suddenly involved. We get our news from "Special editions snatched and read abruptly". This picture of the frenetic attempts most men make to keep pace in a world of 'news' is contrasted with MacNeice's view of the problem as so all-embracing as to be well-nigh insoluble; he saw it as too great for the ordinary citizen.

Auden in the memorial broadcast of 1966 said that political commitment could be a serious threat to the integrity of a writer but "Louis MacNeice, to his eternal credit, resisted . . . better than most". This detachment was denigrated by W. H. Mellers in *Scrutiny*, because MacNeice's feelings did not "differ materially from those of the average sensible 'man in the street' " (a strange basis for adverse comment); nor was it later appreciated except as a kind of "evasive honesty". Perhaps now, when we are more accustomed to the intellectual difficulties of acceptance and have seen the public martyrdom of men like Oppenheimer, we may have more sympathy and more quickening of the pulse for the poetry of one who is not prepared to make a choice. So we are not surprised when we come to Canto VII that

> one – meaning I – is bored, am bored, the issue
> Involving principle but bound in fact
> To squander principle in panic and self-deception –

an analysis which does indeed come close to that of the man in the street, or the taxi-driver who says "It turns me up/When I see these soldiers in lorries". The taxi-driver makes immediate contact with the intellectual whose mind hears the "rumble of tumbrils/Drums in the trees/Breaking the eardrums of the ravished dryads". In four lines MacNeice explains his boredom with the age-old repetition of the same war theme. We pass from 1938 to the French Revolution, to the war drums of the Ashanti, to the destruction of classic Greece. If these are the feelings of the average sensible man in the street, and they may well be, then they are fit subject for poetry. What else should he feel in the face of "Conferences, adjournments, ultimatums" and Chamberlain's "Flights in the air"? MacNeice's perspective is true.

In the midst of these threats, these impossible certainties, it is the small things that remain in the memory and make, sometimes, the deepest scar. In Canto V MacNeice has remembered that Primrose Hill, which he can see from the window of his flat, was once a gun emplacement. Now in Canto VII: "I hear dull blows on wood outside my window;/They are cutting down the trees on Primrose Hill" and in an image of stark distaste: "The wood is white like the roast flesh of chicken". (He was sensitive to the bareness of trees; in Canto XXIII "The white plane-trees were bone-naked.") He goes to St John's Wood police station to reclaim his dog. The horror is that from this normal placid background we

> must, in order to beat
> The enemy, model ourselves upon the enemy,
>> A howling radio for our paraclete.
> The night continues wet, the axe keeps falling,
>> The hill grows bald and bleak
> No longer one of the sights of London but maybe
>> We shall have fireworks here by this day week.

MacNeice designs the next canto (VIII) so that the sour moment of repeal when

> The crisis is put off and things look better
> And we feel negotiation is not vain –
>> Save my skin and damn my conscience.
> And negotiation wins,
>> If you can call it winning,
> And here we are – just as before – safe in our skins;

is enshrined in a nostalgic review of life as it had been in the few previous years:

> Sun shines easy, sun shines gay
>> On bug-house, warehouse, brewery, market,
> On the chocolate factory and the B.S.A.,
>> On the Greek town hall and Josiah Mason;

On the Mitchells and Butlers Tudor pubs,
On the white police and the one-way traffic
And glances off the chromium hubs
And the metal studs in the sleek macadam.

The "bug-house" was the semi-affectionate term for the Birmingham local cinema, not used so frequently now, and one hopes with reason. Cadbury's of Bournville was an all-pervasive influence on the south of the city, and the Birmingham Small Arms factory dominated the area to the south-east, while the Aston area smelt of malt. Birmingham Town Hall is in neo-classic style and is overlooked by a statue of Josiah Mason, built in Chamberlain Square outside Mason College, then housing the Arts and Medical faculties of the University, and now demolished. 'M. & B.'s' pubs were all very much in one mock-Tudor style. The compressed picture is evocative, as is that of the "prison-like lecture room". If a reference to "Homer in a Dudley accent" appears class-conscious, the pervasiveness of the Black Country intonation is some defence and it certainly has (or had) odd, though not necessarily displeasing, effects when deployed poetically. The essence of those times, for MacNeice, for many other young people, is summed up in:

But nobody cared, for the days were early.
Nobody niggled, nobody cared,
The soul was deaf to the mounting debit,
The soul was unprepared
But the firelight danced on the ply-wood ceiling.
We drove round Shropshire in a bijou car –
Bewdley, Cleobury Mortimer, Ludlow –
And the map of England was a toy bazaar
And the telephone wires were idle music.
And sun shone easy, sun shone hard
On quickly dropping pear-tree blossom
And pigeons courting in the cobbled yard
With flashing necks and notes of thunder.
We slept in linen, we cooked with wine,
We paid in cash and took no notice

Of how the train ran down the line
    Into the sun against the signal.
We lived in Birmingham through the slump –
    Line your boots with a piece of paper –
Sunlight dancing on the rubbish dump,
    On the queues of men and the hungry chimneys.

So he looks back on 1931 from 1938; and now he has "No
wife, no ivory tower, no funk-hole"; it is from the subjective
standpoint of private desolation that he regards the possibility of
dislocation of normal life in war. He goes to the music hall
"packed to the roof and primed for laughter", seeking, as so many
did, a temporary escape from reality, and he listens to "the
ukelele and the comic chestnuts" (of George Formby perhaps?)
until the next day he can say

    Glory to God for Munich.
And stocks go up and wrecks
    Are salved and politicians' reputations
Go up like Jack-on-the-Beanstalk; only the Czechs
    Go down and without fighting.

This betrayal he underlines at the end of Canto XVIII in which he
is considering the philosophical and religious implications of the
time, when he says

No wonder many would renounce their birthright,
    The responsibility of moral choice,
And sit with a mess of pottage taking orders
    Out of a square box from a mad voice –

R. L. Cooke says "No other modern poet has depicted the dying
throes of the life that was swept away by the war as directly or as
vividly as MacNeice" (*Poetry Review*, May/June 1947).

Rarely has the frenetic attempt made by so many in the 'thirties
to hide from themselves the present horrors and the threatened
future of which they were more than half aware, been so fully
expressed as in Canto XV. The canto is a picture of frustrated
despair half-buried in a round of pastime. The pastimes range
over the field of pleasure, amusement and escapism, from Shelley

to hymn tunes. They draw on the literature of the past and of the
world, "Rome and Ionia/And Florence and Provence and Spain".
They include the sheerly sensuous:

> give me a new Muse with stocking and suspenders
> And a smile like a cat,
> With false eyelashes and finger-nails of carmine
> And dressed by Schiaparelli, with a pill-box hat.
> . . .
> Give me a houri but houris are too easy,
> Give me a nun;

and the sensational such as motor-racing, strip-tease, all-in
wrestling. This is nearly 30 years ago, but we may well wonder
whether if we looked over our shoulders from the midst of
similar diversions, we should not see, as MacNeice saw, those

> Walking in file, slowly in file;
> They have no shoes on their feet, the knobs of their ankles
>   Catch the moonlight as they pass the stile
> And cross the moor among the skeletons of bog-oak
>   Following the track from the gallows back to the town;
> Each has the end of a rope around his neck. I wonder
>   Who let these men come back, who cut them down —
> And now they reach the gate and line up opposite
>   The neon lights on the medieval wall
> And underneath the sky-signs
>   Each one takes his cowl and lets it fall
> And we see their faces, each the same as the other,
>   Men and women, each like a closed door,
> But something about their faces is familiar;
>   Where have we seen them before?
> Was it the murderer on the nursery ceiling
>   Or Judas Iscariot in the Field of Blood
> Or someone at Gallipoli or in Flanders
>   Caught in the end-all mud?
> But take no notice of them, out with the ukelele,
>   The saxophone and the dice;
> They are sure to go away if we take no notice;
>   Another round of drinks or make it twice.

If like the poet and his contemporaries we decide to take no notice, but to return to another round of drinks and the songs of the negroes or the Greeks, we shall find that whatever our denials these men and women will still be there. We cannot surely agree with the critic in *Scrutiny* that this is "a lot of 'Come on boys, we aren't afraid of the bogies give us another drink stuff, with the bogies winning on points all round, despite the handicap of a coil of rope round the neck.' " It is more than that. It is no invocation to action. Its anger at our inability to rise above "Pearls in wine" is the anger of frustration. It is savagely critical and the poet includes himself in his condemnation. That it offers no solution is its limitation.

MacNeice in his attitude to the international complications of his day, and to the political situation, mirrors the attitude of a large section of the contemporary intelligentsia. Despairing of achieving action, or influencing political thought, the critical analysis is drained of hope and foreshadows only the inevitability of disaster. It is not enough to say "there will be sunlight later". There is an overriding sense of failure. Though this has made poetry in *Autumn Journal*, there will always be those who find its lack of positive idealism a factor which limits their appreciation. There are two schools of thought. The anonymous critic of *The Times Literary Supplement* in 1949 obviously did not feel it enough to be left with the "unhappy ruminations of the average intellectual man" about the "discouraging days of Munich", even if they look at times oddly like 'Maud'. But Cyril Connolly is probably nearer to the truth when he finds *Autumn Journal* preserves "for ever the uneasy atmosphere of Munich", or Larkin when he describes it as "brilliant quotidian reportage". And the last word may well rest with R. L. Cooke: "the future will be able to turn back to find vivid documentation and a truer guide to 'Munich time' than most of the prose that has since been spawned by biased politicians and others can offer."

IV

Perhaps MacNeice was infatuated with Mariette, rather than in love with her. Perhaps in place of a crusading urge he felt only a moral obligation to be politically conscious. Certainly when he considers the philosophies of this world, his attitude is ironical and verges on the cynical. He is not really capable of reverence for any system of thought solely because it exists. Although a classical scholar of ability, he felt that he had become an "impresario of the Ancient Greeks" and he contemplated them and their philosophies with no scales on his eyes. "They plotted out their life with truism and humour". He sees them after the heroic age as a race of professors, secretaries and clerks whose world is chopped by "the humanist in his room with Jacobean panels" to "turn a sermon/To the greater glory of God". This is a bitter analysis of verbal scholarship and says little for the glory either of scholarship, God or Greece. Yet strangely enough, it is in the envoi to Canto IX that the classical scholar brings the world of Greece to life, and in so doing displays his own viewpoint on society in all times. Although he concludes "It was all so un-imaginably different/And all so long ago", he must have been aware that he was describing the world of his own day in confessing that when he should remember the paragons of Hellas, he thought instead of

> the crooks, the adventurers, the opportunists,
> The careless athletes and the fancy boys,
> The hair-splitters, the pedants, the hard-boiled sceptics
> And the Agora and the noise
> Of the demagogues and the quacks; and the women pouring
> Libations over graves
> And the trimmers at Delphi and the dummies at Sparta and
> lastly
> I think of the slaves.
> And how one can imagine oneself among them
> I do not know;

It was all so unimaginably different
And all so long ago.

In the face of this he cannot enthusiastically chop "the Ancient World to make a sermon/To the greater glory of God".

As the poem shifts and turns, as MacNeice pursues his task of composing a metaphoric portrait of himself, so in *Autumn Journal* from time to time he makes a tentative examination of the philosophies which set out to reconcile man and his universe. In Canto II he shows us that he is familiar with the Hegelian philosophy of Being and with Schopenhauer's Nirvana. As we should expect from one so affected by the impact of the physical world on the senses, he finds that "Becoming is a match for Being". He is a creature of the combination of time and place. He cannot live as pure essence and so he comes to the conclusion, banal perhaps, that

I must go out to-morrow as the others do
And build the falling castle;
Which has never fallen, thanks
Not to any formula, red tape or institution,
Not to any creeds or banks,
But to the human animal's endless courage.

This is surely poetic expression of the bourgeois ethic (which others beside Ian Hamilton have found "frigid"). It is the outlook of those who know that "None of our hearts are pure, we always have mixed motives" (Canto III), but can say (Canto XII)

All that I would like to be is human, having a share
In a civilised, articulate and well-adjusted
Community where the mind is given its due
But the body is not distrusted.
As it is, the so-called humane studies
May lead to cushy jobs
But leave the men who land them spiritually bankrupt
Intellectual snobs.
Not but what I am glad to have my comforts,
Better authentic mammon than a bogus god;

If it were not for Lit.Hum. I might be climbing
   A ladder with a hod.

This is very understandable, indeed humdrum, thinking, but is
none the less admissible and in its way admirable. He spoils the
effect when he concludes Canto XIII with

They don't want any philosopher-kings in England,
   There ain't no universals in this man's town.

and gives vent to a kind of pettish anger, as though he blamed
society for his own failure to comprehend. He comes nearer to
his true agnostic attitude in Canto XVII when he admits

the mind that did not doubt would not be mind
   And discontent is eternal.

This is the canto in which he comes closest to a clear explanation
of his fundamental attitude:

even the sense of taste provides communion
   With God as plant or beast;
The sea in fish, the field in a salad of endive,
   A sacramental feast.

Our virtue, he says "is invested, the self put out at interest", but,
and here for MacNeice is the crux of his eternal disillusion, "the
fact compares/So badly with the fancy". Perhaps it was not
always so. Day-Lewis writing on *The Poetic Image* uses some lines
of Canto XVIII to illustrate his point (which concerns the
universality of poetic images) that the modern industrial world
has robbed mankind of mutual understanding. MacNeice, with
no great originality, feels that

Things were different when men felt their programme
   In the bones and pulse, not only in the brain,
Born to a trade, a belief, a set of affections;
   That instinct for belief may sprout again,
There are some who have never lost it
   And some who foster or force it into growth
But most of us lack the right discontent, contented
   Merely to cavil.

In a metaphor that reminds us of forceful Christian sermonizing he says

> Spiritual sloth
> Creeps like lichen or ivy over the hinges
> Of the doors which never move;

Are these perhaps "our own clay shuttered doors" of Thompson's 'Kingdom of God', are they Milton's "living doors" of heaven, or the doors in Holman Hunt's painting, 'The Light of the World'? Perhaps they are all three, since we cannot remember who is behind them or even if they conceal a fairy tale, the Holy Ghost or utilitarian philosophy. He can find no comfort in any of these and in fact will go so far as to say

> If everything that happens happens according
> To the nature and wish of God, then God must go;

His Christian upbringing hangs round him like a cloak whose folds he cannot escape, its imagery is always with him, he finds "the trees are naked/As the three crosses on the hill". This is a compromise between his sensuous approach and his apprenticeship to Christian imagery, and in so far as there is compromise rather than conflict, the poetry is robbed of force and diminished in stature. It is on this muted note that *Autumn Journal* ends.

In Canto XXI he returns in part to the experience of the diversity of the world he describes in 'Snow'. Once again we have the flowers, this time "chrysanthemums and dahlias". He tries to take the view of Marcus Aurelius that we must appreciate both the world of man and the world of the gods, but he does not find this easy and can only ask

> Can you not take it merely on trust that life is
> The only thing worth living and that dying
> Had better be left to take care of itself in the end?

> For to have been born is in itself a triumph
> Among all that waste of sperm

And it is gratitude to wait the proper term
  Or, if not gratitude, duty.
  . . .
We shan't have another chance to dance and shout
  Once the flames are silent.

V

There is nothing startling or inspiring in MacNeice's philosophizing in *Autumn Journal*. It is the common sense escape from
the apparent rigours and restrictions of schematic and abstractive
thinking. There is nothing extraordinary in his personal story of
infatuation and lost love. There is nothing outstanding in his
social comment and criticism and his half-hearted attempt at
political contributions. With so little original material in three
major themes of this personal chronicle, what are the qualities
that make it a success? Rees in the 1966 broadcast described it as
a "masterpiece of sustained inspiration". Ian Hamilton feels "there
is a range and accuracy of observation, a lively grasp of the
frenetic bored excess of a threatened social order which are
quite admirable" and that "it is the range and variety of social
experience, the details of its surface, that delights him". The
appeal of *Autumn Journal* surely lies in the concept of engaging us
by means of a poetic journal in the poet's personal reaction to his
environment. MacNeice's gift was his extreme sensitivity to the
world in which he lived allied to a craftsmanship which translated
his apprehension and his physical perception into poetry. It is this
capacity which entrances us from the first canto, which is, after
all, not very original in its subject matter. We are immediately,
and almost physically, translated to the counties where "close
clipped yew/Insulates the lives". The observation is acute and
descriptive, immediately evocative, "spyglasses hung in the hall
and the prayer-books ready in the pew" and "bacon and eggs in a
silver dish for breakfast". There is the realistic and yet nostalgic

description of "Farmyard noises across the fields at evening/
While the trucks of the Southern Railway dawdle . . . shunt/Into
poppy sidings for the night – ". By comparison his own conception
of what living should be is in sensory terms:

> Following the curve of a planet or controlled water
>   But a leap in the dark, a tangent, a stray shot.

We then have our attention shifted to

> Surbiton, and a woman gets in, painted
>   With dyed hair but a ladder in her stocking and eyes
> Patient beneath the calculated lashes,
>   Inured for ever to surprise;
> And the train's rhythm becomes the *ad nauseam* repetition
>   Of every tired aubade and maudlin madrigal,
> The faded airs of sexual attraction
>   Wandering like dead leaves along a warehouse wall:

This is a strong compassionate description rendered all the more
effective by the inevitable recollection of the dead leaves of
Shelley's 'Ode to the West Wind' – "ghosts from an enchanter
fleeing". Then comes a love song of bought love which is full of
imagery that relates it both to fantasy and modern life, "I loved
my love with a platform ticket", prosy companion of lovers'
meetings, and "A jazz song", the eternal seeking for the background cinematic angelic choir. "Till life did us part I loved her
with paper money/And with whisky on the breath". This is
scathing realism, and if it contrasts with the unreal "peacock's
eyes and the wares of Carthage" and with "the wings of angels/
Dipped in henna, unearthly red", we are brought back sharply by
the line that reduces it all to nothing, "And lots of other stuff"
and by the practicality of the last line of this catalogue, in which
he tells us that he loved his love

> With my office hours, with flowers and sirens,
>   With my budget, my latchkey, and my daily bread.

This has the painful honesty of one who cannot deceive himself
and is aware of the ultimate lack of value in an association which,

while itself on the lowest level, is touched by the wings of a romance which it can but mimic. The last two lines of Canto I close on a modern image to which he often returns; the moving staircase of the Underground seems to him, with the evanescent relationship of those moving up and down upon them, to be a particularly apt allegory of modern life, in which men are so much together – and never more solitary:

> And so to London and down the ever-moving
>   Stairs
> Where a warm wind blows the bodies of men together
> And blows apart their complexes and cares.

We get close to MacNeice's strength as a poetic observer and his dilemma as a man unable or unwilling to forego the appearance for the essence in Canto XVII, where he is describing the early morning in his flat overlooking London and says:

> I light my first cigarette, grow giddy and blink,
> Glad of this titillation, this innuendo,
>   This make-believe of standing on a brink;
> For all our trivial daily acts are altered
>   Into heroic or romantic make-believe
> Of which we are hardly conscious –

This is a shrewd observation indeed; this is a daily, frequent unregarded act, caught for all time in poetry, and more nearly explained then than in a wealth of panegyrics on and counter-blasts to tobacco. He continues with a sensuous (truly the word here) description which recalls such occasions and is the very quintessence of enjoying a bath. As one reads one can feel the "strata/Of cold water and hot" on the skin, see "Ascending scrolls of steam" (an excellent word, 'scrolls', for the wisps that roll, unform and reform) "between tiled walls". We actually 'feel', physically, "feel the ego merge as the pores open" so that "responsibility dies" and does so because thought is surrendered to sensation "and the thighs are happy/And the body purrs like a cat".

These are direct, sharp, sensory descriptions and there are

many others throughout the poem. Conrad Aiken, writing in 1941, speaks of "the bright rush of nominal images, the gay prodigality of scene". One recalls the carpet-sweepers in the Corner House that "Advance between the tables after crumbs/ Inexorably, like a tank battalion/In answer to the drums", a simile which is apt at any time, but more so when war threatened. One recalls "The housewife with her shopping bag/Watches the cleaver catch the naked/New Zealand sheep between the legs – ". It is the "posters flapping on the railings" that "tell the fluttered/ World that Hitler speaks". It is when "the meter clicks and the cistern bubbles" that "the gods are absent". He describes "these bald-at-thirty Englishmen whose polished/Foreheads are the tombs of record sales". The physical fear of war, "The heavy panic that cramps the lungs and presses/The collar down the spine" has rarely been more immediately described.

Almost everywhere we look, we find the image is immediate, civilized, even scientific, and related to the life around MacNeice. It is this immediacy which misleads critics like D. S. Savage who finds in MacNeice "a failure of that deep seriousness which might have enabled him to set life in its perspectives". This is the age-old difficulty of the critics endowed with 'gravitas' to realize how close to truth the higher levity may come. Why did Mac-Neice succeed where others, more involved in the issues of the day, failed to convey its special poignancy? Day-Lewis was then a card-carrying Communist, though one who had already commended MacNeice's poetry as "a salutary corrective" to the facile political optimism of the poets of *The Left Review*. Auden in the 'thirties, as he later explained to Spender, was basing his politics and the political aspects of his writing, on the conviction that the anti-Fascists could really stop the war. In *The Strings are False* we have a wry glimpse of Spender in glorious disagreement with his fellow Communists. Day-Lewis was disillusioned. Spender soldiered idealistically on, Auden found himself in America after his Far Eastern journey and in the end became an American citizen. Only MacNeice maintained his position. A little with-drawn, a little cynical, sensuous, critical, not in the least willing to allow either compassion, or dialectic, or emotion, to lead him to conclusions of which he was not convinced, he never believed that salvation lay in any system either religious, philosophical, or political. *Autumn Journal* is a personal testament. The world was judged in personal terms.

The attraction of *Autumn Journal* lies in this: it is a predominantly romantic poem by a predominantly romantic poet. In the last canto he speaks of "my various and conflicting/Selves I have so long endured". From this stems the seriousness which Savage could not appreciate. Here is the poet composing a symbolic portrait of himself in his metamorphoses. And his language is to him the common language of his urban world, as surely as, perhaps more surely than, Wordsworth's was the language of rural inspiration. His aim, as he says in his prefatory Note, was to write what he felt at the moment. He succeeded; that very special moment is caught for all time.

CHAPTER THREE

Poems of the war years

The outbreak of war, even the development of the conflict, brought no change in MacNeice's personal approach to poetry. In the next three books, *Plant and Phantom* (1941), *Springboard* (1944), and *Holes in the Sky* (1948) the influence of the war is not greater than the other and more permanent influences. The dominant themes are still first, self, studied and pored over in the light of a recollected childhood; secondly, society, seen for the most part subjectively, but in these volumes, in the light of war-time work and consequent new experiences and of the aftermath of war; and finally, philosophy, the continuous emotional half-sincere, half-intellectual and insufficiently dedicated search for a meaning to life, and death.

Slight as it is, 'Autobiography' is the epitome of the despairing nostalgic contemplation of his childhood which cast a net over MacNeice's mind, which "amounted almost to an obsession" and from which he tried to escape by writing (also in 1941) the manuscript of *The Strings are False* "as a necessary act of catharsis". His sister points out that this poem expresses his feelings at the death of his mother 27 years earlier, when he was seven, and we perhaps owe to his recollected emotion the plangent refrain *"Come back early or never come"*. Whether the poem has in itself the depth that can be attributed to it from a knowledge of *The Strings are False* is open to doubt.

Opening with a statement of childish simplicity which conjures up the enormously large garden of the second home, the poem moves to the other element in the Oedipus triangle in which MacNeice found himself permanently trapped, "My father" who "made the walls resound". In *The Strings are False* he tells us "I could hear his voice below in the study . . . and I knew he was alone – intoning away, communing with God". When in the poem MacNeice says "He wore his collar the wrong way round" he is exorcizing with flippancy the impression on his childish mind of one whom he found somewhat alarming.

Yellow seems to have been for MacNeice a colour associated with the people of his childhood. In *The Strings are False* he says "My sister wore yellow shoes", "my mother made cakes in a big yellow bowl". Then he adds "My mother kept being ill, and at last was ill all the time". So when he sees her in his poem, he says of her "My mother wore a yellow dress;/Gently, gently, gentleness." When his mother, with whom he had spent so much of his time, fell into melancholy and then left, the little boy, not unnaturally, suffered a period of "black dreams". "Oh God" he would pray "I do not want to have any dreams". "When I was five" he says in 'Autobiography' (do we need to be pedantic about his actual age?) "the black dreams came;/Nothing after was quite the same." We are reminded of the "black racks" of 'Prayer Before Birth'. Death, another dominant theme of his poetry, was an early acquaintance for MacNeice. In *The Strings are False* he says "and the other side of the hedge was the cemetery, you could hear the voice of the minister tucking people into the ground." So, in the poem, "The dark was talking to the dead". Sharing a room with his father, who arrived with "the lamp and his own gigantic shadow", he found "The lamp was dark beside my bed". The adults of a world without his mother were not concerned about his night fears and indeed, when a child he was scolded for causing his father to come and comfort him. His terror was silent because he was, as he says in *The Strings are False*, "frightened to say he was frightened". The last three verses of 'Autobiography' are desolate:

When I woke they did not care;
Nobody, nobody was there.

Come back early or never come.

When my silent terror cried,
Nobody, nobody replied.

Come back early or never come.

I got up; the chilly sun
Saw me walk away alone.

Come back early or never come.

for, he said "I wanted to be rid of my family and start making good".

'Christina', another almost macabre nostalgic recollection of childhood, is also a potted psychological case history. The event which inspired it is related in *The Strings are False* and derives from the same period of his early childhood which inspired 'Autobiography'. It is simple: he built brick houses for his sister's doll, which one day fell and broke and was seen to be hollow. The poem retells the story, but in it the doll which

smiled while you dressed her
And when you then undressed her
She kept a smiling face.

becomes "a lady/Somewhere seen before". We read of

Building motley houses
And knocking down your houses
And always building more.

We are reminded of the home he established with 'Mariette' and

which they "modernised". She left him and explained that everyone "had always treated her as a freak or a doll". So

> He heard the name Christina
> And suddenly saw Christina
> Dead on the nursery floor.

This little episode told both in prose and poetry casts an interesting light on his infatuation for 'Mariette' as an indirect mother
substitute, a substitute for his sister's doll (with her "yellow"
head) with which he played at houses and which had been a
comfort to him as his mother withdrew into illness. In a Third
Programme broadcast E. R. Dodds said of Louis and 'Mariette':
"They played an endless, innocent game of keeping house". So
when MacNeice "went to bed with a lady/Somewhere seen
before", it was in one more of the "motley houses".

The postscript to 'Christina', 'The Old Story', the first of the
'Novelettes', describes another actual experience told in prose
in *The Strings are False*. "The shore of a cold sea in winter" was
Atlantic City where he met 'Mariette', now remarried after their
divorce. He found her

> The same but different and he found the difference
> A surgeon's knife without an anaesthetic;
> He had known of course that this happens
> But had not guessed the pain of it or the panic,
>
> And could not say 'My love', could hardly
> Say anything at all, no longer knowing
> Whom he was talking to but watched the water
> Massing for action on the cold horizon.

The bitterness of 'Christina' and 'The Old Story' makes a
sharp contrast with the excitement of 'Meeting Point', a lyric
poem celebrating the moment at which love is recognized. It is
also the meeting point of two of MacNeice's major themes, the
personal and the philosophical. It is a love poem: the realization
of love has placed their meeting "At the still point of the turning
world". In MacNeice's words: "Time was away and somewhere

else". The experience of suspended time at some emotional moment is not unusual. The rendering of this in 'Meeting Point' has its philosophical background in Eliot's *Burnt Norton* of which the last few lines of Part II and the final 20 lines may well have been in MacNeice's mind. The modern idiom heightens the age-old experience, and "My true-love has my heart and I have his" becomes "two people with one pulse" (Man, remember, is described in 'Plant and Phantom' as "a pump of blood"). The "moving stairs" which so often imaged for MacNeice the remorse-less passage of time were now "neither up nor down", like the armies of the noble Duke of York. Although they sat in a coffee shop where others, he would remember, had "measured out their lives with coffee spoons", for them "The stream's music did not stop/Flowing through heather" and (like coffee) is "limpid brown". The stillness of time is fixed by the bell (again with memories of *Burnt Norton*):

> Holding its inverted poise –
> Between the clang and clang a flower,
> A brazen calyx of no noise:

and we remember the phrase "calyx of ice" from 'Plant and Phantom' as one discipline that Man had imposed on flux. So here it represents triumph over the flux of time. As the experience places the lovers apart from time, so it places them in infinity of space which was still their Meeting Point:

> The camels crossed the miles of sand
> That stretched around the cups and plates;
> The desert was their own, they planned
> To portion out the stars and dates:
> The camels crossed the miles of sand.
>
> Time was away and somewhere else.
> The waiter did not come, the clock
> Forgot them and the radio waltz
> Came out like water from a rock:
> Time was away and somewhere else.

Her fingers flicked away the ash
That bloomed again in tropic trees:
Not caring if the markets crash
When they had forests such as these,
Her fingers flicked away the ash.

Forests and deserts were theirs and for this, he says in existentialist terms, may God (a long step indeed for his agnosticism,
but he qualifies it by adding "or whatever means the Good") "Be
praised that time can stop like this", and

That what the heart has understood
Can verify in the body's peace
God or whatever means the Good.

Conrad Aiken places 'Meeting Point' among the best of the
lyrics and notes in particular the "very skilful use of a vernacular
refrain to dignify a sentimental theme".

It is not perhaps too fanciful to think that 'Meeting Point'
referred to an early occasion with Hedli Anderson whom he
married in 1942 and to whom he dedicated *Springboard*. In this
dedication he says:

Because the velvet image,
Because the lilting measure,
No more convey my meaning
I am compelled to use
Such words as disabuse
My mind of casual pleasure

As if to prove it, he opens the volume with 'Prayer Before
Birth'. This is a poem so consistently misunderstood that the
B.B.C. in 1966 permitted its use most inappropriately in the
prologue to a Christmas service. Anthony Thwaite finds 'Prayer
Before Birth' one of MacNeice's "most ambitious and technically
adventurous poems" and feels that "the shape of the poem itself
is an expression of its theme – the slow hesitant urging forth of
the child from the womb". This may well be to mistake liturgical
rhythms for anatomical ones; but it is true that it is a poem which

originated in MacNeice's obsession with his own life and especially his childhood. Its greater merit is that it contains the universal in the particular and reflects the despair and resentment of mankind trapped in the inescapable toils of war.

The opening phrase, "I am not yet born", repeated as a refrain at the beginning of each prayer, is a revulsion from the traumatic experience of entering the world and a desire for a return to the womb, a desire exaggerated for MacNeice by the early death of his mother. As we know from *The Strings are False* the influences to which the imaginative child was exposed from that time onward encouraged fantasies and the irrational fears that spring from them. Escape back to the womb concentrated all these fears, and the more rational fears of later life, into the greater fear of facing birth again.

To return and face the world again the poet needs reassurance and as the son of a clergyman he seeks it in prayer. He calls it 'Prayer Before Birth' and chooses for it a liturgical form; but it is noticeable that even in these circumstances he does not escape from his agnosticism. He must pray, he feels the need for prayer, he prays; but he never at any point in the poem exposes the object to which he appeals.

His first prayer is for protection against the vampires, rodents and ghouls that menace childhood from a myriad fairy stories, and inform folk tales and black magic. (Did he ever see the popular poker-work charm of the 'twenties known as the 'Cornish Litany' – "From ghoolies and ghosties and long-leggity beasties, Good Lord deliver us"?) He asks for consolation because he fears that the human race may "with tall walls wall me" (it was a time of concentration and prisoner-of-war camps), or that he may be drugged and lured with "wise lies"; and one is reminded again that in *Modern Poetry* he lists as one of the "things" that conditioned his poetry "A liking, now dead, for metaphysics". He fears, in prosody reminiscent of Hopkins, that the "human race" will with "black racks rack me" and that it will "in blood-baths roll me". This was perhaps not only a fear of war, but also a recollection of that unpleasant aspect of Christianity which demands "Wash me in the blood of the Lamb", a ritual concept he must, as a rector's son, have heard many times, but from which, with his clear apprehension of the sensory world, he must have revolted. His recent reading of Eliot must have reminded him of

> The dripping blood our only drink,
> The bloody flesh our only food

a stark, indeed horrific, rendering of the puritan complex of guilt and hope.

The third verse of 'Prayer Before Birth', the only hopeful stanza in the poem, is the only one which seems to provide any real reason for birth. Even here the imagery is overlaid with psychology of the womb. In a uterine image he asks that he be provided with "water to dandle me", using in "dandle" a word with a Miltonic connotation of innocence:

> Sporting the lion ramped, and in his paw
> Dandled the kid

He turns the pleasure of nature inward to himself:

> provide me
> With water to dandle me, grass to grow for me, trees to talk
>   to me, sky to sing to me, birds and a white light
>   in the back of my mind to guide me.

Why does the sky sing and whom do the birds guide, and is MacNeice's "white light" a memory of Vaughan's "white, celestial thought"?

In the next verse he asks for forgiveness; but this is ironical, for even his sins are those to be committed by the world in him; while his words and thoughts strictly condition him, a Pavlovian, or behaviourist outlook. He prays for forgiveness at the same time foreseeing that he will need it because he cannot fight against the forces that will lead him to sin. "Treason" and "traitors" are wartime images. He is afraid, as many were afraid in those days, that "They", the impersonal forces, will "murder by means of my hands". In Freudian terms he is now trying to resolve his moral anxiety, in itself an outgrowth of the subjective fear of the parents. This fear is betrayed in the next liturgical phrase, which is "rehearse me", an image continued with reference to the "parts I must play" and "the cues I must take". It is an appeal to a 'director', to a father figure, even though his first request is for instructions as to his proper reaction "when old men lecture me", itself a father fear ("My father made the walls resound").

The central emphasis of the next phrase must be on "the white waves call me to folly", perhaps a direct reference to the birth of Aphrodite and the Uranus myth. This casts back to the "mountains frown at me", a symbol for the forbidding father figure, a rival for the affections of the adored mother and therefore linked with the Uranus/Aphrodite image through the castration complex. This castration fear transferred from father to himself by identification makes more poignant the intermediate phrase: lovers laugh at me".

The desert, as we have seen in 'Meeting Point', has classical and biblical associations for MacNeice (who might justifiably have been thinking of Marvell's "deserts of vast eternity"). The cursing of the father by the children is both Freudian psychology and age-old myth. The phrase "the beggar refuses *my gift*" [my italics] has biblical associations, but it is also a strong description of alienation.

He prays

> O fill me
> With strength against those who would freeze my
>   humanity, would dragoon me into a lethal automaton,
>   would make me a cog in a machine,

These are immediate fears arising from the times, and the words and ideas are contemporary. Deep freezing, automation, cogs, machines are modern, if unlovely, concepts. He may have had in mind the line from 'Intimations of Immortality': "And custom lie upon thee with a weight/Heavy as frost".

He prays for strength against those who would make him "a thing with one face". In *Modern Poetry* he writes of "a mood of terror when everything seems to be unreal, petrified" and how, in a mirror in this mood, he thought his own face looked like a strange face. Then comes the greatest fear of all, the fear of depersonalization, of becoming "a thing", a dreamlike and hideous state, close to death, that is part of the experience of shock, and which he describes in 'Jigsaws' IV – "Fresh from the knife and coming to/I asked myself could this be I". If he remembered also Lear's words to Edgar: "Thou art the thing itself; unaccommodated man is no more but such a poor, bare, forked animal as thou art", he would also have had in mind his mongolian brother so tragically – and from the womb of the same mother – "a thing".

Finally he asks for strength against those who would

> dissipate my entirety, would
> blow me like thistledown hither and
> thither or hither and thither
> like water held in the
> hands would spill me.

The fear is of not being born, of being 'spilt' (with its connotation of Onanism and "seed spilt upon the ground"). He underlines this fear in the last two lines, where the carelessness of man to what is precious in another's life is contrasted with the malice of nature, or of witchcraft:

> Let them not make me a stone and let them not spill me.
> Otherwise kill me.

Although the appeal of the poem lies in its comment on universal experience, to be able to write it is self-exposure of the most ruthless kind. It is not naïve or accidental, for MacNeice's absorption with his own life left him in no doubt that it had meaning for others. He had a little, but probably superficial, knowledge of Freud, enough perhaps to believe that he was portraying the real anxieties from which the foetus might pray to be spared, in terms of general experience in a frightening world. What he exposes is a neurosis of moral anxiety, based on feelings of guilt, shame, and fear derived from childhood experiences of helplessness, plus a regressive desire to escape back to the womb.

This self-revelation is ennobled by the liturgical form in which it is presented. This gives it an ironical overtone from the guilt element derived from his familiarity as a child with the ritual of a religion in which he can no longer believe. His wish to find belief is shown by the prayer-like nature of the poem although he cannot address it to God. The language owes much to the Book of Common Prayer and the rhythm, basically anapaestic, is suitable for intonation, but unlike the true litany, it is skilfully alliterative and employs assonance and both internal, external, and every variety of weak, as well as strong, rhyme, as in

> I fear that the human race may with tall walls wall me
> with strong drugs dope me, with wise lies lure me,
> on black racks rack me, in blood-baths roll me.

or:

> forgive me
> For the sins that in me the world shall commit, my words
> when they speak me, my thoughts when they think me,
> my treason engendered by traitors beyond me,
> my life when they murder by means of my
> hands, my death when they live me.

The poem cannot be read without thinking of Eliot's 'Animula', of which the keynote is compassion, and Wordsworth's 'Ode' of which the keynotes are innocence and enthusiasm. The first is as clear-sighted as MacNeice about "The pain of living and the drug of dreams". The second can find from "the meanest flower that blows" . . . "Thoughts that do lie too deep for tears". Babette Deutsch finds an association between 'Prayer Before Birth' and one of George Herbert's "most touching lyrics 'Sighs and Groans' " which are to her "the groans out of the depths of his guilt, that comes from a man and a Christian", and which she compares with MacNeice's poem. This she thinks "is the cry, from the dark cavern of self, uttered by the threatened innocence and translated by a humanist who knows more intimately than Herbert against what worldly and fiendish powers, without and within, the soul must contend!"

This is not the MacNeice that Fraser sees as one "who is out at once to enjoy life and to shoulder his social responsibilities". It is however a poet who gives Fraser's "decent plain man" a ruthlessly straight look at some of the fears that occasionally stir within each one of us. To say as *The Times Literary Supplement* did in October 1949 that 'Prayer Before Birth' "asserts an attractive faith in human values" is to substitute perversity for criticism. It is truer, if no more profound, to say with Anthony Thwaite that "MacNeice has achieved in this poem something which is timeless".

II

Although he is not mentioned in R. N. Currey's *Poets of the 1939–1945 War* Louis MacNeice is occasionally quoted in anthologies of war poetry, but his war inspiration is not direct. It was in 1941 that he joined the B.B.C., and he remained in its employ to the end of his life. Although in his article on his friend in *Encounter* in November 1963, Auden wondered whether teaching would not have been a better breadwinner for him than writing for the radio (a typical if fruitless speculation), he is forced to admit that the B.B.C. certainly did all it could to lessen the pressure and tedium of his regular job. It is arguable that during the war years he was provided with an opportunity to serve the country in a way that made most use of his talents, and contributed in some measure to his development as a poet. His experiences with the B.B.C. and in air raids were absorbed into the general texture of his life. They widened the field for his already acute powers of observation. War as an all-embracing experience, war as a temporary but terrible way of life, the emotional impact of war on the inner personality, the deeper contacts between men and women in wartime, is not to be found in MacNeice's poetry as it was in the poetry of others who served in the ranks, with men, and on the field of battle.

In *Plant and Phantom*, which covers the years 1939 and 1940 (the twilight period of the 'phoney' war) and which he wrote in London, Ireland and the U.S.A. (where he was lecturing at Cornell University), the war intrudes mainly as the death of peace. His attitude towards it had not crystallized. First he felt despair at what had happened ('Débâcle'), then indignation against those who did not share the common peril ('Bar-room Matins'), and finally nostalgia for the past ('The Return').

'Débâcle', a lament that all should come to naught – "not for this the lean/And divinatory years", reminds us of the years of the lean kine and of Joseph's divination of Pharaoh's dreams of years that failed in their promise; "Not for this" the years during which the "red-eyed pioneers" made "the desert green" (cf. "the desert . . . shall blossom as the rose"). The word 'pioneer' may have entered his thought from Walt Whitman (he had gone to Cornell to teach poetry and Whitman was sufficiently familiar to him to provide the prefatory line to *Autumn Sequel*) whose "Pioneers,/O Pioneers!" sang the founding of the New World and of those who "Facing the dark" were allowed but "a passing hour . . . to pause oblivious" even when "the night descended". The next two lines list some of the pioneers: the "pale inventor", the miner, those who with "Vision and sinew made it of light and stone" (is "it" a faint recollection of the "city" of the *Book of Revelation* which, as a child, he was allowed to read during the sermon?). Their "heirs", having the inter-war years as their world, took it for granted and enjoyed the windows that had "gone gold/For half an hour". Then in an image of typically shrewd observation: "a quick/Chill came off the brick/Walls and the flesh was suddenly old and cold". "Their world" crumbles and "something twangs and breaks at the end of the street", a line which, with its simile of the overtight string which on breaking 'twangs' (an onomatapoeic word for

an unpleasant sound), and with its sense of suburban surprise and
untouchability (what has happened is "at the end of the street"),
catches the resigned despair of the times. We think of Eliot's
"This is the way the world ends/Not with a bang, with a whim-
per".

'Bar-room Matins' is a bitter little poem that follows naturally
on 'Débâcle'. MacNeice places us immediately among the heirs
of the "red-eyed pioneers", "Popcorn peanuts clams and gum" – in
one line we are in the United States, where we stay for "Pretzels
crackers chips and beer", as well as for "Anchovy almond ice and
gin". We are concerned not with "Thy Kingdom" of the Lord's
Prayer, but 'our' Kingdom which still has not come. The immediacy of life in the States, and its subservience to commercialism, is pilloried as the "sponsored programme". With remarkable
economy of words he mocks the confusion of thought of a
materialist world which pays lip-service to a religion of sacrifice,
"And yet the preachers tell the pews" (not the empty pews or the
congregation in the pews, just "pews"):

> What man misuses God can use:
> Give us this day our daily news
>
> That we may hear behind the brain
> And through the sullen heat's migraine
> The atavistic voice of Cain:
>
> 'Who entitled you to spy
> From your easy heaven? Am I
> My brother's keeper? Let him die.'

Recollection of the Anglican service of his childhood combines
with bitterness of feeling:

> Mass destruction, mass disease:
> We thank thee, Lord, upon our knees
> That we were born in times like these

a prophetic verse in view of the atomic and biological warfare
that was to follow. The comparison of individual death, the

"journalist's commodity", that "titillates the ear" with "doom tumbling from the sky", conveys impatient disgust. So he says "Let the Untergang begin", let everyone suffer, "Die the soldiers, die the Jews", but, in the words almost of the Lord's Prayer, "Give us this day our daily news".

'The Return' is a poem of more involved imagery. He seems to be saying that, with the onset of war, doubt returns such as "All the lost interpretations" (from textual emendations on-wards) and "All the unconsummated consummations" (including that awaited by the Church of "peace for ever more"). The clear sky of peace is filled again "with the shadow of thy wings" which in Psalm 57 "shall be my refuge until this tyranny be over-past", but which, here and now, is a "shadow on our patience". Then he sees, in one combined image, the world of the Old Testament, of the New Testament and of today "desolate . . . cobwebbed, mute". But even in this winter of our discontent ("icicles round the landing") we know that, sooner or later, the good things of life will triumph. MacNeice's vision of these good things is typically temporal and sensuous. "The lolloping vulcanite of sea-lions" not only catches the colour and texture of the skin, but conveys an atmosphere of circuses and fairgrounds, while Roman Vulcan contrasts with the Christian "Birth" of the previous stanza and with the fairy-tale harlequin picture of "waters through a sluice/Tigers in the air". There is still some hope. In the "teeth of science", the science of war, the science that denies mythology, we shall acclaim "earth's returning daughter". This is Persephone, daughter of the earth-goddess, Demeter, amongst whose attributes was the narcissus or jonquil, and who comes back once a year with "Jonquils out of hell". After hell will come the "imperative of joy", which is (ironically in a poem looking from peace to war and back to peace again) a fusillade: "the dancing/Fusillade of sunlight on the water".

Of the remaining war-time poems in this first volume, 'Death of an Actress' is a not unpleasing exercise in sentiment, with a neat comment on the old pro's appeal to her audience and with a sharp image of war-time: "Now on a late and bandaged April day". 'Jehu' is a not entirely successful attempt to combine satire and parable; and sections IV and V of 'The Closing Album' note the declaration of war and the extraordinary effect it had of distancing one from what, a moment before, had been reality:

> And why should the sea maintain its turbulence, its elegance,
> And draw a film of muslin down the sand
> With each receding wave?
>
> And why, now it has happened,
> Should the atlas still be full of the maps of countries
> We never shall see again?

In *Springboard* and *Holes in the Sky*, published in 1944 and 1948 respectively, we might expect to find the bulk of MacNeice's war poems. In *Springboard* it is true that there are more poems devoted to the war theme than to other subjects. They share the volume with matters of perennial interest to Louis MacNeice (and indeed to other poets too). By the time we reach *Holes in the Sky*, the war occupies an inferior place. His own life, the imminence of death, people observed, the problems of agnosticism are, as ever, the main sources of inspiration.

In both volumes the direct war themes (mainly of air raids, fires, travel in wartime) are those that civilians experienced. In 'Brother Fire' for example, he seems to say that the London blitz meant for him an appreciation of "the Will/That wills the natural world but wills us dead", a human and perceptive comment from one who could not fight back. The final stanza reflects the psychological pleasure of identification with the agents of destruction:

> Did we not on those mornings after the All Clear,
> When you were looting shops in elemental joy
> And singing as you swarmed up city block and spire,
> Echo your thought in ours? 'Destroy! Destroy!'

This attitude is a classic example of the Freudian reaction of which the purpose is obedience to the demands of a potential enemy; it is not disassociated from MacNeice's ambivalent attitude towards his father, the symbol of authority.

'The Trolls' which he tells us was "Written after an air-raid, April 1941" somehow fails to convey the impact of enemy bombers. The image is wrong. Few who heard the intermittent throb of engines overhead would accept the idea that they were "humming to themselves", even qualified by the phrase "like morons". This falls far short of the intellectual honesty and emotional discipline of Eliot's *Little Gidding*.

The last six lines of 'Whit Monday' with their reference to "familiar words of myth", catch something of the combined despair and courage of war-time, and the line "*The quiet* (Thames, or Don's or Salween's) *waters by*" distils the terrifying geographical scope of modern war. 'Swing-Song' is frankly sentimental and 'Nuts in May' tries, but fails, to echo the speed and catchiness of 'Bagpipe Music'. Of 'The Springboard' he himself says in *Experiences with Images* " 'The Springboard' . . . though rational in its working out, begins with two irrational premises – the dream picture of a naked man standing on a springboard in the middle of the air over London and the irrational assumption that it is his duty to throw himself down from there as a sort of ritual sacrifice. This" he adds "will be lost on those who have no dream logic." Certainly this attempt to combine in one image the universal sacrifice with the innumerable small sacrifices of war-time strike one as forced and there is no identification either of self, or of an ideal, with the "naked man", this Christ-like substitute "for each one" of us.

The impact of the war upon MacNeice may be better gauged by considering a series of poems which, for want of better classification, might be described as 'Men Observed' and which, if put together, might form a small collection of characters reminiscent of those in Earle's *Microcosmographie*. The first of these, in *Springboard*, is in 'Bottleneck' and may well be a portrait of Stephen Spender, perhaps with his poem 'Port Bou' in mind. MacNeice was fascinated by Spender's features, his lean ascetic profile which he describes again in *The Strings are False* as "his enormous craggy apostolic face". In 'Bottleneck' it is a very perceptive picture:

> When I saw him last, carving the longshore mist
> With an ascetic profile, he was standing
> Watching the troopship leave, he did not speak
> But from his eyes there peered a furtive footsore envy
> Of these who sailed away to make an opposed landing
> So calm because so young, so lethal because so meek.

It is an unkind picture; "furtive footsore envy" emphasizes slyness and physical ineptitude and an 'un-Christian' lack of virtue contrasting with the Christian 'meekness' of the young soldiers. It catches both the watcher and the watched. The analysis of his victim's earnestness, noble, yet somehow ridiculous, is shrewd:

> yet in his mind
> A crowd of odd components mutter and press
> For compromise with fact, longing to be combined
> Into a working whole but cannot jostle through
> The permanent bottleneck of his highmindedness.

'The Conscript', true enough as comment, is over-elaborate and a little pretentious, but the next of the 'character' poems, 'The Mixer', has merit both as charactery and poetry. The observation is true; the image is familiar, and yet normally escapes comment. It is an unusually objective poem for MacNeice. First the clear and brilliant description, the "pert" moustache; pert, a word usually referring to speech or conduct ('pert as a schoolgirl') is here applied to an adornment, and the effect is immediate, accurate and a précis of character almost complete in itself. The two adjectives conditioning "smile" – "ready" and "candid" – contrast with the "played" of the next line. The places, "pubs,/Deckchairs, lounges, touchlines", define exactly the happy hunting-grounds; "junctions", yes perhaps, in the sense of meeting-places; "homes" is probably a false note. The skilful use of "Far and narrow" (echoing the cliché "far and wide") pins the Mixer in his small world. His unreality is stressed by "other people's leisure" of which he mimics the style, and the last two words of this stanza, "scattering stubs", with a final evocation of cigarette ends, and the implication of useless litter, cut him down to size.

The second verse is an odd mixture of clear observation and conventional analysis; "self-accused" is not convincing, but that "He is only happy in reflected light" is a shrewd description with its reference to moonshine. The last three lines are trite, for here we have a stock explanation of a stock situation lifted from films rather than life. Here MacNeice not only missed a point but laboured an unconvincing explanation. If the poem is read with the second verse omitted, we are nearer the truth: that there were those, and the Mixer was one, whose only real existence had been during the First World War and so they came to life again only in the Second. They felt that they should, but they did not, fit. The Mixer cannot "away with silence". The Mixer is a cypher, he is "like a Latin word/That many languages have made their own/Till it is worn and blunt and easy to construe/And often spoken but no longer heard". This is a poem of surgical compassion, a feat of humane description repeated in 'The Libertine' where MacNeice's response to observed stimuli is used effectively in the lines:

> a scent-spray
> Beside the bed or a milk-white telephone
> Or through the triple ninon the acrid trickle of day:

The next of these poems, 'The Drunkard' is, to those who know the terms of reference, truly observed. The bitter irony of building the whole poem on a framework of religious dogma heightens the clash between conscience and experience with which the poem is concerned. MacNeice uses the train image that had haunted him from childhood:

> His last train home is Purgatory in reverse,
> A spiral back into time and down towards Hell

The next four lines compress the swaying, sickening, unbalanced but determined effort of the drunk to clutch his "quizzical strap", while the "sickly wind" (which is his own) drives the wraiths "Through tunnels" of the Underground to their "appointed, separate places". The emphasis is on separateness, the complete antithesis of, and revulsion from, the "communion" which he had just experienced. He had but now *ascended* (hence the descent through purgatory to hell) in Heaven "Wearing his halo cocked", a delicious cartoon-like phrase like an illustration to *The Little World of Don Camillo*; this is "the panarchy of created things". "Panarchy" is a good word compounded of nature and chaos. From this point we get a realistic picture of the attractions of drinking. MacNeice, we learn from his friends, liked the life of pubs where "time stood still". Here the walls of which, in 'Prayer Before Birth', he was afraid, "have wings" and "instantly" (the fairy-tale "Lo!") all religious mystery is clear. "God was uttered in words", was no longer the mysterious Javeh of the Old Testament, but was "gulped in gin", not sipped in blood-like wine. The barmaid, that mother-wife substitute, was "a Madonna", and the simple companions ("the adoration/Of the coalman's breath was myrrh, the world was We") were elevated to the level of the Magi. Finally in two lines reminiscent of Housman, he finds

> pissing under the stars an act of creation
> While the low hills lay purring round the inn.

a perceptive image of the hills crouched cat-like in the dark. The poem should have ended here. Some future editor of MacNeice may well increase the stature of his poet by denying him his chance to "point a moral and adorn a tale". The last verse describes the inevitable revenge that time takes on the drunkard; it is a cliché redeemed only by the last line – "That hour-gone sacrament of drunkenness." – which completes the religious imagery of the opening of the poem. This last verse may have been intended to reflect the anticlimax of the hangover, but becomes in itself an anticlimax. As a whole this is a lyric which comes well from a man who, as Auden remarks (surprisingly enough in the obituary notice he wrote for *Encounter*) "spent more time than he should pub-crawling."

It would be necessary to include in a volume of MacNeice's poetic 'characters' the portraits collected in 'The Kingdom' of those who are in "an underground movement,/Under the crust of bureaucracy", the people, he says, "Who vindicate the species". We are given a portrait of the "old man with the soldierly straight back" who is "A country-lover and very English", of "Our Mother", of the soldier, of a "Doric river-goddess", a scientist, an old preacher. The list is a very proper one, the poem is properly done, and we are intended to be properly elevated. It is a little like Earle at his most pedestrian rendered into poetry by Crabbe; our verdict on it can only be, surprisingly enough, that its purpose is worthy.

Ian Hamilton in his article in *London Magazine* feels that these poems are an attempt by MacNeice to "synthesise the rhetorical and documentary aspect of his work". This may be true of 'The Kingdom' but is surely a wrong approach to the other poems which are not an 'attempt' to synthesize anything. Each is a rendering into poetry of sharp observation allied to human but not sentimental understanding. Ian Hamilton finds these poems of character too complacently "punch-lined". He goes on to comment that "their solutions intrude too glaringly". This is a criticism that, in regard to subject and content, cannot totally be accepted. 'The Mixer', 'The Libertine', 'The Satirist', were characters of the times, far more than those in 'The Kingdom'. It was right and proper to portray them even in miniature. The portraiture is sharp and vivid, as miniatures should be, and of necessity selective. To complain of the "punch-lines" is to complain of MacNeice's capacity for vivid phrase; and to accuse them of "complacency" is to use the easiest and handiest of weapons to belabour anyone who dares to make a human judgment.

When the war ends MacNeice finds more inspiration in poems which reflect an aspect of war too often forgotten. The otherwise denigratory *Times Literary Supplement* criticism of the *Collected Poems 1925–1948* admits that they contain "sensitive, if not profound" reflections on returning peace. In 'Hiatus' MacNeice touches on the tragedy of "The years that did not count" in that period of suspended time:

> – Civilians in the towns
> Remained at the same age as in Nineteen-Thirty-Nine,
> Saying last year, meaning the last of peace;
> Yet eyes began to pucker, mouth to crease,

By comparison, he says:

> The schoolboys of the Thirties reappear,
> Fledged in the void, indubitably men,
> Having kept vigil on the Unholy Mount
> And found some dark and tentative things made clear,
> Some clear made dark, in the years that did not count.

In 'Aftermath' he summarizes in three lines that feeling of disillusion that came with peace:

> the bandaging dark which bound
> This town together is loosed and in the array
> Of bourgeois lights man's love can save its breath:

He himself was more inclined to pride himself on the image from poker in this poem:

> The joker that could have been any moment death
> Has been withdrawn, the cards are what they say
> And none is wild;

He says in *Experiences with Images* "To my present taste this sort of economy – the *twist* of an ordinary phrase, the apparently flat statement with a double meaning – is far more exciting than the romantic elaboration of glamour images", but he admits that "It is of course hard for me to tell whether such conceits 'stick out' too much."

Perhaps the most outstanding of the 'return' poems, written with deep compassion and from a human viewpoint, is 'Bluebells'. For those in love "parting is such sweet sorrow" that the tragedy of being parted is not hard to imagine. The emotional difficulties of reunion are unforeseen. "She", of the poem, has become accustomed to waiting for peace, but "This Easter has no peace to be waiting for". The sentence construction conveys that she neither has it, nor has it to anticipate. For the same reason she no longer needs to play 'he loves me, he loves me not' by "coining dandelions" (turning them to account either by tearing off their petals or blowing away their seeds) because, to continue the 'value' image, it has "lost the old enrichment of surprise". (How natural it is to think of golden dandelions in this way.) But all is not well: "though her man is back", he has brought with him an experience she has not shared. Here MacNeice uses "The Desert", so long in our minds as a battlefield, as the synonym for war experiences and by extension, an image of discipline, repression and solitude. Now the desert that her man has brought back with him makes "her cheeks taut", an accurate physiological observation of the outward effect of surprise and disappointment verging on fear.

Rarely has the psycho-physical difficulty of return to normality been better portrayed than in the next two verses. They, "she" and "her man", lie together, in the early morning "without words", because communication is not only difficult but will be dangerous. They listen to the "badinage of birds" (a pleasantly ironic phrase contrasting with the wordlessness of the human beings). Worse, in the evening, now so still that one is aware of the flight of bats, they "miss those engines overbrimming the sky". How much better "overbrimming" conveys menace than "humming to themselves like morons" did in 'The Trolls'. How truly he catches the extraordinary unreality of return to peacetime life from a life of constant menace. So the poem continues "For all green Nature", green both as contrasting with the desert and green in the sense of the youth lost during the war, "green Nature" has, in a vivid modern image, "gone out of gear" since the time they were "apart and hoping".

The next verse is one of high lyrical intensity. It starts with a phrase that reminds one of Donne's 'The Sunne Rising': "Sun is too bright and brittle". What a heart-breaking word is "brittle", and how cunningly it catches that time when the bright day is over-clearly defined to the puzzled mind. The line continues: "wheat is too quick". The word "quick" is not only contrasted with "slow" in the next line, but carries the connotation of life (as in "the quick and the dead"). Linked with wheat it brings to mind the allusion to the classical goddess of love. The whole line reflects the difficulty of resuming a longed-for relationship, which should be full of sunshine and harvest. So she turns to the shade of the wood: "slow thick/Shade" which is "becalmed and chill". We are back in the Garden of Proserpine where "life has death for neighbour", as it has in time of war, and where we find the "fruitless fields of corn", and where, in consequence, wheat is not "too quick". Then comes an unusually pure and vivid visual simile. The poet remembers, perhaps from his pre-war Icelandic trip, a glacial stream entering the sea. He remembers how it "inlays" the "dark waste" of the sea and "weaves a milky gleam" through it, rather as "Alph the sacred river ran/Through caverns measureless to man/Down to a sunless sea". In a way it 'impregnates' the sea and serves as an image of conception. Similarly the bluebells flow through the undergrowth ("athwart", never a melodious word, would be a false note but for the undertones of 'Kubla Khan' and a remembrance of "that deep romantic chasm which slanted/Down the green hill athwart a cedarn cover") and are a "merger" of blue snow. Perhaps he remembered Day-Lewis's "Later within the wood sweetly reclining/On bluebell and primrose we loved". Here the frustrated sensuousness, and consequent despair that comes from inability to release emotion too long pent up, are brought together. The bluebells contrast with the "glacial stream" and yet they are the stream. She then describes the inability to escape from the repressions they have acquired during parting as "this dark beneathness", where they live, and from which they cannot achieve reality. So the bluebells must serve for the sky they "cannot face". Then in a series of words which have overtones of frigidity and contraception ("my ice-cap"), the womb ("that brine so deep and yet so dim"), the Oedipus complex ("my cold gentleness") and atomic guilt ("irradiate") and of MacNeice's permitted juvenile reading in

church (the "pure river of the water of life"), we have a prayer –
to whom or what we do not know – that might be the prayer of
all frigid but loving women:

> let a delta of flowers atone for the sky
> Which we cannot face and from my ice-cap, oh,
> Let one river at least unfreeze and flow
> And through that brine so deep and yet so dim
> Let my cold gentleness irradiate him.

III

In *Modern Poetry* MacNeice, as we have already noted, lists among
those "things" that "had conditioned my poetry . . . a liking (now
dead) for metaphysics." The parenthesis may be disregarded if we
consider the quantity of his poetry after 1938 devoted to philosophic themes. In *The Strings are False* he says "Metaphysics for
me . . . was an account of reality, but an artistic account not a
scientific one." In 'Plurality', originally published in *Plant and
Phantom*, he expresses his criticism of systems of metaphysics,
explains his doubts, and offers a solution which makes the poem
unusual. The solution is based on his own experience which, for
MacNeice, meant based on his awareness of the physical,
sensuous, personalized world in which he lived. He begins with a
strong physical image, "It is patent to the eye that cannot face the
sun/The smug philosophers lie". These are philosophers such as
Parmenides, who considered the senses deceptive, or like
Spinoza, the "modern monist" who believed that "the world as a
whole is a single substance, none of whose parts are logically
capable of existing alone . . . that relations and plurality must be
illusory". MacNeice says "only change prevails" and whether he
knew it or not, shows himself to lean towards existentialism, that
"anti-intellectualist philosophy of life holding that man is free and
responsible" and which is based on the assumption that reality as
existence can only be lived, but can never become an object of

thought. We can "stake a claim/Only to what a bird can find within the frame/Of momentary flight". In spite of this, his philosophy is coloured by a residual Christianity: "you and I/Can only live by strife . . . /A species become rich by seeing things as wrong/And patching them, to which I am proud that I belong". So he concludes with a kind of hedonist, pantheistic, evangelical existentialism.

Francis Scarfe draws attention to the similarity of subject of 'Plurality' and certain passages of Eliot's *The Dry Salvages*, and criticizes MacNeice for abandoning his subject as soon as it becomes difficult. The comparison is between a poet in whose work feeling and emotion is achieved through hard intellectual discipline, and an intellectual magpie with a predisposition for the sensual world. When the comparison is made between the achievement as poetry, of an analysis of the "point of intersection of the timeless with time", then Eliot's poem is of greater stature, because of its consistency, its clarity, and its human insight into the higher sensuousness, as when he speaks of "music heard so deeply/That it is not heard at all, but you are the music/While the music lasts". MacNeice's poetry is not on so tight a rein. It contains, as Scarfe says, "an inadequate proportion between the cerebral and sensual elements". If in doing so it avoids the single-mindedness after which Day-Lewis struggles, we can only be grateful, for though we do not have either a poet of close intellectual reasoning, or of high and resolute purpose, we have instead one who rejoices that

> he must continue, raiding the abyss
> With aching bone and sinew, conscious of things amiss,
> Conscious of guilt and vast inadequacy and the sick
> Ego and the broken past and the clock that goes too quick,
> Conscious of waste of labour, conscious of spite and hate,
> Of dissension with his neighbour, of beggars at the gate,
> But conscious also of love and the joy of things and the power
> Of going beyond and above the limits of the lagging hour,
> Conscious of sunlight, conscious of death's inveigling touch,
> Not completely conscious but partly – and that is much.

'Plant and Phantom' is the title poem of the first of the three wartime volumes. As for some other volumes, he selects for the whole the title of the one poem which has particular significance for him, though not necessarily as poetry. In 'The Springboard', for example, he is concerned with 'dream-logic' (a near-flirtation with surrealism). In 'Plant and Phantom' he is concerned with the theme he also treats in 'Plurality'. The "Plant" of the title is fairly clearly a recollection of 'Essay on Man': "Fix't like a plant on his peculiar spot/To draw nutrition, propagate, and rot", but the "Phantom" is a poetic image used sufficiently frequently to tease us with its many implications. We are reminded of Arnold's "Phantom of ourselves" or the early Yeats's "Beauty in a mist of tears". Perhaps the dominant recollection is of Shelley's 'Adonais' who, "awakened from the dream of life", has left us to "keep/With phantoms an unprofitable strife"? When in the poem MacNeice comes to describe "Man", it is in his own terms of sentient awareness and struggle against an unknown power which elsewhere (as in 'Prognosis') he so frequently identifies as "Death". He dismisses prophecy, divination, metaphysics, in the first two lines, for Man himself is a "flutter of pages,/Leaves in the Sibyl's cave". "Leaves" is a pleasant pun with its play on pages and on dried leaves in a witch's cave "like ghosts from an enchanter fleeing". The rest of the verse is a series of vivid contrasts between man as a part of nature, "murmuration of corn in the wind" and "a pump of blood", and Man as a "chaos" of superstitions. In the third verse Man is all sensuous, mysterious and beautiful things, "a dance of midges", "a gimcrack castle", "Seaweed tugging the rocks"; and in the fifth he becomes "a riot of banners", "A rampant martyr", "a forest fire". As the poem progresses, so does the scale and grandeur of the images used to describe this creature, this "spider". And as the poem is organized, it is in the alternate verses between these descriptions that we find the intellectual development portrayed. Man "cheats the pawky Fates/By what he does, not is,/By what he makes" ('pawky' is a striking adjective for the Fates, but in its meanings of 'sly' and 'shrewd' is not inappropriate, if diminishing of stature by implication). He imposes on flux "Loops across the void,/Stepping stones in the random", all of which are described as "architectonic", a word which has both an architectural meaning and also refers to the systematization of knowledge. In the fourth verse we find that Man's life is, in the vernacular, "a bluff", because he is in revolt against Nature, "Smuggling . . . a sense of value" into the world "over the frontier/Of fact", which is the sum total, the "Metabolism", of the changes wrought in living matter by the existence of death, and is for Man a "Re-orchestration of world". His last two verses epitomize Man's dichotomy as a carnal being gloriously able both to reflect the world about him and to "keep with phantoms an unprofitable strife".

'Plant and Phantom' is a well-organized poem with the sensory and spiritual inspiration developing side by side to the crescendo of the last verse which yet stops short of faith. The tightly packed images, the economy of words, the strong stresses on the short lines, the controlled alliteration and assonance, the lack of rhyme, reflect with more than usual discipline the agnosticism (in the true sense of the word) which is one of MacNeice's major themes.

The longest of MacNeice's philosophical poems, 'The Stygian Banks', is also one of the most tantalizing. Ill-organized, discursive, loosely phrased, it ambles through a maze of sentiment and half-digested metaphysics. It is a lazy and self-indulgent philosophic soliloquy, and yet it has the appeal of a friend's post-prandial talk. Once we begin to read it, the poem engulfs us; we are trapped like flies in honey by its inconsequence; we take heart at its occasional flashes of brilliance; we submit to the seductive thought that we, together with the poet, are within an ace of revelation. As a poem it has little development of thought. Its argument runs thus: everything in the world is new and exciting to the innocent and ignorant, so we have children to renew this awareness in ourselves. But although we can dream of being other than we are, we cannot merge with other lives. We are only one in a pack of cards with little more than superficial contact. We do not know what will happen after death, but we can recognize our inability to understand and to die acknowledging ignorance is noble. We must, in existentialist terms, distil value from mere existence. The existence of death makes life real; beyond death we may at times think there is something that makes life worth living though in all probability a mechanistic system is all we can admit. But we can in the meantime be both lyrical and despairing.

The core of the poem is in the fourth part, which develops a sense of nearness to the infinite unknown in an image which perhaps had its origin in the childhood experience described in *The Strings are False*:

"We were walking along a road between high walls and I could see nothing but the road and the air on the road was quiet and self-contained. On the top of the walls, on the contrary, there were long grasses growing in the stonework and these were blown out, combed, by a wind which I could not see. I wondered what was over these walls and I thought that it must be space. Not fields or roads or houses but an endless stretch of a windblown something, something not I nor even my father and mother could ever, however we tried, walk to the end of."

In Part IV of 'The Stygian Banks' this becomes a lyrical passage in the romantic tradition:

> Drilling the peas and beans in the garden but not seeing over
>   the wall,
> The mellow grass-grown wall encircling and forbidding
> Too high to climb and no birds fly across it;
> Only an incoming wind which unlike the winds of the garden
> (The winds which threaten the new-born child in the tree-top
> But only can share the name of This by analogy)
> Flutters no paper tag on a stick in a plot,
> Moves no leaf; the dandelion puff balls
> Ignore it and we often.

(Note how this is interwoven with his constantly recurring "rockabye baby" concept.) When however in the next few lines

he tries to personalize the incoming wind by describing its effect
on the lover:

> Not one hair on his head
> Is blown out of place but he ceases to give, give out;

and on

> that tired man in the queue
> In whom fatigue dulling the senses has rendered
> Some other part of him sensitive

he is only a mite short of bathos. On the other hand the world
itself is painted in strong contrast:

> Arkwright and Hargreaves are busy changing England,
> The hooter sounds at eight, Darwin will sweep away
> One code and give us a new one;

and:

> So take London to-day: the queues of itching minds
> Waiting for news that they do not want, for nostrums
> They only pretend to believe in; most of their living
> Is grinding mills that are not even their own.

So we have the world as it is on the one hand, and on the other
the mystery of the infinite void beyond the wall. Of this he is
lyrical:

> Can it be that the wall
> Is really a stepping-stone? So that what is beyond it
> (That which as well perhaps could be called what is Not)
> Is the sanction itself of the wall and so of the garden?
> Do we owe these colours and shapes to something which seems
>   their death?

He cannot follow this train of thought; he can find no system
there: "It does not bear thinking of".

Although MacNeice arrives always at an agnostic conclusion,
his voyage to its expression is bedecked with a kind of brave
non-conformism, of middle-class moral courage:

    smuggling in
  To a world of foregone conclusions the heresy of choice,

and:

    it is our privilege –
  Our paradox – to recognize the insoluble
  And going up with an outstretched hand salute it.

This is all the nobler because we are solitary heroes in this difficult progress towards the unknown:

    I am alone
  And you are alone and he and she are alone

but there is no escape from this loneliness:

    We must avoid
  That haunting wish to fuse all persons together;
  To *be* my neighbour is banned – and if I could be,
  I could neither know him nor love him.

(Notice the Christian ethic of 'love thy neighbour', here taken casually for granted and not explored.) This dilemma forces us to consider what object there can be in living. His only solution is:

  It is your birthright never to be grown up
  But always growing, never yourself completed
  As are the brutes and therefore, unlike the brutes,
  Able to shape something outside yourself
  Finding completion only in othernesses
  Whether perceived started without you
  Or conceived within you, ending beyond you;

These lines are reminiscent of Eliot, but stop short of Eliot's more fearless thinking on the same theme:

    Either you had no purpose
  Or the purpose is beyond the end you figured
  And is altered in fulfilment.

MacNeice seeks for the purpose of life, not through resignation, but by trying to conquer time and therefore death. He tries to feel that immortality rests in the "line of men", that there is much of the past in us and that we share the future through the part of us which is in our children. Since this leads him to consider once again the sensual world in which he took so much pleasure, we have some of his characteristic flashes of insight:

> The very limitedness
> Of childhood, its ignorance, its impotence,
> Made every cockcrow a miracle after the ogre's night
> And every sunbeam glad –

and:

> Munching salad
> Your child can taste the colour itself – the green –
> And the colour of radish – the red;

These are two understanding analyses of perceptive childhood culled from his own recollections.

As MacNeice seeks for the purpose of being alive, the basic teachings of the Christian Church, however disguised, inevitably intrude:

> To raise a value gardens must be gardened
> Which is where choice comes in. Then will. Then sweat.

One is reminded of the nonconformist insistence that "In the sweat of thy face shalt thou eat bread". He still feels that life, as he had learnt it in the parsonage, is a protracted and arduous search:

> The well-worn symbols
> Of quests and inns and pilgrims' progresses
> Do correspond;

His conclusion is a despairing one. We are alone:

> No communion
> In sex or elsewhere can be reached and kept
> Perfectly or for ever. The closed window,
> The river of Styx, the wall of limitation
> Beyond which the word beyond loses its meaning,

Are the fertilizing paradox, the grille
That, severing, joins, the end to make us begin
Again and again, the infinite dark that sanctions
Our growing flowers in the light, our having children;
The silence behind our music.

Nevertheless, as Ian Hamilton says, "his love of bright particulars persists" and he would like to believe that from the silence beyond the wall, from infinite nothingness

Are borrowed ear and voice and from that darkness
We borrow vision,

From the unknown comes the sanction to savour the known which once gone is gone for ever.

This is neither fully realized intellectual poetry, nor emotionally religious poetry. It contains one of his worst lines: "The remembrance of an effulgence that was illusion". It is a poem enshrining

The paradox of a sentimentalist
Insisting on clinging to what he insists is gone;

It covers a great deal of his feeling about life, its sensuous attraction, lack of meaning, lack of hope, its fundamental anarchy. Despite its negative criticism, it commands respect. It conveys accurately the poignant despair of the intelligent man imprisoned in his complexes, his common sense, his inability either to respond with deep feeling to religious concepts, or to compromise with them because of instinctive fears. It sets out his longing without hope for life beyond life. John Press has compared MacNeice to Clough as being "hurt and self reproachful at his inability to accept the Christian Faith". MacNeice found no way of escape from this situation. In a repetitive, discursive, unrhymed poem calling on the medieval, classical and homely analogies of the ordinary educated man, he recreated the ordinary, intellectually lazy, educated man's doubting, reprehensible agnosticism, "half-blind questions that still lack their answers" ('Dedicatory Poem: To Hedli').

It is at this bleak point that Eliot found, in *East Coker*, what passed for faith:

> I said to my soul, be still, and wait without hope
> For hope would be hope for the wrong thing; wait without
> love
> For love would be love of the wrong thing; there is yet faith
> But the faith and the love and the hope are all in the waiting.

In 'Prayer in Mid-Passage' MacNeice is both "lyrical and despairing" more effectively than in 'The Stygian Banks'. The background of this poem lies in the hymns and psalms and religious observances of his childhood at the rectory, of his boyhood at Sherborne, and of his adolescence at Marlborough. Constant use of Hymns A. & M. and the Public School Hymn Book gives to all of us an endless variety of menacing or comfortable rhymed and rhythmical clichés (often little to do with Christianity) which can, if we wish, be used as talismans, and which have power of deterrence or of solace reminiscent of that of Tibetan prayer wheels. Phrases and rhythms from this background seep into much of MacNeice's poetry (we have already noted this in 'Prayer Before Birth') but it is at its most obvious in 'Prayer in Mid-Passage'.

This poem has emotional effectiveness because it contains an unresolved conflict between the disparate elemental need of reassurance, parental denominational Christianity, and intellectual agnosticism (expounded at length in 'The Stygian Banks') against a background of physical fear on a wartime journey to America. The conflict is sharpened by the ironical device of using a rhyme pattern and a metre easily recognizable as being similar to a number of well-known hymns (e.g. Heber's 'I praised the Earth', Oxenham's 'Lord God of Hosts'). It begins, as so many hymns begin, with an invocation, but an invocation designed to shock: "O Thou my monster", a word chosen perhaps from Psalm LXXI: "I am become as it were *a monster* unto many" and transferred in the verse from man to God. If we glance forward to the last stanza, and note the final invocation: "Thou my death", we may recall the comparison in *Romeo and Juliet* of "unsubstantial death" to a "lean abhorred monster". The second part of the opening takes us back to the hymnary, "Thou my guide", with its reminder of lines such as "Lead us, Heavenly Father, lead us . . . Guard us, guide us . . ." and "Where Thou art guide no ill can come".

"Be with me where the bluffs divide", beside being a clear picture of the ship leaving shore, reminds us, with its enfolding image, of "Rock of Ages, cleft for me". At this point the poet asks to be prevented from thinking about returning to "where my backward chattels burn". His thoughts may be with the burning London of the Blitz, which he cannot bear to contemplate. But the phrase is made arresting by the use of "backward" in its adjectival form (cf. Vaughan's "But I by backward steps would move") applied to "chattels", a word usually associated with a last will and testament; he is looking backward and asks that he be prevented from going back to "The Cities of the Plain of Youth", here described as "haunts of friendship and untruth". Ironically in relation to Sodom and Gomorrah "haunts" takes the mind back to Milton's "Towered cities", and "the busy haunts of men". "Untruth", coming so soon after "friendship", is a bitter word. What then are the "backward chattels" that now burn? – perhaps they are those of casual pleasure of which he speaks in the dedication of *Springboard*, 'To Hedli'. Perhaps he feels, in the mood of the poem, that false friends in the "Cities of the Plain of Youth" led him to misuse his talents and in this prayer he asks to be led no further into temptation.

How great the temptation may be is underlined by the invocation of the second verse. We are back to the hymn book of 'Once in Royal David's City' from which is recalled "For He is our childhood's pattern". How many intelligent children have felt with MacNeice "O pattern of inhuman good", as they go on to sing "Christian children all must be/Mild, obedient, good as He", or in Heber's hymn, "O good beyond compare". There is ironical ambiguity in the word "inhuman" applied to the God of the Old Testament and of the Litany, the Monster Silence, Guide, who

135

now becomes "Hard critic of our thought and blood"; and where one phrase "critic of our thought" may have relevance to the harder standard of thought and content MacNeice had consciously (if not always successfully) set for himself. Then with reminiscence of a further hymn dealing with the sea, he speaks of the "decree" ("Hath 'stablished it fast by a changeless decree") by which there is no "zone" (a wartime, a political and psychological word) "Where man can live by men alone", an admission in Biblical phraseology which is the nearest MacNeice comes to admitting the necessity for faith. He calls now on "the monster", the "guide", "the pattern of inhuman good" to "Unveil thyself that all may see/Thy fierce impersonality", recalling the irresistible force of "the changeless purpose" from the same hymn.

Then MacNeice speaks for himself and those like him who "were the past – and doomed [like Odysseus] because/We were a past that never was", a line that catches all the malaise, combined with nostalgia, of the years between the wars, of the 'lost generation', including those friends he was crossing the war-riven Atlantic to see again.

Nevertheless, he says "Yet grant to men", still, in spite of all, permit men to "climb/This time-bound ladder out of time". The "time-bound ladder" is life itself that leads to death, which is "out of time". "Grant", he continues, that by "our human organs", by our own efforts (with an implied reference in "organs" to our own powers of reproduction) "we/Shall thus transcend humanity", which ironically recalls the Wedding Hymn, "O perfect love, all human thought transcending".

The final prayer is for understanding:

> Take therefore, though Thou disregard,
> This prayer, this hymn, this feckless word,
> O Thou my silence, Thou my song,
> To whom all focal doubts belong
> And but for whom this breath were breath –
> Thou my meaning, Thou my death.

This is the poem of an agnostic humanist who cannot but feel that we are granted only human means by which to transcend the

human and who finds the equipment inadequate to the task.
Throughout his work he was concerned with the brevity of life
and the imminence of death. For MacNeice "the point is the
assertion in the teeth of dissolution", said Blackburn in *The Price
of an Eye*, "and this assertion colours all his poetry". Life itself,
MacNeice thinks, would lack value but for death. In 'The Trolls'
he says:

> Death has a look of finality;
> We think we lose something but if it were not for
> Death we should have nothing to lose, existence
> Because unlimited would merely be existence

and in Stanza IV:

> and the value
> Of every organism, act and moment
> Is, thanks to death, unique.

Perhaps Hamilton and *The Times Literary Supplement* have been
misled by the dedication to *Springboard* and demand too much. A
mind "disabused of casual pleasure" is not under an obligation
either to turn philosophy into poetry or retain an adolescent
gusto, or fail. The powers of recollection, observation and
craftsmanship that produced 'Trains in the Distance', 'Turf-
Stacks', 'Sunday Morning', 'Snow' and 'The Sunlight on the
Garden', produce in these volumes serious poems of great depth
of feeling and wide understanding. 'Prayer Before Birth', the
'character' poems we have noted, the sensitive poems about the
return of peace such as 'Bluebells', the mood of the impossible
wartime Bank Holiday in 'Whit Monday', 'Prayer in Mid-
Passage', 'Elegy for Minor Poets', and 'Slow Movement', to
name but a few, are 'typical' MacNeice poems in their use of
imagery, their power of versification, their sensuous perception.
They are something more. They are an individual view of familiar
but infrequently noted psychological experiences. When they
explore an *emotional* situation to the limit of which the poet is
capable, as in 'Prayer Before Birth' and 'Bluebells', we have

poetry of stature. He understands alienation. He is emotionally aware of failure ('Elegy for Minor Poets'). When the poems philosophize as in 'The Stygian Banks', they are weaker, for they lack hard intellectual discipline. When they attempt to weigh social values ('The Kingdom') they fail, for he is psychologically unable to identify. We must see to what extent his later work is constrained by, or escapes from, these limitations.

CHAPTER FOUR

Ten Burnt Offerings and Autumn Sequel

I

Immediately we read *Ten Burnt Offerings* we are conscious of a sense of surprise, even of shock. The change in both the tone and texture of the poetry is so marked, and is so complete that it can only be deliberate. We must ask ourselves why MacNeice made this change; what forces caused him to modify so noticeably both the style and content of his work? Each of these poems (and we are not now considering *Autumn Sequel*) is of some length but discursive, and for the most part, inconclusive. They are, perhaps, searching for an answer to some of the eternal questions, which he had already tackled, for example in 'The Stygian Banks'; they are philosophical, as was 'Plurality', or have a personal responsiveness to place and history like 'Valediction'; but while each of these earlier poems gives the impression, whatever its faults of loose thinking, that it springs from an impulse that is both emotional and irresistible, rather than intellectual, the first impact of *Ten Burnt Offerings* reverses this impression.

There are one or two clues to the forces that led MacNeice to this change in the nature of his poetry. 'Nature' may not be entirely the right word, since lurking behind *Ten Burnt Offerings*, and there to be discovered by analysis, is still the poet of the early works. Perhaps we should speak of the new aspect of his poetry or of a change of tone. He writes now in a 'key' which does not always suit him; he takes 'subjects' which he might previously have avoided; but as we shall see, the concepts that are struggling for expression remain unaltered. What then led him to this change of tone?

Released by the B.B.C. for a spell with the British Council in Athens, he might have been expected to profit by the freedom from the demands of preparing and producing radio programmes to a time-table. Instead he found that inspiration did not come easily. The appointment was, in all probability, not without its difficulties and it is likely that there were personal problems for him both at work and at play. He says himself in 'Day of Renewal':

> This middle stretch
> Of life is bad for poets; a sombre view
> Where neither works nor days look innocent
> And both seem now too many, now too few.

It would be simple to assume (and it has been suggested) that no other explanation of the change is necessary; but surely the universal validity of loss of inspiration at 44 years of age remains to be investigated. We can only accept this as a comment on the difficulty which he was experiencing. We can, however, take note of the quotation with which he prefaces the first poem in the volume, 'Suite for Recorders'. Against this feeling, this "inner flagging", as G. S. Fraser expresses it, he set "an obstinate ambition". As an epigraph to 'Suite for Recorders' he quotes from Touchstone's complaint to Audrey: "it strikes a man more dead than a great reckoning in a little room", a line which some commentators think refers to the murder of Christopher Marlowe. But it may be of interest to recall the context of these words. What is it that "strikes a man more dead"? It is "when a

man's verses cannot be understood, nor a man's good wit
seconded with the forward child, understanding".

It is not easy to appreciate which of MacNeice's verses had
hitherto not been "understood", except that the act of understanding has a subjective element and will vary from person to
person. There had already been criticism of his poetry which had
appreciated the music and colour but, as we have seen, had been
deficient in depth of understanding. Perhaps however the thrust
was intended to be nearer home; perhaps he felt that understanding was lacking amongst his friends and those he loved, and
above all where, as a mother-fixated man, he most expected and
hoped to find it. If this were so, and the quotation at least gives us
some cause for speculation, then his response seems to have been
somewhat perversely, but not unexpectedly, to try to find subjects for poetry which would win the approval of the more
intellectual of his critics. Poems such as 'Areopagus', with layer
on layer of reference to the mythologies of Ancient Greece, the
Old Testament, the Gospels, the Acts of the Apostles, as well as
to the poems of T. S. Eliot and of Tennyson, are a challenge to
'understanding'; so is 'Didymus' with its demanding knowledge
of the Gospels, allied to a comprehension of the broad outlines of
Indian folklore and mysticism. So is 'Cock o' the North' with its
assumption that the reader has an intimate knowledge of Byron's
works, of his last days, of the domestic politics of the early nine-
teenth century, and of the legends of Ancient Greece; so is 'Day
of Returning' with its challenging fusion of the sagas of Ulysses
and Jacob. So, above all, is the poem which the quotation pre-
cedes. 'Suite for Recorders' is one of the most objective of his
poems, so objective in fact that, as we shall see, it might almost
be a deliberate scholarly exercise.

Something, but not necessarily the onset of middle age, had
stopped the flow of music and imagery which had characterized
MacNeice's poetry hitherto. With a career of some distinction
at their finger tips, many men might have been content to rest on
past achievements. MacNeice elected (and if we bear the 'text'
to 'Suite for Recorders' in mind, that is not too strong a word) to

continue the struggle. Much of interest, and a little of note, was the immediate result, and we may be allowed to doubt whether the melancholy mastery of the last three books could have been achieved without this middle stretch.

II

Taken as a whole, the poems in *Ten Burnt Offerings* reflect both the classical scholar and the son of the manse. The collection is more cerebral, more contrived than his previous poetry and the philosophical element predominates. The three aspects, self, society, and thought, are of course still there, and though often very closely interwoven, they serve as threads on which to string our analysis of this volume.

'Day of Renewal' is a poem devoted to personal contemplation. The occasion is his birthday. To be far from home and alone on a birthday is a common enough experience, but it has its own nostalgia and a bitter-sweet reality not to be forgotten and not to be despised. On any birthday it is not unusual to look back over the decades; on a lonely occasion it is, as he finds, irresistible. He begins by asking: "Do I prefer to forget it?" and never answering his own question, plunges *in medias res*. Then follow the lines on "This middle stretch/Of life" with which, as we have seen, *Ten Burnt Offerings* has too often been dismissed. The quotation has been applied to the whole volume, when in fact it is the main theme of this one poem. Whether he looks back or forward over his life, neither his work nor his future content him; but this is no new discontent. As a child he "felt sad to end each fairy story" and so then invented a dream world where "children were reborn each night". This childish escapism recalls the haunting problem of reality, the eternal struggle "Not to become but be", a fleeting ideal whose skirts he had so nearly touched in the second canto of *Autumn Journal*. Now he realizes that only "Death is, but life becomes". So he passes on to the relationship of time and place which becomes a major theme in his later poetry:

> This day a year ago
> Or thirty years lies rooted in one spot
> Which in itself has changed but in our mind
> Does not become but is; is what it now is not.
> Thus for me Cushendun is war and frustrated
> Love, Dieppe an astringent idyl, Lahore
> Blood, cholera, flies, blank eyes, becoming forty:
> Each birthday placed and each place dated.

In the last stanza of Section I we have perhaps the most complete statement of his feelings of imprisonment in body, in habit, in inescapable training (compare 'The Habits' and 'The Truisms' later) and in determinism:

> Such and such my beginnings, launched and engined
> With such and such a tackle of nerve and gland
> And steered by such and such taboos and values,
> My What and How science might understand
> But neither the first nor last page tells the story
> And that I am remains just that I am.
> The whole, though predetermined to a comma,
> Still keeps its time, its place, its glory.

The last lines have an element of unconvincing defiance.

Part I of 'Day of Renewal' is a sad and truthful and universally recognizable salute to a birthday in middle age when memories are tinged with regret and the future with apprehension. Though there are interesting elements in the remaining three sections, they do not add to the first and even, as so often in *Ten Burnt Offerings*, diminish the effect by repetition. In the second he uses reference to nursery rhyme and folk tale to underline exactly the same point – that there is no escape: "Same changes./ Same. Is life. Changes. Is life." (a portentous reliance on short words and short phrases to convey a meaning beyond their weight, like an orator beating the table before him.) Suddenly the poem lights up: from this unpromising beginning we have 15 lines of swinging phraseology based on nursery rhyme, proverb, folk lore, cant phrase and fairy tale, interwoven with echoes of *The Dry Salvages* and which is reminiscent, in a more restrained way, of 'Bagpipe Music'; equally it is fun to read aloud:

> One-Two-Three-Four-Five-Six-Seven-Eight:
> This year, no year, ever, never, next time,
> Eat your cake, have your cake, last time lucky,
> Ace high, bottoms up, cut again, turn again,
> This year, next year, a pocket full of plumstones,
> All the white horses and – turn again, Whittington –
> All the King's aldermen sweating on the bellropes
> Cannot put together again, by no means whatsoever again,
> What time and tide have parted – brickbats and dividends.
> Orange flotsam, lemon jetsam, Tower Reach is bobbing with it
> And never put together again. Bow bells and coster carts.
> I'm sure I don't, the bell says, the great bell, the tenor bell
> Booming out of the brine trough, swinging on the world's wheel,
> Mouth up in ribaldry, I'm sure I don't, an oracle
> For lord mayors and beggar boys, I'm sure I don't know!

He brings us down from this exciting excursion with a bang to "Bits and pieces". We are now back with the thought that memory fades and that we do not know the future. Only the imagery is different. Now the past lies in the reminiscences of "Ancient brogues/Caught in a wrinkled grin" or of "a hat/With a bent black brim". These are the past. The future is a nursery rhyme again and all the pent-up longing to find out "what is that light at the top of the well".

So now the third section takes us painfully over the "Milestones" of his life, and the nightmares that have marked it; and we are back again to a consideration of past birthdays, distinguished it is true by the striking image that they are marked out by "Shorthand of wavering shadow on white icing/Scribbled by tiny candles".

The fourth plays every variation on the plumstone theme; but the truth lies in a line and a half:

> For all my years are based on autumn
> Blurred with blue smoke,

and in those we recognize the true MacNeice.

In so far as a love poem concerns self, 'Flowers in the Interval' belongs to the category of personal poetry. It is extremely difficult to place in the gallery of love poems. It is long; it traces the original joy of discovery of the loved one; in a kind of inverted pathetic fallacy it outlines the emotions of travels shared and of the pleasure of places. It sings of colour, movement and physical pleasure; and in the final series of six-line stanzas it hymns the actress and singer who is now "on the edge of the world/In the wind". It has a certain fragile verity that compels attention. It has also a hysterical over-emphasis that casts doubt on its ultimate sincerity. There are here felicitous phrases and descriptions, which strike true:

> you my galactic
> Marvel of ivoried warmth, with your warm hair curled
> Over the cool of your forehead and your ambivalent
> Tigercat eyes, which are amber and javelins,

but there are banal images, as of the sleeping princess. There is the happy concept "you are all the places/That I have been in with you", but catalogued they are too many. There is the eye-catching

> Because your colours are onyx and cantaloupe,
> Wet seaweed, lizard, lilac, tiger-moth
> And olive groves and beech-woods,

but the list is too long, and the loved one disappears into too many colours and sounds and qualities. There is the true subjective moment:

> And thus when the winds begin to whisper
> Which lurk in the night and trouble space
> I cross my fingers, grit my teeth,
> And wait for the moment when your face
> Appears from nowhere,

which is spoiled by the forced image that follows:

> Appears from nowhere, as beneath
> The frozen earth the bulbs burn upward.

So, sadly, because there are moments that come near to success, we are left with a poem that fails to convince, perhaps because it was written to convince above all others, the poet himself.

If this is true of 'Flowers in the Interval', it is not true of 'Didymus'. Here is the anomaly of a poem about doubt which is totally convincing. The core of the poem lies in the entrancing study of doubt embedded in the first four verses of Part III, spoiled in its entirety as a metaphysical poem by an over-clever use of punning internal rhymes, assonance and alliteration. The doubt that always assailed Thomas is anchored in biblical comment: "To me those tongues of fire were fire, not light", or "Blessed are those who believe and ask no leave/Of hand or eye". The impact lies in the sympathetic understanding of a believer's need for reassurance, a step beyond MacNeice himself in his intellectual incapacity to achieve faith. The tragic force of the poem lies in this ability to understand doubt by one who suffers because he cannot achieve even the degree of belief which is implicit in doubt:

> Oh but my doubt is a sea harsher than this that I see,
>   Oh but my hands tremble fumbling the night,
> To all of my questions I know the reply must be No;
>   To me those tongues of fire were fire, not light.
>
> Blessed are those who believe and ask no leave
>   Of hand or eye, for whom all water is wine,
> Who whatever the weight on the heart have the heart to wait
>   For the clouds to lift – a gift that was never mine.
>
> Whatever the clime, my task is ever to climb
>   Foothills that never are mountains; this Indian sky
> Is bowed with the dour monsoon and I doubt but soon
>   All of my converts and most of my work must die.
>
> I doubt that I have the least right to preach or write
>   In the name of Christ, I doubt that my doubt can find
> One hint that my terrible role could aspire to roll
>   The stone from the door of the tomb of the Indian mind.

Unfortunately the inspiration that makes a lyric of these four verses fails at the fifth. The predominant weakness of *Ten Burnt Offerings* is the impulse to continue and contrive beyond the limits of genuine feeling. This weakness is inevitably exposed and conviction sacrificed by needless repetition; verse six takes our mind straight back to verse nine of Section III. Who can believe that the images of the fifth verse are anything but mechanical?:

> I doubt and I doubt; in a crumbling exposed redoubt,
>   Enfiladed by heathendom, here to the end
> I watch in the endless rain to herald the reign
>   Of the Friend of Man – but can he be Thomas's friend?

What relation had the "redoubt" to any possible train of thought of which St Thomas, his Master, his contemporaries, or those among whom he found himself, were capable? Having used such a word, does it excuse the military image of "enfiladed"? That the rain is endless is not true, the last two lines are a forced return to the purpose of the poem, while the last two verses have a simplicity that is unconvincing to the point of banality. It may be objected that it is too easy to say of a poem that the poet should have stopped at this or that point; and it is not difficult to understand the desire to take so complicated a verse form and show that it could be used to convey simplicity of mind. Sadly the attempt fails. Here was a subject which gave every opportunity to explore the agony of an intellectual agnosticism fighting against the emotional weight of inherited beliefs. Apart from the four stanzas we have noted, the opportunity is sacrificed to an over-elaborate prosody, and surrendered to an elaborate form of word play that, far from crystallizing genuine emotional conflict, dilutes it with artificial and pretentious tricks. If these temptations had been resisted, these first four stanzas might have been developed into a poem of the same stature as Herbert's 'Frailtie' or 'Confession'.

III

The analysis of St Thomas's doubt and the portrait of the meek, doubting man are somewhat repetitously inserted into a picture of the teeming continent to which myth says that the saint went. The second part reads like a guide-book introduction to the story of Didymus by means of a visit to his chapel in Madras, and the description of the saint's doubt is more effective in the third part which we have already examined. The last section harps again on the same theme, and the introduction into the un-rhymed poem of two rhyming songs of temptation, while perhaps deliberately intended to recall St Thomas à Becket by its similarity of thinking to Eliot's *Murder in the Cathedral*, contributes nothing new into the poem and is therefore of only limited effectiveness. Apart from the highly wrought craftsmanship of the third part, the main pleasure of this poem is in the description of the teeming Indian world. The references to Hindu mythology are superficial and the concept of the god uniting both birth and destruction or death (surprisingly for one whose own philosophical thinking was along this very boundary) is never exploited. What are immediately and recognizably right are the odd lines and phrases that convey the sheer multiplication of life, the smells, the strangeness. The first three lines set this scene admirably:

> A million simmering kettles: in the Destroyer's shrine
> The world is on the boil, bats in malodorous dark
> Under a pyramid of writhing sculpture

If later the reference to the shrine of Indra above the Himalayas as the granite axis of India is a little forced, still "The whole of India jinks and twitters", allied to the phrase "monochrome under her motley" reproduces the endless restlessness of so many people. The surface colour and variety is contrastingly caught in the lines:

> Roses and sandalwood,
> Red spittle on the flagstones of the temple,
> Green flash of parrots, phosphorescent waves,
> Caparisoned elephants and sacred bulls,
> Crystal-gazers, navel-gazers, pedants,
> Dazzling and jangling dancers, dazzling lepers,
> Begging unfingered hands and mouthing eyes,
> Faces on faces each like a blind end,
> Lives upon lives bubbles of jewelled scum

If the last line lacks compassion, it does not lack the force of observation and the same may well be said of the sharp comment that

> even doubting,
> For those dark and sly and chameleon minds,
> Was a technique they knew.

Similarly in Part IV the pictures are clear and true:

> The last light purples the mirrors of paddy, the tracks
> Become dark rivers of peasants with brushwood on their heads,
> Rivers which all day long flowed out of sight
> Leaving the world to children. Now the palmtrees
> Grow dark like gigantic fly-whisks

MacNeice had visited India several times, and as one might expect, the colourful, malodorous, restless, remote sub-continent made an impact on his senses which he was capable of expressing in verse. He was constitutionally unable to achieve belief and might therefore be expected to understand doubt. Here there was an opportunity, as he obviously appreciated, by seizing on the subject of Doubting Thomas to bring together two strong elements of his understanding. If the poem only partly succeeds, or succeeds in part, it is perhaps because it established no real relationship between Thomas, whose problem would have remained the same irrespective of place and time, and India and its people. The poem might have gained unity and stature had MacNeice explored the possible relationship between Christian doubt and undogmatic Hinduism in greater depth.

'Suite for Recorders' may well be, somewhat belatedly, cathartic. It gives intellectual form to MacNeice's awakening from the Romantic time when his view of history was conveniently false, and when he thought of Elizabethan England as "through-and-through glamorous, ignorant of its appalling chicanery and crudity and ignoring the cheeseparing old harridan who sat on the throne, starving her navy, double-crossing her favourites and giving the lie to the myth of Gloriana".

Strangely if 'Didymus' takes a central figure and fails clearly to relate it to its place and time, 'Suite for Recorders' mirrors a time and fails to relate it to any central figure; and perhaps in consequence it also suffers from repetition and disunity. It is a little out of tune with the collection of poems in *Ten Burnt Offerings*. Whereas most of them draw some inspiration from places visited on his working travels the theme of this poem, with which he begins the volume, he develops later and more poetically, in 'Visitations' I. His argument is concerned with the paradox of Elizabethan culture, "the dung and the flower", as Fraser expresses it in *Vision and Rhetoric*. Herrick's lyrical mood of "gather ye rosebuds" is contrasted with the savage remnants of medievalism in political life, a contrast which the Elizabethans themselves had not failed to notice. Our outlook is naïve if, in contemplating our Elizabethan forebears:

> We envy what we think an innocent ardour,
> What in fact was staged revolt upon a tightrope, a creative
>   Despair, a blithe despair of youth,
> Which in that swivelling dubious web essayed its white lies in
>   defiance
> Of the black void of truth.

Nor should we think the Elizabethan picture is accurately painted in echoes of Chaucer's "Smyler with the knife under the cloke". It was that, and much else beside:

> Courtier with the knife behind the smile, ecclesiastic
> With faggots in his eyes, tight-lipped scholar with forbidden

Fruit in his back garden, all were conscious in their bowels
    Of the web and whose it was
And beneath it of the void where not old faith nor yet new
    learning
    Dare breathe the word Because.

It is only when MacNeice turns to a theme, perhaps best expressed by Eliot in *The Dry Salvages* – "I have said before/That the past experience revived in the memory/Is not the experience of one life only" – that the poetry begins to sing. Even then 11 stanzas in Part III are more than MacNeice's own development of this thought can sustain, but there are lyrical and striking verses. The continuity of life through the generations is well put in:

Pride in your history is pride
In living what your fathers died,
Is pride in taking your own pulse
And counting in you someone else.

Which someone, though long dead before,
Scrabbles and chirps on your own floor;
The orange he can hardly hold
Contains a world of Spanish gold.

The chilling vacuum in the truly agnostic attitude:

The windblown web in which we live
Presumes a yawning negative,
A nothing which cries out to see
A something flout its vacancy.

is a summary of intellectual despair, the other side of Eliot's "deep unbelief of the intellectual convert". And the final attitude is agnostic, tolerant, grudgingly admiring:

Yet read between those lines and peer
Down through the mesh of gossamer
And you will sense the darkness which
Made either guttering candle rich;

And you, a would-be player too,
Will give those angry ghosts their due
Who threw their voices far as doom
Greatly in a little room.

The 'Suite' is redeemed by the coda. Here, in singing of his
muse, MacNeice rounds off the poem by bringing us back to the
land of shepherds by way of Ireland and the Crucifixion, the
maypole, May Day and Judgment Day. We are allowed, as were
the Elizabethans, our pastoral dreams but our flocks must "shun
the rusty wire, the tank-traps". This is the conclusion of his
argument and in the end he finds the reason to continue even
"When a man's verses cannot be understood":

Come, this pipe is only on loan, I only a hireling,
    Yet, though my hire be due
And always unpaid, and my songs, heard by you only,
    Must needs be always unheard,
Come, my flocks, where this twilit wall still holds the
        noon-heat;
    Now I will sing of Her.

It is this note of courage which carries him through to his final
songs.

The historical theme, and the associations of Greece where
MacNeice, as he tells us on the title page, wrote these ten poems,
turned his thoughts to Byron, the philhellene, in whose work he
had taken an interest since the Audenesque parodies of *Letters
from Iceland*. Steeped in the stories of the last years, he starts off
'Cock o' the North' in swinging ballad metres and fills his lines
with appropriate references. The ill-fated helmet which Byron,
in a fit of enthusiasm, had designed for himself, and the two dogs
(Lion and Moretto) who were such a nuisance throughout the
abortive campaign, figure in the first line. Princes and generals,
leaders of opposing parties, lend their names for the sheer enjoyment of the sounds. Those unreliable brigands, Byron's favourite
Suliots in their white kilts, join with the provincial governors
and local bankers to give us hurrying syllables that are so enjoy-
able to say aloud:

Bad Lord Byron went to the firing, helmet and dogs and all,
He rode and he swam and he swam and he rode but now he
   rode for a fall;
Twang the lyre and rattle the lexicon, Marathon, Harrow
   and all,
Lame George Gordon broke the cordon, nobody broke his
   fall;
Mavrocordato, Colocotroni, faction, fiction and all,
All good fellows in fustanellas but all good fellows must fall.
Fall, fall, the kodjabashis! Snuff, douse, the Turkish moon!
Dollar credits with Barff and Hancock, conches in the sick
   lagoon!
Don John had fought Lepanto, Don Juan will dare it too;
Knaves and slaves are burning Sappho – hubble-bubble,
   hullabaloo!

We are reminded of Byron's own descriptions in his letters and of his sense of despair; we are reminded of that incredible political enthusiast, Leicester Stanhope, and of Braham's pet word for over-enthusiasm, in the delightful scurry of:

   'Flies and lice and fleas and thieves', Jeremy Bentham and gin –
   Scusi! Scusi! Entusymusy! How did I ever get in?

At this point inspiration seems to fail. "The Pilgrim came down like a wolf in the cold" is an unnecessary echo of 'The Destruction of Sennacherib', and the malquotation from *Hamlet* "he knew a hawk from a handshake" is a pedantic way of describing Byron's basic shrewdness; the opening section of the poem concludes too slowly in a welter of references to Meleager of Calydon, Leonidas who held the pass of Thermopylae, Byron's perpetual financial doles to the Greek forces, the London Committee for the Liberation of Greece, as well as to Castlereagh who was so savagely satirized in *Don Juan*, to Byron's own letters and to the celebration of Easter by the Greek Orthodox church. It might have been a jolly swinging satirical ballad on "Bad Lord Byron", but it is diminished by over-elaboration.

The second part compares the Missolonghi of Byron's day in phrases collected from contemporary letters and journals and the not so different Missolonghi of today with its statue of "Veeron"; and both this and the third continue the Meleager comparison which merges into the scene of Byron's death, with its emphasis on the unfortunate poet's demand to his two futile doctors to "Close the vein". To a reasonable knowledge of the last days of Byron the poem adds too little to bring a sense of tragedy to a sorry tale.

The analogy between Byron and Meleager is pursued in the fourth section which opens with a line deliberately reminiscent of Burns: "Bards wha hae for Hellas bled" echoes "Scots, wha hae", and then continues the nightmare reflections of the dying Byron in Scots (he was, of course, a Gordon on his mother's side and had been reared in Aberdeen). It is clever, but though possible, lacks conviction. As poetry it remains pedestrian.

There are among these ten poems one or two which have this appearance of being over-contrived, as though MacNeice had sat down at a café table perhaps, and looked around for inspiration. 'Our Sister Water' is of this kind; the idea of writing a poem to water seems to have occurred to him as he was served a tumbler of water with his Turkish coffee:

> Here on this grid of cemented heat
> We wilt at a table and order a Turkish
> Coffee. To pay for. Water is free.

From this point he takes us on a conducted tour of all the associated ideas conjured up by the thought of water. We are reminded of Thales, with whom philosophy is thought to have begun about 585 B.C., who held that everything is made of water and who is supposed to have said "water is best". We are reminded of Pindar, who five centuries before Christ wrote in praise of athletes and compared their virtue to water. We have the merits and beauties of water described.

The resulting poem is too precise, too reminiscent of a learned catalogue. The degree by which it fails to associate water with life, and desire for water with a passionate need for living, is underlined by reading again the second section of Part V of *The*

Waste Land – 'What the Thunder said'. The fourth part of 'Our
Sister Water' (which has, in its opening, echoes of Eliot, this
time of *East Coker* and *Little Gidding*) develops again the comparison between humanity and water. A few lines recall the
felicity of the earlier poems:

> Even now we contain an untold
> Capacity for sliding, rippling, filtering under the limestone hill,
> Moving in order under ice, charging in combers, lying still,
> Reflecting faces, refracting light, transparent or opaque,
> Can be wind-curled fountain, tigerish weir, garrulous rain or
>   tongue-tied lake,
> Can be all shapes or shapeless, assume all voices or none,
> Can alchemise rock and pavement, flatter and fleece the sun,
> Maraud and mime and bless. Such is water, such are we,

MacNeice falls into the fault of repetition and the next few lines,
in saying again what has already been said, are over-wrought:

> Termagants and trulls of froth, virgins in the naked heart,
> Bombardiers of breaker and bore, who in the end sidle apart
> Into still cells of crystal.

The third section explores water geographically from the bogs
of Ireland to the paddy fields of India and the second is a Ballad to
John Watt. It is Auden who has the last word on the subject:
"Thousands have lived without love, not one without water".

'The Island' is yet another poem that seems to come from a
deliberate attempt to find inspiration, and certainly its beginning
is not entirely without it:

> First the distant cocks. A hairfine
> Etching on silence, antiphonal silver,

and this is contrasted, both in description and in prosody, with:

> Then the donkeys; clumsily splicing
> Coarser hausers – Haul away, bullies,
> For all your grumps and catarrh.

but apart from a few moments of colourful vision:

> The grey stones breathe in sky, a slim and silent girl
> Gathers salt from the sea-crags, green among green leaves
> Figs, kid-soft purses, bulge, on low stone roofs
> Figs, grapes, tomatoes, dry in the sun and sweat
> Pastes the hair to the forehead, a tall woman
> Strides out of Homer over the pine-needles, mule-droppings,
> Holding a distaff while the swallowtail butterflies
> Fly, or seem to, backwards. Seem to. Backwards.

(and in passing, it may be noted how even this is spoilt by the portentous mannerism of repeating "backwards. Seem to. Backwards."), it is dull. The poem has a homely logic, a comment on the world of today in which a simple village has associations with the civilization of the West, and the measure of MacNeice's lack of true and irresistible inspiration lies in the kind of unconscious plagiarism of, for example, "a brown leaf clanks from the green tree/Dry on dry ground like a subpoena" with its immediate recollection of "While the dead leaves still rattled on like this/ Over the asphalt where no other sound was".

Of 'The Death of a Cat' it is better for a critic who is by nature indifferent to the deaths of cats, and finds anthropomorphism displeasing, to say nothing. In these circumstances it is not possible to distinguish between sentimentality and proper feeling.

IV

Since *Ten Burnt Offerings* constitutes a more contrived and intellectual approach to poetry than was customary for MacNeice, it is a triumph of its kind that the most successful poems are the two which are most intellectually complete. Each is based on the association of place with history, myth and the eternal conflicts of the human spirit; both suffer from repetition.

'Areopagus' is a very demanding poem. It requires of the reader that he has a fair working knowledge of classical Greek history and mythology, and of the early history of the Christian church. The 'Areopagus' itself had both associations. It was a rocky promontory to the west of the Acropolis, which gave its name to the Council that met there (originally) to try cases of homicide, murderous wounding, arson and religion. It was here in consequence that St Paul was brought to explain "what this new teaching is, which is spoken by thee".

The opening section of 'Areopagus' is a welter of cross references. In essence it brings the Christian faith, dependent equally on the subtle Roman convert, Paul, and the determined Hebrew, Peter, into direct contrast, both with the sophisticated, and in that period, decadent, thought and wit of Greece, and with the whole of the mythological concepts which were the original inspiration of that thought. We start with Christ whose history is "a tall story" ending in a "dark sanctum" and who was "That Hebrew riddling in a land of olives". With the use of the verb, we think of Donne's "riddling, perplexed, labyrinthical soul". Then we are reminded of Peter, the Apostle to whom Christ said "Put up again thy sword" but who with "all the disciples left him and fled". So we have an extraordinarily vivid picture of Peter carrying the word:

> The saint on the run had a sword in his mouth
> And his feet on the rock were rock;

In the last line we are reminded of St Matthew again: "thou art Peter and upon this rock will I build my church". We are allowed no pause in our thinking, for now we are with Paul. "As it were scales had dropped in Damascus" refers to the *Acts* and we cannot doubt that it was Paul who provided in Athens "Iron faith in the city of irony". The hill of Ares, the original site of the Areopagus, this "Outcrop of judgement", overlooked the temple of the Eumenides (fertility earth-dwelling spirits) who derived (by a confusion of popular thinking) from the Erinyes, or Fates. So MacNeice saw the conflict between those who belonged to

157

Athens, the city of irony, and those with "The foreign accent/ Souring their salt", as taking place above the cave of the Medusa-like Furies, the Erinyes, the Kind Ones. In so doing he is directing our attention to the consistency of mythical and religious association with place; the passing of religion based on myth; the rise of philosophy, the birth of a new myth; and the coming of a religion with a new philosophy, but yet having around it (in the dark sanctum) the trappings of the old dreams. Finally the impact of Paul on these subtle philosophers is well described: "they nudged and doubted./Diamond cut diamond. Something new." One of the few occasions perhaps in which the sudden introduction of a one- or two-word phrase is fully justified prosodically. To accompany the packed references we have a spare hard unrhymed stanza of five lines with the stresses reading 5.5.3.5.3. There is considerable use of alliteration emphasized by short, sharp words:

> Was an appetiser for a tired mind.
> With a stone in it too. A sharp titillation
> With a snub, if not threat, in it too.

The cunning use of 'ti' and 'it' as well as 't', the use of words beginning with 's' for contrasts and the repetition of "in it too", all contribute to a feeling of unease that reflects the impact of new thought on established ways. Assonance is used to contribute to the unity of the stanzas: "outcrop", "souring", "tousled" in verse 3, and "limestone", "sliced", "prides", "diamonds" in the last, are but two examples. So we have a learned, metaphysical, craftsmanlike poem in a prosodic form that is modern, but traditionally based. It sets a scene, and by implication poses a problem. Is it answered in the other three sections?

The second one starts with a splendid word (not in most dictionaries) "Spermologies", which, with the Miltonian use of 'sperm' to mean offspring, can be taken as a cynical comment on that type of religion based on love of mankind; and that it has fallen on stony ground recalls the parable of the Sower. The word "stone" itself is used to suggest the stone before Christ's tomb, and the altar of sacrifice and the tablets of the law; the hard words that flow in the dark flow in the voice of God to Moses, yet we are reminded of those other gods, the Titans (themselves the offspring of Cronos), who sank to the lowest depths of Tartarus.

We are unprepared by the breadth of reference and comparison in these four lines for the sudden change in tempo that follows. Suddenly we have a recollection of *The Waste Land* and it is disturbing because it reminds us of Eliot's economy of verse and the universal nature of his understanding as he says:

> After the torchlight red on sweaty faces
> After the frosty silence in the gardens
> After the agony in stony places

By comparison MacNeice is too much concerned with the paraphernalia of change, and he attributes significance to the ephemeral:

> And the torches hissed where now, ringed round with
>   mountains,
> Flow seas of electric light.

That he cannot resist the cry from Aladdin, "New lamps for old", brings him perilously close to bathos. The next three verses traverse the same ground. The simple people celebrating Easter are only a step away from the Furies, and we are again reminded of Eliot, speaking of the power of words:

> Shrieking voices
> Scolding, mocking, or merely chattering,
> Always assail them.

MacNeice comes near to an understanding of Eliot's kind of Christianity in:

> Hide if you choose in Stoa and Garden,
> Your own crisp words will begin to hiss
> In key with our torches, in step with our snakes,
> And your own sharp eyes, at home to doubt,
> Will blur with a greater despair: belief.

It is here perhaps that MacNeice should have stopped; but he continues and he comes to no conclusion. Man will have myth and if he is offered a new religion he will convert it to myth, and the myths will have much in common:

> Not fez and hookah (there is no God but God),
> Not tommy-gun and brochure (there is no god but Man),
> Could cancel out Christ's death or prove the Furies dead.

and so our choice is between

> Christ, if we could, having Christian fathers;
> But Furies, if we must.

He can educe no argument to convince of either. In the fourth section of the poem, written in verses each of three rhyming lines of uneven length, we arrive nowhere. We are back with both Paul and the Erinyes, and with Leda, and with Orestes (who was acquitted by the Areopagus, and may be compared to Paul who was heard without condemnation) and so by implication with the whole story of Clytemnestra and Agamemnon. We are reminded once more that the Erinyes are also the Eumenides and we are invited (with a passing reference to their cave and Christ's tomb) to propitiate these "Nurses of fear and hope". It is a pagan conclusion; and it is a weak one. The opening promise of the poem is not fulfilled, even in the verse.

'Day of Returning' is the poem which of all those in *Ten Burnt Offerings* shows most understanding, conveys a sense of greatest *rapport* with its subject, and has therefore most integrity. The basic subject is nostalgia. MacNeice was the poet of nostalgia, of that longing for something that is lost, or impossible, or not attainable now, or unknown but just around the corner. The first speaker is Odysseus during the period when he is in thrall to Calypso on the Island of Ogygia; and Odysseus weeps for return to home as MacNeice longed for the return to childhood and mother. The phrasing of the opening is reminiscent of the Greek, or of translations of the Greek, from which it is derived, with its adverbial and adjectival clauses preceding the main verb:

> Crouched upon sea-chiselled gravel, staring out and up at the
>   sea,
> The gnarled and glorious twister, seasoned in danger, wept

The thrusting of the mind over the seemingly impassable ocean is
well conveyed by "terrace on terrace of waves" and by "he rode
his mind at the hurdles of ocean". The psychology is accurate.
Odysseus wept,

> But not as of old when he half enjoyed the weeping
>   For shared sorrows in company.
> But this was not tragic, this was frustration; infertile as the
>   foam
>   That creamed around his sandals, listless as the hope
> The sweet voice held out sometimes of an immortal
>   Life, but life here, not Ithaca.
> For here his bed was too soft and the wine never rough and the
>   scent of the flowers
> Too heavy;

Perhaps the next section is the most successful of the attempts
in *Ten Burnt Offerings* to show that "Time past and time future . . .
point to one end, which is always present". It is successful because it is based on the universality of men's sentiment for home;
which is the one great similarity between all homes in all ages.
So MacNeice paints the simple home, clear as a Dutch interior:

> On scrubbed white deal two hands, red from the sink, are
>   clenched
> On the hope of an after-life; there is dirt in the cracks
> Of the table and under the nails for all their scouring
> And the golden walls of Jerusalem the Golden
>   Have black cracks in them too.

Zion is compared to Calypso's isle, out of time. The picture is
completed, with more affection than is usual for MacNeice,
with:

> On Sunday perhaps the alarm is stilled and the red hands
> Reposed on a Sunday lap in the just-so room
> Which does not exist on weekdays, where the Penates

Are no more jug nor clock but family photos
  Of a family not to the life.

Stiff collars and a harmonium. White and black. Stiff keys.
A creaking lock in gates of mother of pearl.

One can smell the dusty, too-sweet smell of the Sunday parlour.
The question that MacNeice now asks us is whether, if we
successfully reach the top of Jacob's ladder:

    Will Wesley hand us a gold
  Chalice of nectar – immortal and islanded life,
  A home from home?

and will our bliss be a prison, as it was for Odysseus, away from
real people "Who lived"? The third section is a meditation that,
in tone, reminds us of Tennyson's 'Ulysses' and might indeed be
almost a pastiche. In the first half MacNeice falls again into the
besetting sin of this volume and repeats in a new form the
argument of the first section. But half-way comes a description
that is better than any translation and produces a real and human
Odysseus:

    They call me crafty Odysseus;
  I have used my craft on gods and nymphs and demigods
  But it is time, high time, I turned it again
  To the earth that bred it, a new threshing floor
  Or setting up boundary stones, for even the best
  Neighbours encroach – and I like to have someone to argue
    with
  About my rights of grazing or wood-cutting; aye, it is time
  I heard the bleat of my goats and smelt the dung of my cattle;
  Here there is neither dung nor rights nor argument,
  Only the scent of flowers and a too sweet voice which is ever
  Youthful and fails to move me. Here could never be home,
  No more than the sea around it. And even the sea
  Is a different sea round Ithaca.

The poem 'Day of Returning' is rounded off by an implicit
comparison with Jacob, another crafty hero and founder of his
race, but this part of the poem is pedestrian and one feels that

MacNeice has been misled by the resemblance in folk history of Odysseus and Jacob to continue beyond the limits he can sustain.

MacNeice was a reluctant agnostic, never quite able to deploy the emotional or the intellectual force either to make an act of faith, or the final denial of all faith. The consequence of this attitude is a perpetual search in his poetry for answers he is not prepared to find. In *Ten Burnt Offerings* there is a feeling, almost a suggestion, that he has searched for answers to the eternal problems by an attempt at synthesizing, or at least comparing, different religious mythologies. In 'Didymus' we are presented with the deliberate contrast between pious Christian intellectualizing disguised as simplicity and the "sly and chameleon minds" of Hinduism. There is genuine conflict here between MacNeice's intellectual capacity for doubt, and his more superficial but pleasurable capacity for apprehending all the facets of the physical world about him, never fuller and more fascinating than in India. In 'Areopagus' he attempts to show, by his favourite device of identification of idea with place, that all religions are at heart but one, and the apparently savage myths of the past and its more refined philosophies are not without influence and bear much similarity to the subtleties of the new religion of Christ. In 'Day of Returning' he takes us further back, to Homer and the Old Testament tales, and seems to say that the qualities admired in the early folk heroes were, if not necessarily truly praiseworthy, simple, predictable, human and above all, similar for widely different peoples. That nothing finally emerges from this global survey, that it solves nothing for him, and contributes nothing to the development of his poetry, we shall see as we study *Autumn Sequel*.

V

The problem facing anyone attempting a preliminary analysis of *Autumn Sequel* is the poem's lack of form. Its 26 cantos, while occasionally sequential, have no apparent order and develop no consistent train of thought. If the "Parrot" that appears in the first canto was meant to provide some link, its reappearance is spasmodic and therefore ineffective. Many lines are given over to hagiography which is too uncritical to be interesting, though it is sincere. The alternating reportage and soliloquy of *Autumn Journal* has given way to less immediate and less arresting reflections: only here and there do we find some sharp and colourful observation that reminds us of the force and vigour of the earlier poem. The verse form, terza rima, has caused some comment, but it is not as rare in English poetry as might be thought, and was used, for example, by Wyatt, Byron, Shelley and Tennyson. In *Varieties of Parable* MacNeice describes it as being "a yet more severe form" than rhyming couplets, and "therefore, if well managed, more sustaining". Of its nature it gives the impression of continuity.

MacNeice himself describes *Autumn Sequel* as "A Rhetorical Poem". A glance at the dictionary yields the meaning of 'rhetorical' as 'expressed in terms calculated to persuade'. To persuade whom? – and of what? If this is its purpose, then neither the subject nor the object of the persuasion is ever clear. We are forced to conclude that *Autumn Sequel* is defective because its purpose is never apparent. Purpose imposes form, and form presumes purpose. "True rhetoric" he had said 16 years earlier, "presupposes a certain scale of values, certain conceptions of good and evil". Here these conceptions are never clear, nor is any scale defined.

We must not forget that the bulk of the poem was broadcast by the B.B.C. and was doubtless written with broadcasting in mind. Radio has the capacity to bestow a false importance; music and the voice from the loudspeaker can lend emotions to writing that are not implicit in the sense. "Broadcasting" MacNeice says "can give us something unobtainable from print." To some extent radio production can disguise a fair degree of repetition and considerable looseness of prosody. "The radio dramatist", he says in the Introduction of *Christopher Columbus* (and by extension we may apply what he says to the radio poet), "must think in terms of sound rather than words alone."

Because MacNeice was thinking in terms of broadcasting, it is perhaps to the earlier B.B.C. success, *The Dark Tower*, that we owe the sequence in *Autumn Sequel* which is as near as anything may be to the core of such an amorphous poem. It is an attempt at expression by parable much as was *The Dark Tower*. Had this sequence, from Canto XIV to the middle of Canto XVI, been totally successful, it might have transformed the poem by radiating a glow from its centre and providing the missing unity. It surprises, and it has more force in its allegory than there is in some of the penny plain passages; but it is not great enough.

Canto XIV, with little ado, starts us on one of MacNeice's 'quests'. The beginning is not without wit; nature and suburban man are brought sharply together:

> While windblown moons embark
> On seas of cloud and the winds of October scatter
>
> The late night finals round the empty park,
> Young men with dead leaves plastered on their shoes
> Set out with scrip or briefcase through the dark,

They set out on the Quest, not inspired by the hope of the Grail, or like Spenser's knights, in order to submit to a test of their dominant virtue, but doubtfully, "not so sure what it is they stand to gain". The first allegory succeeds in giving a somewhat mealy-mouthed impression of the effects of surrender to drink, and the lower sexuality, and by oblique and biblical references to the importuning of married women and of whores. That the reward is to

> put out the light that shone
> In the back of their mind this morning.

is a perceptive comment. Here, in nullity, ends the first path of the Quest.

Others, like pilgrims, "clutch their amulets and wallets" (a pun here surely, since a wallet is both a pilgrim's scrip and a pocket case for money) and go on to explore the world of politics; and Demos is described as

That show of fat white hands to point the way

To the Better Life for All.

This Quest leads to little more than nothing: "Long live this Status Quo". "Still, some aberrant errants give a miss" – a line which must surely rank among the worst that conscious crafts-manship can do – "to such Utopian Zions" and explore instead "the temple of Aesthetic Bliss", which he describes unkindly as "That blind aquarium of chanting trout/And quivering fins and suckers" (another pun). The mythical figures from Scheherazade to Tristram here surround the youth who hopes to find in art "what others find through science/Or perhaps through God".

Here is surely the missed opportunity to explore in allegory or parable (however he may care to define the words), the causes of man's deeper satisfactions. One may find it in science – and what is that? One in God, however defined. One may be eternally dissatisfied, but for what reason? But no, once again the issue is bilked:

> Outside and inside shift
> Into each other continually. No sieve,
> Not even the finest in the world, can sift
>
> Essence from accident; the muses give
> Nothing for nothing; works of art, like men,
> Must be at least a little impure to live,
>
> And therefore accident-prone. No brush or pen,
> Woodwind or strings, can pledge a constant truth
> That may not lapse into untruth again.

This is the thinking behind 'Homage to Clichés'.

We are now conducted through another allegory in which we are invited to consider the ape which is in all of us and which lurks, and can be seen and pursued (but to no purpose) in the portraits of the great. We break through this experience in a claustrophobic "stillborn hullabaloo". In this nightmare world "Picking his steps among the mummied heads", we are brought to the depths by a line that parodies Yeats: "Treat softly because you tread on the dreams that are not there". The dreams are not there because we are in a society

> Of meaningless activity, of clever
> Means to some stupid end, this endless spate
> Of highly organized yet blind endeavour.

Now we have a satirical allegory of society as a hive of bees, a "blind bustling nation" to which "Let there be!" is an adequate order. In this world it is appropriate that the highest expression of love should be the love that is sacrificed to continue the race, as in the love-flight of the bees. The consummation is also failure: "everything has been said/Of love and freedom".

The image changes and we are now invited into Vanity Fair, an invitation underlined ironically by a cross reference to Walt Disney's 'Jiminy Cricket' in the barker's cry of "Just let your sense of Whatnot be your guide". Once inside, and lured on to the sideshows, we are plunged into a welter of uterine and foetal images:

> Precipitated, immersed
> In a clinging dark, a rubbery blubbery duct,
> Wormlike the young man slithers through its pursed
>
> And elastic coils, its foiled and moiled and mucked
> Byways, its miles of narrowness and juice
> With no more room for his body than a plucked
>
> Fowl wrapped in lard,

Suddenly, at this moment of complete reversion to the womb, we are startlingly reminded of Edgar Allan Poe's

> the play is the tragedy 'Man'
> And its hero the Conqueror Worm.

It is the worm that claims "I am the only Way" and that it lives "both in/And on man's guts and so have conquered man". The Quest has "come to a standstill" at the not very original point of appreciating (however 'poetically' expressed in phrases such as "there are darker cells/Enclosing blinder lives") that "Great fleas have little fleas upon their backs to bite 'em" and the revolt from this reminds us, but on a lower plane, of Hopkins:

> Not, I'll not, carrion comfort, Despair, not feast on thee;
> Not untwist – slack they may be – these last strands of man
> In me or, most weary, cry *I can no more.* I can;
> Can something, hope wish day come, not choose not to be.

Here "the young man" is rescued by seizing on "the worm's" rhetorical quotation "Who would choose life?" and giving an answer in the Bergsonian sense that "we are free when our acts spring from our whole personality":

> 'Then I have choice!'
> The young man cries; 'Most certainly I choose;
> Choose to grow and decay, to weep and rejoice,
>
> To be what I was and shall be.'

This is a position, not of transcendental hope, but of near existentialism. It is a disappointing position, for it has not advanced on earlier thoughts or beliefs, and would not seem to have the seeds of such advance within it. The message is the same as it was 15 years before: "nothing is more proud than humbly to accept" and "All that I would like to be is human", and in the light of this, that "A fire should be left burning/Till it burns itself out". So now:

> The Quest goes on and we must still ask why
>
> We are alive, though no one man has met
> A full or lucid answer; all we can do
> Is answer it by living and pay the debt
>
> That none can prove we owe.

We are not one step advanced from 'The Stygian Banks':

> it is our privilege –
> Our paradox – to recognize the insoluble
> And going up with an outstretched hand salute it.

The allegory is a failure since it does not rise above the concept of mere acceptance, since there is no belief. In *Varieties of Parable* MacNeice deals, not very fully, with "Belief", but he does say that "in a poem, and implicitly an allegorical poem, the beliefs are formalizing elements". The lack of belief, this inability to take up and to hold a position either social, philosophical, or religious, is reflected in Cantos XIV to XVI of *Autumn Sequel*; the allegory lacks form, and the lack is reflected backward and forward over the whole poem.

MacNeice had a lifelong interest in allegory. His basic position was summed up in the Introductory Note to 'The Dark Tower':

Some element of parable therefore, far from making a work thinner and more abstract, ought to make it more concrete. Man does after all live by symbols.

If this is true, and it is reasonably debatable, it is at least necessary that the symbols shall be recognizable, and, for preference, universally recognizable. It is also, surely, essential that what they stand for shall be of universal interest. So it follows that if the poet is to venture successfully into this field his comment, his point of view, as well as his presentation, must be of the order that makes us exclaim that we have seen and learnt something new about the world, about the existence or absence of God, about the human heart, or have at least regarded them with new vision. The parable in the middle of *Autumn Sequel* fails by this standard. Pantheism in the suburbs, disillusion with politics and with art for art's sake, a little anthropomorphism, some philosophizing, the surrender of the personality to the demands of society, ideal love, and the complications born of the Oedipus complex and its associated foetal death-wish, call either for a

transcendental magnificence in poetic treatment, or calm acceptance, or powerful incisive satire. Here the parable at the very
core of the poem is a sustained imagery of the obvious; it fails,
and in doing so it measures the poem's failure, in MacNeice's
own terms, by making it "thinner" and "more abstract".

Inability to achieve faith can communicate passion and provide
the basis for allegory. Who can doubt that the emotional force of
much of *The City of Dreadful Night* derives from the fierce sincerity of Thomson's disbelief? MacNeice was afflicted with a
guilty agnosticism, because to be an agnostic was to be a traitor to
an upbringing that had taken place in an atmosphere of unquestion-
ing belief, and he came to feel that to believe unquestioningly
was to be intellectually dishonest. This dichotomy, obvious
throughout all his poetry, and itself a source of some of the
'metamorphoses' from which he composes the symbolic portraits
of himself (e.g. 'Birthright') takes the heart from the core of
Autumn Sequel. It is an attempt to be sceptical, but the scepticism
is forced and the conclusion lamely Episcopalian, if not Nonconformist:

> And yet those debts accrue
> Which we must pay and pay but, what is odd,
> The more you pay the more comes back to you.
>
> Which some explain by reference to God
> And others find an inexplicable fact,
> But fact it is, as downright as a clod,
>
> As unremitting as a cataract.

It is his troubled lack of conviction that diminishes the stature
of this portion of his poem. Shelley's 'The Triumph of Life',
itself an allegory in terza rima, is unfinished; but its vitality
derives from a river of striking images which hurry one on to
some unknown, inevitable conclusion, unfortunately never
reached, but yet anticipated. The end, once reached, would, one
feels, make both plan and purpose clear, and the emotional unity
of Shelley's great uncompleted poem compels belief in its

subjective truth. In the allegorical cantos of *Autumn Sequel* the goal is neither obvious nor achieved. The mainspring is neither belief nor unbelief, nor is it desire for belief; it is an uneasy lack of ability to believe or disbelieve in any hard, definite and final way. This unease robs the poem of strength to carry its burden. Many of the images chosen to carry the allegory (of bees and apes and tunnels and trains) are banal and others are forced. Even if we attempt to interpret the allegory as illustrating the despair that comes from quests attempted but doomed to inevitable failure, the final sense is that of mild frustration which shrinks to its proper size when compared with the bitter and defiant force of Thomson's poem.

As one examines MacNeice's thinking throughout *Autumn Sequel*, the same inability to reach any conclusion overshadows the too occasional inspiration. His philosophizing is generally too tentative. In Canto VII we are given a touch of the *Rubáiyát*:

> All other colours run,
> All other guides abscond; its countless rays,
> Could we but count them, would add up to One.

followed by a few stanzas of what John Press aptly calls "agnostic sermonising":

> Then clutch that thread of light and seize the days
> Opening; which, opening, will not let you out
> But lead you in, to the blind heart of the maze
>
> Where your antagonist waits, unknown, though all about
> Him stand your too well known and too triumphant foes,
> Each horned and crooked greed and spite and doubt
>
> With small red virulent eyes which presuppose
> Eternal malice; but behind them all
> Stands the eternal bride like a half-opened rose
>
> In a hedge of spears and horrors.

The final section of this canto, intended as a song to creative achievement and as a confession of faith, a "Fanfare for the Makers", comes close to bathos. To write

> Merely to tighten screws or sharpen blades
>
> Can catch a meaning,

or

> as workers work and can take pride
> In spending sweat before they draw their pay,

is to say little more than that "if anything is worth doing, it is worth doing well", and though the penultimate line is not without its psychological interest, it is too suddenly negative, and in consequence, slightly ridiculous:

> As life can be confirmed even in suicide

The concept fits in well enough with the despairing comment in Canto XXI:

> And, if it comes to the worst, let us have the Devil
>
> Rather than mere negation.

This takes but a little further the thought expressed in *Autumn Journal*, although the mood is entirely different:

> Can you not take it merely on trust that life is
> The only thing worth living and that dying
> Had better be left to take care of itself in the end?

For whereas *Autumn Journal* is still informed by hope, or at the least acceptance, *Autumn Sequel* can find that acceptance only in the devil himself.

In Canto XIII he has recognized that "To be devout/Or scholarly would help" and that scholarship might well have helped him to a true philosophical synthesis, and devotion would have led him to belief. Either would have rescued him from the limbo of doubt. Indeed in Canto XXIV he makes a conscious effort to deceive himself into belief with a lyrical outburst which is more

convincing than all his efforts to solve place-time relationship in
Ten Burnt Offerings. These few verses shine from their context:

> Can we sever
> Two thousand years ago from here and now,
> Or Bethlehem from say Birmingham? I never
>
> Can make of history what the dates allow
> Or clamp historic places to the map;
> Gas Street seems old as Memphis and the brow
>
> The foundry worker mops beneath his cap
> Seems wrinkled deep as Joseph's. By outmoded
> Canals beneath black piles of slag and scrap
>
> One still can find a stable. And if corroded
> Iron makes room for steel and glass, what then?
> Statistics in the end must be decoded
>
> Into the works, and days, and lives of men
> Who still are born and die. Profit and loss
> Will not prevent the robin and the wren
>
> Mourning the babes in the wood; no chromium gloss
> Could ever disguise a manger, no transmitter,
> Gantry or pylon dare replace the Cross.

For that moment, since faith in anything transcends its expression, the poetry sings and the poet recognizes how close he has
come to faith:

> While I, brought up to scoff rather than bless
> And to say No, unless the facts require
>
> A neutral verdict, for this once say Yes.

The final canto of *Autumn Sequel* is both the most revealing and
the most disappointing. We are back, as so often with MacNeice,
in the train, to him so evocative and so symbolic of life and time.
We have (omitting once again the hagiography) the same seeking

to break down the isolation of the individual that we find in his earlier poems:

> let the wall
> Of isolation crumble and the light
> Break in, but also out, the black scales fall
>
> From all their eyes together in one white
> And final annunciation.

This recalls the difficulty of human relationship he had always experienced, and which he expressed in *Autumn Journal* XVII: "Why not admit that other people are always/Organic to the self" and in 'The Stygian Banks', "I am alone/And you are alone and he and she are alone". Suddenly we are reminded of Canto IV of *Autumn Journal*. Now these "people with blank faces that are yet familiar" are identified (with stirrings of his essentially Christian and puritan conscience) as "The wrongs I have done, thought, said". "Pat cliché" though it is, he is here "for your sins" as any Christian might be. Next the sins of the world are personalized:

> I mark a huddle of men with coloured skins
> Had they not lost their skins in the scorch and blast
>
> Of new and clever bombs;

(The lack of cohesion here results in a welter of sentimentality and conventional horror. There was no need to add consciousness of colour to a tragedy sufficient in itself and then underline it by such a crude negation.) His own shortcomings contribute equally to the nightmares:

> Each meanness, blight, spite, doubt, guilt, hate, remorse and
>   fear
> Fills carriage after carriage.

The equation of personal sin and global guilt is too facile and forfeits the 'willing suspension of disbelief', nor is it regained by the tepid credit list he offers in consolation. The philosophers, poets, Lords of Misrule, and visitors from the "Kingdom" are vague abstractions. So we have once again the familiar assertion that there must be something for which to struggle, since we are here. Once again he presses "an anxious ear against the keyhole,/ To hear the future breathing", and as he ends *Autumn Sequel*, we are aware that in his thinking he has progressed nowhere:

> To discern
> The future is not easy since those fires
> That warm us are the selfsame fires that burn
>
> Our guts, and since the wood of our desires
> Consists of single yet entangled trees
> Which maybe form a wood the world requires
>
> But yet a wood which none distinctly sees
> Or fully finds his way in.

VI

Indecision may well be the philosophic fate of the intelligent suburban man. If MacNeice would have scorned this description of himself, at least, as we know from 'Sunday Morning', he fully understood the suburbs. So Canto III begins with yet another uterine image verging on anal eroticism, effective because of the shock of recognition for a fierce description of a too-familiar experience:

> A suburban train
> Squeezes me through the black wood of Saint John
> By intestinal tunnels like a pain
>
> That London would get rid of,

This is followed by a not unpleasing descriptive journey through the suburbs to a job of preparing the film of the Everest expedition, a job which gives rise to a series of questions, and experiences, and impressions. To what extent, he asks, are we justified in turning ideals and achievements into entertainment:

> What price
> Should we demand for turning what was rare
> Into a cheap couvade or proxy paradise,
>
> Just one more travelogue to make the groundlings stare?

"Groundlings" is an intellectual class description (though also a reminiscence of the Elizabethan theatre) and MacNeice's use of it reminds us that, fighting against this current of his nature, he had in *Autumn Journal* III declared:

> There is no reason for thinking
> That, if you give a chance to people to think or live,
> The arts of thought or life will suffer and become rougher
> And not return more than you could ever give.

This was intellectualizing. In his heart, and 15 years later, he is unconvinced:

> Groundlings will never see why Mallory answered why
> Men should climb Everest: because it is there.

Then follows one of these moments in MacNeice's poetry when the logic of his thinking on matters of social behaviour, or of ethics, is sacrificed to a straightforward statement of his own experience:

> The target that we almost hoped to miss
> Is what we hit and what we hate we pardon
> And only kill what we have failed to kiss.

This, if not original, is psychologically well-observed and well-expressed.

As if the word "kiss" inspires him, we are brought suddenly on to another small parable to show that to do things 'because they are there' is an impulse as old as original sin. It contains perhaps the best lyric stanza of the sequence:

> A glimpse of golden breasts, a mat of hair
> Thrown back from the eyes; a naked arm in a ray
> Of sunlight plucks an apple. Because it is there.

The whole canto is an analysis of the three-stage impact which adventure has on modern suburban civilization. There is the adventure itself. There is its photographed and recorded image. There is the edited version of this record produced by men like MacNeice whose critical sensibilities were aware of the innate falsity of the final impression:

> Who can blame
> The middleman for leaving some things out?
> What's in a peak that is not in a name?
>
> Middlemen all, we labour like devout
> Lay brethren whom our Rule allows to talk,
> Not knowing what the silence is about.

The residual effect on the poet himself of all this activity is amusingly and convincingly conveyed in the remainder of the canto. On his way home

> chasms abound
> Under each plot and path; commuters hurrying back
> Ought to be roped together – could a fit rope be found.
>
> I leave them to their fate, enter again the black
> Tunnel of gentle or was it headless John,
> Suffering a little from my bivouac
>
> At such high altitudes, my breath is gone,
> My wits are going; I shall cure all this
> Down there at my base camp in Marylebone.

He is still touched by high romance and this gives a lyric quality

to his vision and so we have a description of unusual charm
(almost in the W. H. Davies manner, but individual enough):

> The mild September evening blows a kiss
> In ripples over the lake, a sky of peach
> Explodes its pulp – a metamorphosis
>
> That leaves a stone. And stony-grey trees reach
> Down to the water where like landing craft
> Low-draughted ducks whiten their wakes as each
>
> Duck's whim directs but never land, a daft
> Moorhen crosses their bows, its clockwork head
> Going forward, backward, forward, while abaft
>
> Over the silver shimmer and sombre lead
> Sail two great swans, ghost-white, and between them two
> Birds trying to be ghosts, still brown, still birds instead.

A more discouraging contrast between an appreciation of the
ideal and romantic, and a sense of the mundane world in which
we live, inform Canto IX. He describes the sudden return to
reality after the magic of the ballet and we are reminded of *Les
Sylphides*. This time we go "Forth from this magic circle" to, of
all drear images:

> a Saturday night
> Past closing time, an interim of flat
>
> Refusal and discouragement; the white
> Tiles in the public lavatory deny
> The whiteness of the skirts that bloomed in flight.

Immediately, and with immense discouragement, the image of
the escalator follows:

> And the stairs carry us down and we do not try
> Even moving down to move; an endless file
> Of faces flows up past us, brassy or coy or sly,
>
> Boosting each gadget, gewgaw, stunt or style,
> All with the same self-love,

This is in despairing contrast to the image in *Autumn Journal* I, with its implicit feeling for his fellow men:

> And so to London and down the ever-moving
> > Stairs
> Where a warm wind blows the bodies of men together
> > And blows apart their complexes and cares.

and also of 'Belfast' and 'Birmingham'. These latter echoes are even more insistent in Canto X where he describes the closing of the pleasure gardens in Battersea Park, and, appropriately addressing the mistress of Spenser's Bower of Bliss, he says

> > Acrasia grieves
> Her fluorescent joys, her papier mâché rocks,
> Her arches that lead to nowhere, her unbound sheaves
>
> Of imitation corn, her filigree box
> Of knick-knacks and false bottoms, her swans in plastic
> And all her inanimate creatures. Antirrhinums and phlox
>
> Have yielded to candy floss, the heavy fantastic
> Toes have tripped on a cocoanut, the last
> Fun of the fair will snap with a snap of elastic

The reference to 'L'Allegro' brings us flatly down far short of 'Il Penseroso'.

At the level of poetical description this is an outward expression of the meretricious political aspect he has described in Canto VI:

> What is the news? Big business and small beer,
>
> Meat and eggs expensive, life still cheap,
> Divorce and juvenile crime, while peace on earth
> Is muttered away by statesmen in their sleep.

This is observation but there is apparently nothing to be done about it. It is a superficial and silly world and we are the impotent dupes of incompetent rulers. Our technology is put to trumpery

use, but there is nothing MacNeice can do but turn in Canto XXI
to some ill-defined deity with the prayer:

> Pity us for the follies we have lost;
> Pity us for our learning, who can count
> In light-years by the million, but not the cost
>
> Of even a broken toy.

The broad social picture in *Autumn Sequel* is ironical, critical,
despairing. The private social picture consists of cosy and
uncritical tributes to friendships, termed 'hagiography' by one
reviewer. It is an attempt, not always successful, to pay a pious
tribute to his friends. It will not avail us much to equate "Gavin"
with Graham Shepherd, "Wimbush" with Herrickx, "Aloys" with
Stahl, and "Boyce" with Dodds, to name but a few. The tone is
uniformly adulatory, and perhaps for that reason disappointing.
Rarely can a prized and cherished friend, and obviously a man of
charm and courage, have been so ill-served as "Gavin". A grubby,
snobbish little boy in *The Strings are False*, "swapping gags in
winking bars" in 'The Casualty', an unconvincing and unsym-
pathetic figure in *He Had a Date* (first broadcast in 1944 and
revived in October 1966), here in *Autumn Sequel* he is as so many
are, "on the beam/Which ends in real buttocks" and speaks as so
many do, "in the innocence of his lust". Only once does the real
forlorn loss of someone dear come through this inadequate
attempt to convey the depth of friendship:

> His sister called and came upstairs and stood
> Quietly and said quietly 'We have lost
> Gavin';

In the light of this quiet acceptance of death, one can see more
truly the validity of:

> Wild, witty, randy, serious, curious, kind,
> And boisterously loyal to his five
>
> Senses and his one life,

MacNeice had apparently a capacity for some few and deep friendships. He had little ability to do much except alienate when describing his friends; and there is no greater disappointment in *Autumn Sequel* than that which stems from his incapacity to recreate the presence of Dylan Thomas except as a jester:

> with the first pint a tall
> Story froths over, demons from the hills
> Concacchinate in the toilet, a silver ball
>
> Jumps up and down in his beer till laughter spills
> Us out to another bar followed by frogs
> And auks and porpentines and armadills.
>
> For Gwilym is a poet; analogues
> And double meanings crawl behind his ears
> And his brown eyes were scooped out of the bogs,

Nor does the rest of Canto II convey the unique qualities of Thomas's poetry. Canto XVIII, the "Lament for the Makers", does little to repair this omission. The flavour of Thomas's poetry, its surrealist force, find no echo in:

> He made his own sea-shells
> In which to hear the voices of the sea,
>
> And knew the oldest creatures, the owl that tells
> How it has seen three forests rise and fall,

One is left with the impression that true recollection for MacNeice is not of the poet, but of the good companion:

> Debonair,
> He leant against the bar till his cigarette
> Became one stream of ash sustained in air
>
> Through which he puffed his talk.

The funeral described in Canto XX would serve for the funeral of any friend lost from one's favourite haunts, and only the description of the train as

> that moving belt of doom
> That grinds through small dark stations of despair;

really rises above the normal homage of friendship. The measure of MacNeice's failure truly to show his understanding in mourning Dylan Thomas can be measured by comparing this section of *Autumn Sequel* with Auden's memorial poem to MacNeice, *The Cave of Making*, which combines recollection with dignity, a sense of companionship, respect and critical appraisal, and which contains in the last lines of *Postscript* a *cri de coeur* of the poet who cannot but realize how far from the idea is the expression. To include these lines, overtly self-critical, in a poem written 'in memoriam' is the deep compliment of one artist to another from whom he is sure of understanding:

> God may reduce you
> on Judgment Day
> to tears of shame
> reciting by heart
> the poems you would
> have written, had
> your life been good.

Professor Dodds says MacNeice failed in *The Strings are False* fully to convey "the rich flow of fun and fantasy, the mercurial gaiety, the warm vitality and love of life" which endeared him to his friends. Equally it might be said that he failed fully to convey in *Autumn Sequel* the qualities other than those on a hail-fellow-well-met basis that endeared them to him.

VII

Strangely, the element that is least to the fore in *Autumn Sequel* is that which in other volumes informs the most lyric aspect of his work, concern with himself, his impressions and his life. In Canto XXIII we have an unusual analysis of the individual's identification with the mass through the cathartic power of sport, to which he had always been susceptible:

> those muddy but unbowed
>
> Players are me, this crowd is me, that undinted
> And indestructible mischievous ball is me,

Something of the same, rather unusual detachment is to be found in his description of "the worst of my dreams" in Canto XXII. The nightmare picture of the crucifixion cast in modern times where

> newspaper scraps
> Capered around the foot of three tall black
> Crosses

is sharply etched. The moment of truth comes at the end in the deep concern which he felt in his dream for the effect of this on his father:

> I had the worst of it, in the lack
>
> Of my own faith and the knowledge of his, the accursed
> Two-ways vision of youth.

This is an unusually shrewd analysis of his attitude; but the rest of the canto tails off into a foetal image and not very well developed value comparisons of Stone Age Man and modern schoolboy.

Most of his personal explorations in *Autumn Sequel* are at this level of intellectual analysis backed up by surrealist imagery. In Canto VIII he speaks, somewhat disrespectfully, of his Muse:

> Nor is she the best of employers; it being beneath
> Her pride to pay on the day or sometimes at all,
> She can pay a thousandfold with a funeral wreath.

Anyhow it is employment, stand or fall,
And all I am fit for now, which is saying little
But claiming almost everything;

This is pedestrian enough and probably mock-modest to boot,
but this Muse is described with more typical vigour than is usual
in *Autumn Sequel* and real conviction brings the verse to life:

Where science, ethics and politics stand aloof
The arts eat meat and paddle around in dung,
They tear off women's knickers and raise the roof

With thump and rump and kickshaw, they blow the bung
From the cask and the corpse from the casket, they mount the
    ladder
Of Jacob and toss it behind them rung by rung.

And the arts are unpredictable, like an adder
They sting you in the heel, like a drunken ape
They daub your belly and brow with woad and madder

And chop your logic by half and change your shape
And, when you might prefer a string quartet,
They give you a drum and muffle it in crape.

Reading this, and considering at the same time the longueurs of
Autumn Sequel, one understands why in Canto V MacNeice could
say

        I sometimes think
    That I am an actor too, that the Muse has defaulted

    And left me an apparatus, rivet and link,
    With nothing to link or rivet, and I lament
    The maker I might have been;

and though in the event this may be thought to be too early a
despair, nevertheless it is reiterating his feeling that "this middle
stretch of life is bad for poets". Certainly some factor had
diminished his lyric powers until he rediscovered them in the
last three books. Perhaps the clue lies in Canto XI and its oblique

approach may hide one of those wearing and unrewarding relationships that can neither coalesce nor dissolve. The background is
once again nostalgia. He remembers "Legendary girls" when "to
think/Meant to feel and to feel meant to be/And being meant
pure joy". Now the truth is different:

> This is that greater doom which bodes and bides
> In time till it burst the clock. This is the point
> In the crooked and narrow path where romantic love collides
>
> With brute and practical hate; where a witch's oils anoint
> Our hands with numbness and our eyes with pain.
> The strings, my lady, are false. Each minute is out of joint.

This seems definite and final enough, but:

>   At other times
> Dawdling down that same lane we found a happier lot
>
> Between wild hedges where the dogrose climbs
> With Chloe or Nicolette, whose magic was white and pink
> And no false note could spoil the varied chimes
>
> We heard with them at midnight, when to think
> Meant to feel and to feel meant to be
> And being meant pure joy and no weak link
>
> Impaired the daisy chain which a not impossible She
> Had tied our hands and hers with. We did not call
> On God or Time to free us; nor did we want a free
>
> Hand, nor would we imagine a world at all
> Outside our present chains. Nor did we know
> That heavens, however green in leaf or gold in fall,
>
> Are not for ever, and yet can be heavens even so.

In spite of the calm fall of the conclusion of this canto, it is not
easy to forget the savagery of "brute and practical hate"; it is
possible to imagine that in the emotionally consuming dichotomy
of this feeling, inspiration may have faltered.

By choosing the title *Autumn Sequel*, MacNeice deliberately challenges comparison with *Autumn Journal*. He underlines this challenge in the "Prefatory Note" to *Autumn Sequel*:

In the autumn of 1938 I wrote a long occasional poem, *Autumn Journal*, hinged to that season. Its sequel, fifteen years later, though similarly hinged to the autumn of 1953 and so also by its nature occasional, is less so, I think, than its predecessor.

Although comparison is challenged, is it appropriate? In the first place, *Autumn Journal* is written in lines of unequal stresses and varying syllabic length and with (for most of the poem) only the alternate lines rhyming. This is a loose and pleasing prosody appropriate to the ranging recollections, the day-dreams and the personal but not profound political and philosophical thoughts natural in a diary. *Autumn Sequel*, on the other hand, is written within the quite sharp disciplines of *terza rima*. To be successful, discipline must be imposed on enthusiasm, and this, as we have seen, is the element that is missing from *Autumn Sequel*.

The last words of *Autumn Journal* are "there will be sunlight later/And the equation will come out at last". Here was hope; but there is little hope in *Autumn Sequel* or at its conclusion, but thoughts of death kept in check only because he is returning to "one person" – "Who takes the ancient view that life is holy".

Unexpectedly, *Autumn Journal* has more 'form' than *Autumn Sequel*. It has the unifying theme of the poet confiding in his Journal. He takes such liberties with time as are humanly permissible; recollection is part of experience and mingles with immediacy; there is none the less a sequential unity from calf love, through parting, to first job and then to the individual facing global disaster. The only unity of *Autumn Sequel* is the unity of despair, or, if that is perhaps too strong a word, of hopelessness. Nothing is inspiring; the allegory leads nowhere. Friends are good fellows and die, our jobs produce false impressions; mankind has failed to make use of its opportunities. MacNeice's view of society here, and of his place in it, falls short of cynicism only because he retains the faculty of criticism and the capacity to catch and describe the passing impression.

MacNeice was born in autumn and he says himself "all my years are based on autumn". The nostalgia of autumn had attraction for him. He felt that both *Autumn Journal* and *Autumn Sequel* were "hinged" to autumn. He perhaps wished to 'cash in' a little on the success of the earlier poem. There are great differences. The poet of the 'fifties writing 15 years and one world war later, chronicles disillusion and despair.

We have looked at *Autumn Sequel* seeking the same three motifs that we have noticed in MacNeice's poetry to this point: self, the world about the poet, and that attempt to find reason in life that we have loosely called 'philosophy'. We have found in the last no advance on his earlier thinking and some floundering in a not very deep psychological allegory. We have found his pictures of his world and his views on social life and politics echoing, though more pessimistically, those in *Autumn Journal* and of poems before *Ten Burnt Offerings*. The pictures of his friends we have criticized either as kindly and pious platitudes, misleading, or superficial. Only in one or two autobiographical references have we found evidence of real feeling, and this a little more controlled and analytical than usual, except in the two passages of surprising outburst in Canto XI, passages which seem to have sprung from a deep malaise, which could not be resolved because the words could not be spoken. One has throughout a feeling that in the deepest sense the poem lacks honesty. The link that runs, however loosely, through *Autumn Journal* was the breakdown of that first gay infatuation, its agony, and the recovery. All else takes its tone from that experience. Whatever the experience was that inspired

> A wall
>
> Of wailing lies at the back of many a tented
> Temple of Love;

it was choked back and not given the freedom that might have informed the poem, either directly, or through imagery, or through allegory.

For a craftsman of MacNeice's stature the word 'failure' is too
strong. There are moments as we have seen, when passages rise
above the general competent level of the verse. There are frequent striking images:

> And one accordion gypsifies the dark

striking comparisons:

> A dive-bombed jeep
> Is no less broken, or old, than a bronze wheel
> From Agamemnon's chariot.

high description such as:

> delicate whippets of fire
> Hurdled the streets, the cockney firmament

> Ran with flamingoes' blood

or:

> The wind braids
> Long strands of brine together; tags of gorse
> Assert their blazing truth as the bracken fades

or again:

> Already the Park is scribbled across with white
> Goalposts and lines, winter's too simple script,
> While empty deckchairs cast a cold grey blight

> Over the cold grey lake.

There is the striking simile:

> The years like small dun oxen crash the ford

and metaphors such as:

> Past walls of broken biscuit, golden gloss,

> Porridge or crumbling shortbread or burnt scone,
> Puma, mouldy elephant, Persian lamb,

These are the lines for which one continues seeking. But they are the occasional pleasure in a poem which does not succeed as a persuasive whole. Its discursive style does not disguise its lack of coherence, and its prosody does not impose discipline. It has no purpose, or more than the vaguest consistency, and thus lacks persuasion, or as Fraser sees, "the beauty of necessity". Even MacNeice's description of it is wrong; it is not truly rhetorical. It is not enough to use as a preface Walt Whitman's

> Do I contradict myself?
> Very well then I contradict myself.

Day-Lewis did better when he chose the same lines to precede 'Transitional Poem' Part 2, but completed the quotation:

> I am large, I contain multitudes.

MacNeice must have known this could not apply to *Autumn Sequel*.

CHAPTER FIVE

The last three books

I

The last three volumes of MacNeice's poetry were written during the nine years remaining to him after the publication of *Autumn Sequel*. With the first volume, *Visitations*, we are back in the MacNeice country of which we were given only distant glimpses in *Ten Burnt Offerings*. The cerebral approach of that work and of *Autumn Sequel*, which seemed to call for an almost deliberate abstention from many of his previous sources of inspiration, is thrown overboard in the first poem of *Visitations*. Addressing "the Public" directly, MacNeice asks "Why hold that poets are so sensitive?" He felt that 'the public', labouring behind the practitioner of art, was still conditioned by the concept of a poet endowed with "more lively sensibility, more enthusiasm and tenderness". Or perhaps he realized the continuing influence of Tennyson's vision of "the passionate heart of the poet whirl'd into folly and vice". Devoted though he was to Wordsworth's high idea of the poet's character, he could not resist painting a practical picture of poets as "A thick-skinned grasping lot who

filch and eavesdrop", a rather shrill way of acknowledging the
debt that each poet owes to his fellows of all ages. He may here
also have been referring to the often disconcerting behaviour of
poets as people, based on those he knew.

With a passing reference to Shelley's *Defence of Poetry* MacNeice
says "legislators or not, ourselves are lawless". Both MacNeice
and Auden were unable to accept the concept of the poet
controlling the destiny of man. In the next line MacNeice says
"We do not need your indulgence", a word with both religious
and an everyday connotation. Poets need neither forgiveness from
the Church, nor patient understanding from the world. So he
goes on to paint a defiant picture of poetic independence, of
poets with more "common sense" than "your Common Man"
(shades of *1066 and All That* and of G.B.S.). He claims more
freedom for poets with a series of metaphors drawn from skills
that cover the range of human activity. They have "burglars' . . .
fingers", lockpicking, delicate fingers that give entry to secret and
private places. They have "gunmen's fingers", quick on the draw
and springing perpetual and dangerous surprises. They have
"green fingers" that deal delicately with growth and birth and
death. With these assets, he says,

> crude though we are, we get to times and places
> And, saving your presence or absence, will continue
> Throwing our dreams and guts in people's faces.

That this poem, which Fraser aptly describes as "agreeably
cantankerous", is a sigh of relief, a declaration of independence
and an overstatement, is underlined by the next in the volume,
'To Posterity'. Having announced his escape from the "distressed
determination" which, as we have seen, he brought to the writing
of *Ten Burnt Offerings*, he now looks ahead to what 'Posterity'
may find as sources of poetic inspiration and he wonders if they

> Will find in flowers and fruit the same colour and taste
> They held for us for whom they were framed in words,

And will your grass be green, your sky be blue,
Or will your birds be always wingless birds?

This is no throwing of guts in people's faces; but we are immediately reminded that in 'Prayer Before Birth' the only
prospect that pleased him was "grass to grow for me" and "sky to
sing to me, birds and a white light/in the back of my mind to
guide me". So now he wonders whether the generation to come
will find inspiration in the "drunkenness of things being various"
or whether their birds will be "always wingless". And the two
poems together 'To the Public' and 'To Posterity' may be taken
as a declaration of intent to return to his original sources of his
inspiration, himself, the world about him, and the problem of
reconciling his *Autumn Journal* view that "Time is a country, the
present moment/A spotlight roving round the scene" with the
passing of the years and the inevitability of death.

II

The poems concerned with 'self' in the last three books deal
sadly with the realization that youth is gone, and examine the
past for the seeds of present failure. If for a moment hope is
raised that love may have been breathlessly rediscovered, it is
only too soon relinquished, and too easily lost.

'Dreams in Middle Age', one of the first poems in the collection he called *Visitations* (1957) is at one level as shrewd an
observation of a psychological aspect of aging as any that exists
in our literature. To a generation fired with the excitement of
Freud's *The Interpretation of Dreams*, the descent (as the years pass)
from dreams worthy of interpretation, to those which are all too
obviously workaday, is a sad experience. From "dreams of
dalliance" we descend to "The debris of the day before", "the
faces" of those who have impinged on our consciousness "Come
stuttering back". We add up again and again "The nightlong

figures of the daylong ledger". Who has not had the tedious experience of repeating in dreams a simulacrum of the events of the day, and of having them "Stick at a point", like a needle in an over-played gramophone record? (but perhaps this doesn't happen to 'discs'?)

If this is all we can expect of dreams, if we cannot "Retrieve our dreams of dalliance", then, he says "Sooner let nightmares whinny", let us have the worst the mind can do in sleep than such tedious stuff. Standing in these more exciting dreams with Rupert Brooke in his "tunnel of green gloom", we may perhaps have been drowned with Ophelia, blinded with Samson, been in the Forest of Arden with Rosalind, escaped with Perseus, have travelled with Orpheus, and seen the Crucifixion in visions. He now feels, defiantly, that if our "dreams", our poems, are to be concerned with petty detail (a reference here perhaps to the Movement poets of the 1950s, "with their lowered but polished sights") it would be better for us to go to hell on Pluto's "black horses, spluttering fire", or for the plague to fall on us "Unless we can be ourselves — ourselves or more".

The same sense of time passing, of middle age supplanting youth, informs 'Time for a Smoke'. It also provides an excuse for indulging MacNeice's endless contemplation of his own childhood. That we are to consider more than one period of time interwoven in his mind is made clear from the first line "Sitting once more outside the British Museum". The line invites us to recall his earlier poem of July 1939 'The British Museum Reading Room'. Now the "stooping haunted readers" have become "seekers for truth perusing a bottomless well". Once again he is "out on the steps" where he prefers to linger "with pigeons and sparrows", pigeons descended perhaps from those that were "courting,/Puffing their ruffs and sweeping their tails" 18 years previously; but this time there is a third element in his time scale. He recalls that some 40 years before when he was "a small boy" he rushed up the stairs of the building opposite (then a hotel) "trying to beat the lift". From the unresolved contemplation of these three times brought to a single moment in the mind, he seeks refuge in a species of disassociation, an almost schizo-phrenic detachment of mind and body, so that he can, for a second, contemplate existence by the impact of the visible world on the sense of touch alone:

> My mind knows less about it than my hand
> To which this town means merely rough and smooth,
> Means moving handrails, knobs, revolving glass,
> Or the swing doors behind me which just now
> It thrust to let its appended torso pass

So we come to a final stanza where all elements are combined, but not resolved. In the Reading Room itself "the buckets [of those who seek for knowledge] knock on the rim of the well" but presumably go no further. He has come down, away from the search for knowledge, in the lift, which as a child he "failed to beat". He prefers to stay among the birds:

> For whom neither truth nor falsehood, heaven nor hell,
> Holds any purport, who have no regrets,
> No ideals and no history – only wings.

The disassociation of the second stanza of 'Time for a Smoke' finds even keener expression in 'Jigsaws' IV, a sharp observation of the feeling of 'depersonalization' which is a psychological effect of shock, and is often experienced on recovering con-sciousness after an operation under total anaesthesia. This experience of being "Fresh from the knife and coming to" which he describes in prose in *The Strings are False* is not unusual, but rarely commented on.

It is interesting that when MacNeice's exploration of self in his poetry begins to enter the phases in which identification in time and place is less definite than it was, when he begins to find that time is all life, and place everywhere remembered, we get a poem describing this experience, which, in his case, occurred some 17 years previously. 'Figure of Eight' on the other hand is an almost too rationalized contrast between time hurried through in youth to a fruitless assignation, and time like a train remorselessly travelling until it reaches the inevitable terminus. This absorption with the passing of time is developed in 'The Slow Starter' and combnied with a feeling of having failed to make use of opportunity. The images are drawn from experiences at various times of life. First there is the childhood experience of warnings against impatience: "nor will the sulking holiday train/Start sooner if you stamp your feet". Secondly we have the youth waiting for the decision of his mistress that never comes, because he obeys her request: "Do not press me so". Finally there is obedience to advice: "Your kind of work is none the worse/For slow maturing". The last stanza begins with the line: "Oh you have had your chance, It said" and the use of "It" in this way is an interesting evasion. He clings to his agnosticism. "It", time and the clock itself, tell him that he has left his chance alone "and it was one". This is probably a reference to life as Tennyson's Ulysses saw it: "Life piled on life/Were all too little, and of *one* to me/Little remains". Now that opportunity is gone, he sees "the accusing clock/Race like a torrent round a rock", a strong neat final simile to a poem notable for neatness, indeed spareness, of language.

'The Slow Starter' is the most cerebral of those of MacNeice's poems (such as 'Birthright') which are inspired by this nostalgic brooding over the past and the passage of time. More 'typical', because it is derived from a sensuous perception of the world about him, is the opening poem of *The Burning Perch*. It is called 'Soap Suds'; the point of inspiration is the odour of soap. Smell has, among the senses, a remarkable power of inducing recollection. From the soap smell springs the memory of a "House he visited when he was eight". With what perception he recreates the world of a child:

> And these were the joys of that house: a tower with a
>   telescope;
> Two great faded globes, one of the earth, one of the stars;
> A stuffed black dog in the hall; a walled garden with bees;
> A rabbit warren; a rockery; a vine under glass; the sea.

How typical of childhood recollection, and of MacNeice, to realize it – "The day . . . is fine" – *of course*!

MacNeice here recalls the past, as he does in other poems, in terms of regret, not so much in the sense of *"Où sont les neiges d'antan?"* as of regret that time passes so quickly and so inevitably and that so little is achieved. As in 'The Slow Starter' there is a sense of failure, an almost hysterical effect of time telescoping:

> Through hoops where no hoops were and each dissolves in turn
> And the grass has grown head-high and an angry voice cries
> Play!
> But the ball is lost and the mallet slipped long since from the
> hands
> Under the running tap that are not the hands of a child.

This is a poem which combines real nostalgic feeling and emotional recollection with a sense of detached observation and mature, if bitter, acceptance.

It is in 'Birthright' that his feeling that life has eluded him and that he has allowed it to escape him is yet more simply and objectively expressed. The opening lines:

> When I was born the row began,
> I had never asked to be a man;
> They never asked if I could ride
> But shouted at me 'Come outside!'

take our minds back to 'Prayer Before Birth' with its regressive wish not to leave the womb, or to Housman's "world I never made". In this poem he says others have thrust the world upon him (the old plaint "I didn't choose to be born")* and immediately demanded that he take charge:

> Then hauled the rearing beast along
> And said: 'Your charger, right or wrong.'
> His ears went back and so did I,
> I said 'To mount him means to die'

This, he feels, is a realization that paralyses the will, and we cannot ride our nightmares. We may compare this poem with 'Dreams in Middle Age' in which some attempt is made to fight off the sense of desolation that comes when youthful dreams are

ended: "Sooner let nightmares whinny". That was written in a
mood of despair with middle age alone; 'Birthright' is written in
almost total despair:

> The minutes, hours, and years went past,
> More chances missed than I could count,

until only death is left. The poem ends with a dreadful punning
inversion; it is in the worst of taste; it is an unpleasing image;
only because death itself is unpleasing and in poor taste does it
escape the charge of being 'smartly' effective: "My gift horse
looked me in the mouth".

Parallel to the introspective poems concerned with loss of
identity in the face of the passing of time, are a series of poems
that deal with the assault on the personality by the beliefs,
conventions and habits that inform our life. The Truisms deals
with those obvious accepted truths with which each generation shackles the one that follows. They have the trappings of
death:

>   a box of truisms
> Shaped like a coffin, then his father died;
> The truisms remained on the mantelpiece
> As wooden as the playbox they had been packed in
> Or that other his father skulked inside.

The truisms are left behind as the young man sets out into the
world of love, war, "Sordor, disappointment, defeat, betrayal".
Then comes the inevitable return. So great are the influences on
our formative years that we inevitably, and not really consciously,
seek refuge in them, and we know what is expected of us.
Because of this, because knowing what to do is ingrained in us,
there is no escape: "The truisms flew and perched on his shoulders" and the triumph rests with the dead: "And a tall tree
sprouted from his father's grave". There is resentment in Mac-
Neice's recognition that he is so inevitably repossessed by the
forces of habitual modes of thought, which compares sadly with

Eliot's calm acceptance, in *Little Gidding*, of a calm and proper certainty, the inevitability of faith:

> We shall not cease from exploration
> And the end of all our exploring
> Will be to arrive where we started
> And know the place for the first time.

'The Habits' is complementary to 'The Truisms' and the similarity is heightened and underlined by the identity of the verse form of five lines each of four stressed syllables with only the second and last lines rhyming. The habits too represent the restrictions that are placed on us by social pressure and which then becomes an inescapable part of our personality. In childhood they are those imposed for simple reasons and we are conditioned to accept them by reward and punishment:

> When they put him in rompers the habits
> Fanned out to close in, they were dressed
> In primary colours and each of them
> Carried a rattle and a hypodermic;

"Hypodermic" is the forceful word here, with its undertone of fear (submission to the unknown), drugs, and interference with the person itself. There is no escape: "His parents said it was all for the best". Then came school: "the barracks of boys" and the full pressures of conformity to a world of wealth, of rule, of privilege, for here the habits "carried/A cheque book, a passport, and a sjambok". "And then came the women" and we must note with wry humour "the habits/Pretended to leave". But they carried "A Parthian shaft" so that they remained triumphant in retreat, "and an affidavit" so that there was no deceit. Now it is the "adgirl" who said "it was all for the best". "Adgirl" is a portmanteau noun that makes of women both an impossible siren and a compulsive liar. It is a fitting addition to the list of parents, masters, computers and the Lord God. With the next sentence we are back to the lament. Now the habits "Make themselves at home" and it is "the computer" that says "it was all for the best", since we are concerned with the arithmetic of time passing. Finally we have a perception deeper than normal into the problems of old age:

> Then age became real: the habits
> Outstayed their welcome, they were dressed
> In nothing and carried nothing.

This is the appreciation of real pathos, that inevitable moment when the habits of a lifetime are irrelevancies. At this point, and it is said with bitterness, "The Lord God said it was all for the best". The import of this line is the greater if we recollect 'The Blasphemies', a poem which underlines the attack which belief can make upon the consciousness which is neither simple enough to accept it nor confident enough to live without it.

Just as 'Soap Suds' takes the sense of smell as the starting point for a lament on the passing of time, so 'Off the Peg' takes the tunes which linger in the memory and are so sharply associated with events. This poem stands between 'Soap Suds' and 'The Habits', and though it also is a lament for the passing of life, there is behind it a sense of pleasure that is missing in other poems on the same theme. It is packed with imagery. The tunes, whether they come from 'Tin Pan Alley' where simple popular songs are forged, or from the respectable world of folksong, or the cultural field of *Lieder*, or from plain memories of nursery rhymes, "hang on pegs in the cloakrooms of the mind". This is a natural extension from the feeling that they were fitting for the moment that caused us to remember them; they

> fitted us ten or twenty or thirty years ago
> On occasions of love or grief;

as clothes are used.

When we look we find the same tunes as "when the weather broke/In our veins", those sad or glad occasions when the blood pounded in our heads like thunder, ran cold with fear, or hot with emotion or anger, or when life itself seemed at an end and

the "golden bowl" of Ecclesiastes seemed to break in our hands
The tunes in "the cloakrooms of the mind" show "Frayed edge:
here and there or loss of nap", but with another rapid change of
image, they are like "Chameleons" that "can adapt to whatever
sunlight leaks" (a sad, bleak little word to use of sunlight,
reminiscent of dark corners and shrubberies and jungles) or to
whatever storms may threaten, or "ghosts of long love strike".
This is a phrase packed with half allusions; to Donne's "old lover's
ghost" to which "I long to talk", to Tennyson's "brief is life but
love is long", to Herrick's 'Love me Little, Love me Long' and
to Othello's heavenly sorrow that "strikes where it doth love".
The allusion is tentative because each word by itself cannot carry
so heavy a burden of overtones; but taken together they set these
echoes ringing in the mind. We can understand how the old
tunes can adapt, like chameleons to the light, to the varieties of
nostalgic regret that the phrase carries.

Then comes an abrupt transition to an image to which Mac-
Neice recurred throughout his poetic career; derived from the
nursery rhyme 'Rock-a-bye baby in the tree top', it was a concept
which in his mind brought together thoughts of birth, chance,
and death. The similarity in the shape of cradle and coffin
haunted his imagination. Now "the coffinlike cradle pitched"
(pitched like a tent, or thrown by chance, or pitching, perhaps,
like a ship in a storm) "on the breaking bough" reveals – and this
is the true horror of it – "some fiend" or some reincarnation, and
does so, not for the first time, but "once more". Here is a nightmare of the mind indeed, but still we reach "for one of those
wellworn tunes". Whatever the circumstances "purgatory or hell/
Or paradise even", their previous association gives to "This chain
of simple notes the power of speech". Once again we have become
creatures of habit, hence the clothing simile, but now, because
we have used these habits so often, they are no longer ready-
made. If they were not made to fit, we have grown used to their
measurements; so there is once more a terse, appropriate, sad,
final line: "And off the peg means made to measure now".

The aura of middle age that looms over *Visitations*, *Solstices* and

CHAPTER FIVE

The Burning Perch is reflected in five short, sad love poems that
straddle the ten years of these volumes. 'The Burnt Bridge' is a
forced little allegory of the passing of life with "a bridge and a
shining lady" towards the end of it. If it is the same "she" as
informs 'Solstice' (which seems unlikely) then the sense of
surprise and wonder has lasted well over five or six years. It is
more likely that he was looking desperately for a love to give
meaning to the increasing sense of passing into middle age, the
midsummer so brilliantly described in 'Solstice' in sensuous terms:

> – the gush
> Of green, the stare of blue, the sieve
> Of sun and shadow, the wish to live.

So he believes he has found the "she/For whom his years were
blessed to wait" and who is making his midsummer which had
"come so soon" now "stay so long".

We are unprepared by this for the assault of 'All Over Again'
upon our senses. *Visitations* is dedicated to Hedli. *Solstices* is not
dedicated and the posthumous *The Burning Perch* is dedicated "To
Mary". It is not too fanciful to believe that 'All Over Again' is his
paean of discovery. This is the love poem to a late love, and
concerned with the amazement of it. He conveys, by omitting all
punctuations, the feeling of being borne along on an unexpected
wave of joy and emotion. The words and the lines jostle for one's
attention and rush bubbling through the mind, assisted by a free
use of internal rhymes sparkling through the loose alexandrines.
Time is still his concern. He feels "As if I had known you for
years", "As if it were always morning". The song of the birds is
for them "Where still time stands" – "And the ripe moment tugs
yet declines to fall". The past has become nothing, "The years we
had not met forget themselves in this/One kiss ingathered world".
He is reminded of Ben Jonson's plea that his mistress "leave a kiss
within the cup" but now it is "skybound" and "timeless". The
world seems to conspire to reflect:

> the sun as if
> This one Between were All and we in love for years.

202

A simple enough theme, but hung about with pictures and references that mirror the wonder that he feels. It is "as if all our tears were earned", as if, that is, we have never been buffeted by an unkind, unreasoning fate. It is like the first moment when we saw the sea. It is as if the dawnsong of the birds were ours alone. It is as though the past years disappear into blue eternity. To speak of it, he says, requires new fires of the tongue (and he finds them in the verse form and rhythm) and he can ask no more from future or past. It is another lyrical musical poem, but his intoxication is with love, and that communicates itself to the words in a way that is not achieved by his most famous poems of word-play.

It is in 'Déjà Vu', a middle-aged title to a poem, that we get the bitter-sweet of middle-aged love, which "must extend beyond time because time is itself in arrears". The very moment of love is no longer unique, as it is in youth. It has been before, and it will come again, though perhaps not for us. Once more we are made conscious of the deceit of time:

> It does not come round in hundreds of thousands of years,
> It comes round in the split of a wink, you will be sitting
>   exactly
> Where you are now and scratching your elbow, the train
> Will be passing exactly as now and saying It does not come
>   round,
> It does not come round, It does not come round, and
>   compactly
> The wheels will mark time on the rails and the bird in the air
> Sit tight in its box

It has happened at a moment when time stood still (as etched over 20 years before in 'Meeting Point' when "Time was away and somewhere else") and Fitzgerald's "bird of time" that "has but a little way/To fly" sits "tight in its box". This is surely Herbert's box where "sweets compacted lie", since it is "compactly" that "The wheels will mark time on the rails". So, by contrast with 'Meeting Point', we have an appreciation of three strata of time. That which is "Déjà Vu" when "I know what you're going to say";

that "when the same bean of coffee be ground/That is now in the mill"; and "now, as you watch". And but for the fact that "you are too lovely by half", "we both", because "we have been" (unlike the coffee bean) "through the mill", "could all but call it a day". This is no rapture. No longer does he say "God, or whatever means the Good/Be praised that time can stop like this". This is wry recognition that above the maelstrom of time past, time present and time future is the occasional flash of love and under-standing that "does not come round in hundreds of thousands of years", but is enshrined in some mundane moment when "you will be sitting exactly/Where you are now and scratching your elbow".

The saddest of these four poems and it may be stretching the term 'love poem' too far to include it among them, is 'The Introduction'. The subject of the poem is simple. A young woman is introduced to an older man and immediately there is that frightening flash of sympathy between them that can only echo what might have been. Once again it is the time that is at fault. She was "too late" because she was young. He was too old, and thus too early. Because of the attraction of young flesh for old, and the repulsion of young flesh from old, "Crawly crawly/ Went the twigs above their heads" while the whole universe derides them, "the larvae/Split themselves laughing". Even the music that accompanies these moments goes "Crawly, crawly" and the introducer has the wit (God forgive him!) to recognize "You two should have met/Long since . . . or else not now". Perhaps the saddest elements in this short poem are the almost derisive echoes of Marvell. Whereas Marvell can say "My soul into the boughs does glide", MacNeice can hear only "Crawly crawly/Went the twigs above their heads". Marvell's "So amorous as this lovely green" and the more famous "The grave's a fine and private place" are echoed in the despairing final line: "They were introduced in a green grave".

In the last three volumes we have the Romantic poet con-cerned still, if no longer invariably 'pleased', with his own passions and volitions. Recollections of childhood are again explored to colour with nostalgia the overriding sense of time passing, which informs even the love poetry. The imagery remains as ever acutely perceptive and grounded in the senses, of smell, as in 'Soap Suds'; of hearing, as in 'Off the Peg'; of touch, as in 'Time for a Smoke'; of sight, as in 'Solstice'; of taste, as in 'Round the Corner'. Yet there is in these poems an assured touch, a sense of mastery that comes from a spare and simple diction, an economy of phrase, a taut versification. It is unmistakable MacNeice. The canon that was broken with *Ten Burnt Offerings* is, as he promised in the introductory poems, now restored, but it has a new authority.

The clarity and restraint of the versification meets a shift of emphasis, a new metamorphosis, as he composes the portrait of himself. In some way his outlook is now more detached, more fatalistic:

> Our lives are bursting at the seams
> With petty detail. Thus we live, if living
> Means that, and thus we dream – if these are dreams.

Where previously we might have expected reproach, or at the least self-reproach, we now have only comment.

The lyrical element in this poetry, which contains so many striking, almost monosyllabic lines, is at its best in the love poems:

> This being last and first sound sight on eyes and ears

and:

> whatever the rules we might be supposed to obey,
> Our love must extend beyond time because time is itself in
> arrears
> So this double vision must pass and past and future unite
> And where we were told to kowtow we can snap our fingers
> and laugh
> And now, as you watch, I will take this selfsame pencil and
> write:
> It does not come round in hundreds of thousands of years.

It is a love poetry of statements, not of promises and it shatters itself on the final irony:

> The string quartet in the back of the mind
> Was all tuned up with nowhere to go.
> They were introduced in a green grave.

III

From the end of the war to his death, MacNeice travelled a great deal on behalf of the British Council and the B.B.C., and these three volumes carry one or two somewhat dull observations about the places he has visited, but in 'Solitary Travel' we have a comment on the sheer dreariness of modern travel, which has become not so much an adventurous progress from one place to another, as the useless passage of time spent in a series of en-closures:

> The hotels are all the same, it might be pawpaw
> Instead of grapefruit, different flowers on the table,
> But the waiters, coffee-coloured or yellow or black,
> All smile, but, should you smile, give nothing back.

The airports are "indistinguishable" and there is always the "Same lounge or bar whose test-tube walls enfold/The self-indulgent disenchanted old". This is the epitome of loneliness. The list of towns should be romantic, but:

> Breakfasting alone in Karachi, Delhi, Calcutta,
> Dacca, Singapore, Kuala Lumpur, Colombo, Cape Town,
> But always under water or glass, I find
> Such a beginning makes the day seem blind.

So there is no distinction between night, which Shelley has invoked to "blind with thine hair the eyes of Day" and the day which has just begun: "Time and the will lie sidestepped". As for the places themselves:

> Though the land outside be empty or man-crammed, oven or
>   icebox,
> I feel the futility of moving on
> To what, though not a conclusion, stays foregone.

The pun is acceptable if one remembers that 'foregone' means both 'what has gone before' and 'what has gone by' and 'time past'! The only movement is through Customs:

> the passport
> Like a chess game played by mail records the latest
> Move of just one square.

It is then that the will is sidestepped, for this one move "is surely seen/By the black bishop and the unsleeping queen". His desire is for escape out into anywhere:

> into icebox or oven, escape among people
> Before tomorrow from this neutral zone
> Where all tomorrows must be faced alone. . . .

'Old Masters Abroad' has its roots in the nature of MacNeice's travels as a missionary of the British Council, desperately busy exporting the 'British Way of Life' to soils ill-suited to its cultivation. If we pause to imagine the servile intelligence necessary should we be forced to pretend appreciation of Sanskrit tales expounded by lecturers of Gujarati extraction, we can fleetingly imagine the impact of an Irishman lecturing on English Romantic poetry to a Tamil audience. This capacity for realism, which in a poem full of fierce and humorous satire is so successful, if taken to extremes, denies all idealism.

It is as merciless as Pope. "Painfully grinning faces like dogs' " is a realistic description of the intellectual lip-service to a culture that must be assimilated to achieve immediate practical ends. "Inattentive like cats' " catches the soft Asian capacity to slide away from real contact. MacNeice implicitly asks if we have the right to expect the world to be static, and listen to "the singing birds of unknown England". In fact the races of the world do nothing of the sort. They "affect to be lectured". To show that the attempt is ridiculous, and an exercise in self-deception, is the whole object of the next four stanzas. "Shakespeare flaunts his codpiece at dhoti" is a line in which the mental image of the two garbs and their confrontation conveys a sufficient sense of the ridiculous. Who could expect Indonesian understanding of "Sir Plume, of amber snuffbox justly vain/And the nice conduct of a clouded cane"? Who could believe that in the heat and marshes around Lagos the finer transcendental implication of the lesser celandine could ever be conveyed? Shelley, eternally sacrificed to the schoolboy intonation hailing his "blithe spirit", must compete with tropical birds of notably harsh call. Keats's nightingale becomes a fighting cock which challenges the red-vented thrush, the nightingale of the East. Burns and Tennyson are absorbed by the geology and geography of the tropics and Browning is brought to nothing by the white ants. Arnold founders in the fires and rivers of Asiatic religions, and Newbolt and Yeats equally sacrifice their silence in the deserts:

> The faces listen or not. The lecturers
> Mop their memories. All over the static
> Globe the needle sticks in the groove.
> It is overtime now for the Old Masters.

In 'Notes for a Biography' there is a more compassionate, if less notable, approach to the East–West relationship (and again some references to parts of his own life-story disguised as the biography of an ex-'burra sahib'). It is a pleasantly perceptive but not notable poem, except that it is one of the few occasions on which he mentions the crucial event of the mid-twentieth century, the dropping of the atomic bomb:

> When I first read the news, to my shame I was glad;
> When I next read the news I thought man had gone mad,
> And every day since the more news that I read
> I too would plead guilty – but where can I plead?

For no one will listen, however I rage;
I am not of their temper and not of this age.
Outnumbered, outmoded, I only can pray
Common sense, if not love, will still carry the day.

That we do not find more references to the potential of the atomic bomb in MacNeice's poetry (and surprisingly little in all modern poetry, taken as a whole) is perhaps explained by Mac-Neice's comment in *Varieties of Parable*:

in fact the one really peculiar thing in our world is the Bomb; and as Arthur Koestler has pointed out, however much we have realised the implications of that with our heads, we have not yet grown into that realisation; the possibility of death for the whole human race is not something we live with as we live with the certainty of our own individual deaths.

'Jericho' is a rather slick echo of the earlier 'Refugees' (1940). Both poems are interesting to compare with the first of Auden's 'Twelve Songs', written in the early 'forties. Auden, by using a simple ballad form in the first person, achieves a high degree of identification with the victims of race hatred: "Yet there's no place for us, my dear, yet there's no place for us". MacNeice in the earlier poem repels this identification in the first two phrases descriptive of the refugees "With prune-dark eyes, thick lips". Compassion is modified by this inability to see through racial differences. So in 'Jericho' the emphasis is repeatedly placed on the cultural background, "And Joshua remembered Moses". The references are to the unlovely books of *Exodus* and *Joshua*: "And the Tables of the Law were broken again". The failure of assimilation is laid equally at the door of the refugee and of society (though the motivation is more emotional than rational), "Refugees from worlds away/Worked out their loneliness in play", and "The Caribbean in spite of cosh/And flick knife wouldn't come out in the wash". The last stanza places the problems of race in a final despairing perspective – and we have one other reference to the atomic bomb:

Neither sense nor conscience stirred,
Having been ultimately deterred,

The reference to the ultimate deterrent is too facile and the escape from a constructive approach to the problem of the poem robs it of anything more than passing interest.

'Rites of War', though a highly contrived and artificial poem (because it is based on the last scene of *Hamlet*, full of the appropriate references, and constructed on a framework of internal rhymes) has nevertheless the true ring of pity and understanding. Addressing Fortinbras he says

> you, sir,
> Have seen far more of gore without this pomp, having heard
> Your dying soldiers cry though not in iambics,

not in "swagged" verse, or verse that is "canopied" with costly state,

> not
> In any manner of speech to reach the future's ear,
> Their death being merely breath that ceased and flesh that
>   slumped

This is true understanding; but the rest of the poem seems to build up almost too cleverly to the final line of *Hamlet* and to the extent that it is so obviously contrived, diminishes its own dignity and sincerity.

In many ways 'Yours Next' (while not reaching the same level of intense awareness of useless suffering as the central lines of 'Rites of War') is a more sustained though more satirical attack on the waste that is implicit in civilization. Here the imagery is from a milieu with which MacNeice was familiar, perhaps too familiar, the world of the bar with its fruit machines and pin tables, and the meaningless camaraderie of drinking. The combination of mechanical amusement, empty ritual, and sheer commercialism, is applied to the great tragedy of our time and in the last verse he makes it clear that the nature of mankind has not altered since the days of medieval tortures:

> Stake and faggot and gas chamber –
> Someone has got to pay for the round.

> Only press the button and all
> The springs will twang, the heads will fall,
> And yet, whatever drinks are downed,
> Someone has got to pay for the round.

In 'Jigsaws' II, the social criticism is more direct though super-ficial and shows little development in outlook since 'Birmingham' written in 1933, in which he says "men as in a dream pursue the Platonic Forms/With wireless and cairn terriers and gadgets". He now extends this thought (perhaps with Tennyson's "Proputty, proputty, proputty" in mind) and brings it up to date with an attack on the accumulation of property "To keep out the neigh-bours and keep us immured". He finds that we live in and with boxes like a Chinese puzzle; the "fruit of our labours" is, like the fruits of the earth, now cold and canned, and we enjoy it alone "In a sterilised cell". It is a fair description of a not uncommon mood arising from a dispassionate and pessimistic observation of the world of our day. His solution is iconoclastic:

> When will it end?
> When will the Poltergeist ascend
> Out of the sewer with chopper and squib
> To burn the mink and the baby's bib
> And cut the tattling wire to town
> And smash all the plastics, clowning and clouting,
> And stop all the boxes shouting and pouting
> And wreck the house from the aerial down

The purpose, to "give these ingrown souls an outing", is not a very clear one, and the poem, cunningly reminiscent in its rhyme, rhythm and use of present participles, of 'The Pied Piper', reaches no conclusion. We are again reminded of MacNeice's discontent with his world, and his inability to contribute, in his thinking and his poetry, to its improvement.

In 'New Jerusalem', written some six years later, MacNeice finds in fact that the rebuilding of London is destroying the old city, even as he had wished, but now he complains that in the process we must "Bulldoze all memories and sanctuaries". In their place he finds the same "sterilised cells", this time "vertical, impersonal" with "walls of thin ice dividing greynesses" and

> we have found an antidote
> To quiet and self-communing: from now on nobody
> Strolling the streets need lapse into timelessness
> Or ponder the simple unanswerable questions.

There is indeed, in these last three books, little in the social scene from which MacNeice derives satisfaction. His series of pictures of the Park, clear though they are, emphasize the "tulips as shriekmarks", the "carefully labelled flower beds/And the litter baskets", and the "empty morning" when the "small clerk/Who thinks no one will ever love him/Sculls on the lake" ('The Lake in the Park'). The park is a place for "The precise yet furtive etiquette of dogs" ('Dogs in the Park') and "the prams are big with doom" ('Sunday in the Park'). Nor is there much left to enjoy in the contemplation of past pleasure. In 'Sports Page' he is reminded that "The lines of print are always sidelines/And all our games funeral games". We have reached the point at which MacNeice found travel an endless and pointless repetitive process when "Time and the will lie sidestepped". He found no satisfaction or comfort in suburban surroundings and the middle-class, middle-aged pleasure of the onlooker. There were now, for him, but few pleasures even in nostalgia.

'October in Bloomsbury' completes the triptych of which the first two panels are 'The British Museum Reading Room' (1939) and 'Time for a Smoke' (1956). In the earliest poem there is understanding and compassion and concern for fellow students: "some are asleep/Hanging like bats in a world of inverted values". In the second there is regret: "We remain apart/While behind us a million books wait to be opened". In 'October in Bloomsbury' there is something near despair: "the Museum/Spreads its dead hands", negroes and children "rummage for culture", while we for whom culture is a heritage miss most "those from the garden", the disciples of Epicurus. This part of London, and the Museum itself, had always invoked strong, descriptive verse. The "hive-like dome" had already given him an image of the honey-comb of knowledge. He was, as we have seen, intensely aware of the surroundings, of the pigeons "Puffing their ruffs and sweeping their tails or taking/A sun-bath at their ease", and confessed he liked to "linger with pigeons and sparrows". Now he notes wryly (in military language) that "a pigeon scores an outer/On a scholarly collar". In the last two lines of 'October in Bloomsbury' he paints a final autumnal picture. In spite of parking meters, and the great new institutes:

> Charles James Fox unconcerned in a bath towel sits on his
> arse in Bloomsbury Square
> While plane tree leaves flop gently down and lodge in his
> sculptured hair.

He stresses the incongruity here, and indeed clings to it as a fixed point in a world of altering values. The lines, although forceful, crude and vivid, lack the natural vitality while retaining echoes of the ironic fun of earlier lines: "the streets run away between the proud glass of shops,/Cubical scent-bottles artificial legs arctic foxes and electric mops" ('Birmingham'), or *Autumn Journal*:

> Sun shines easy, sun shines gay
>   On bug-house, warehouse, brewery, market,
> On the chocolate factory and the B.S.A.,
>   On the Greek town hall and Josiah Mason;

A similar type of observation is at work in 'Pet Shop'. The picture of the shop and its contents is clear, if obvious, but the disillusioned comment:

> But most of the customers want something comfy –
> Rabbit, hamster, potto, puss –
> Something to hold on the lap and cuddle
> Making believe it will return affection
> Like some neutered succubus.

if psychologically perceptive, avoids judgment and in consequence the poem itself lacks the moral force of Larkin's 'Take

One Home for the Kiddies', written about the same time and concluding:

> Living toys are something novel,
> But it soon wears off somehow.
> Fetch the shoebox, fetch the shovel –
> Mam, we're playing funerals now.

There is no lack of force in 'The Suicide', even if there is no moral conclusion either direct or implied. Here the description is vivid, the words tripping over each other to outline a life over-full with the trivia and worries of the day. Maybe he was thinking of his own life when he speaks of:

> the flowery maze
> Through which he had wandered deliciously till he stumbled
> Suddenly, finally conscious of all he lacked
> On a manhole under the hollyhocks.

We recollect his description 25 years earlier in 'Hidden Ice' of those who "have lost their bearings/Struck hidden ice or currents no one noted", and his gloss on it in *Modern Poetry*: "such people in everyday life may end in suicide or the asylum". 'The Suicide' is his final development of the theme. Certainly it seems to summarize his vivid apprehension of the world about him, and the sharp awareness in his poetry of the approaching nullity which is death. Perhaps it was an unexpressed appreciation of this aspect of his personality that made Auden, in his Memorial Address and in the broadcast of 1966, describe MacNeice in a quotation from this poem as "This man with the shy smile". Certainly he has "left behind/Something that was intact".

In these poems dealing with the social aspect of the world of the late 'fifties and early 'sixties, MacNeice comes nearest to despair. It is not only that nothing has been gained in insight and understanding since the pre-war poetry, it is rather that something has been lost. At one time there was a Roman joy in the cities, there was an enthusiasm for technology, there was a sense of its new and special beauty, "narcotic and deciduous". There was a feeling that because it was possible to take pleasure in the world perhaps there was still some hope. There was pleasure in travel: "As gay trams run on rails" ('An April Manifesto'), "Trains like prayers/Radiating from stations haughty as cathedrals" ('Refugees'). All this has gone. Travel is purgatory. 'The Park' is a picture of suburban dreariness. We live in a series of Chinese boxes, in "walls of thin ice dividing greynesses", ('New Jerusalem') among "Thousands of ants in pinstriped pants" ('Jericho') and "the tutelary spirits are hard to please" ('October in Bloomsbury'). The eye is keener now for some of mankind's more intellectual follies and he can then rise to the level of satirical laughter; but the ultimate comment on his contemporary world of "bills/In the intray, the ash in the ashtray" takes us only a step backward from the years of 'Hidden Ice'.

IV

Among those of MacNeice's poems in the last three books which contemplate the mysteries of life and death, we find two or three which range from myth to satire and which have a common merit: they are musical. They are musical as were 'Bagpipe Music' and 'The Sunlight on the Garden' and 'The Jingles of the Morning' (all written in 1937). They share the same delight in the use of words for their own sake, for their effectiveness as sounds, their power of evocation. Defying, as they should, precise analysis, they yet convey their meaning and they charge it with emotion. This meaning hovers around the indefinite borders between MacNeice's concern with his own life, his sensory perception of the sharp world around him, his sense of time passing, and his awareness of the inevitable doom for every man for which he sought in vain to find some reason.

'April Fool', a poem made to be read aloud without pausing to find a precise interpretation, is packed with images and allusions.

The first phrase "Here come I" is habitually used in Mummers' Plays as each character enters (and a further literary reference to it may be found in Thomas Hardy's *Return of the Native*). The Fool has his part in all these plays; and the folk custom of April Fool's Day, when each tries to 'fool' the other, is with us still. (The use of 'fool' in the transitive sense is vital to the poem.) April Fool's Day falls between the time of the March Hare's madness and the impossible "Nuts in May" of nursery rhyme (a corruption of *Knots of May*?). However much we may be fooled, forward or back, time passes. The hares "dance" through their spring court-ship, and the nuts crack in the frosts of autumn.

So to the second verse:

> Here come I, my fingers crossed
> Between the shuffle and the deal.
> Fool me flush or fool me straight,
> Queens are wild and queens will wait.

Superstitious still, with fingers "crossed" to protect against the interference of the devil, the cards of fate are shuffled and dealt, and the terms of poker used to give a wider sense of being at fate's mercy. As playing cards "Queens are wild" – they can mean anything or nothing – or as a woman, the Queen is "La Belle Dame Sans Merci", whose eyes are "wild". In the third verse the fool, the poet, comes in clogs, symbols of work and of dance, but worn out as he dances his way heavily between the burden that must be carried, or the bass part that must be sung, or the meaning of the song ("Love me little, love me long/Is the burden of my song") and the song itself; so fooled hither and thence he would "Keep the sound but ditch the sense".

The next verse moves to deeper waters:

> Here come I, my hair on fire,
> Between the devil and the deep.
> Fool me over, fool me down,
> Sea shall dry and devil shall drown.

Now the April Fool would appear to be playing the part of the red-headed Judas, his hair on fire, unable to find rest either with the devil or in the sea that rejects his traitorous body, until "Sea shall dry and devil shall drown". Then the return to harsh reality, "Here come I, in guts and brass" ("As if this flesh which walls about our life/Were brass impregnable"). But remember, he says, death may not be the end, in spite of Poe and Henley, for "coffins land" like Noah's ark, "on Ararat". So he finally finds comfort in the age-old rediscovery of the Goddess of Spring:

> Here come I, old April Fool,
> Between the hoar frost and the fall.
> Fool me drunk or fool me dry,
> Spring comes back, and back come I.

To have noted some of the more obvious references and meaning of 'April Fool' leaves the poem as a whole a little enriched by the associations that are stirred, but not explained. Perhaps he would no longer answer his own question of 25 years earlier "Shall we remember the jingles of the morning" with so categorical a "No, we shall *not* remember". Perhaps he would say that tradition and customs springing from old religions and half-forgotten rituals remain with us for ever and that, like Persephone, we may return, in some guise, perhaps only in folk memory, with "old April Fool". Perhaps there are other shades of interpretation in other moods and for other people. In essence it is joy of living, joy in myth, understanding of superstition, and an appreciation that Spring and the renewal of life will always be there for the dancer, not necessarily "I", who will also be there, and who will greet Spring, in April, with the age-old magic. The poem must indeed be read aloud.

The impossibility of "coming back", the contrast between "emotion recollected in tranquillity" and the appreciation of the present, the frustration because the place and the moment so rarely seem to coincide (as they do for instance in 'Meeting Point'), is the theme of the last poem in 'A Hand of Snapshots'. 'The Here-and-Never' is a poem of nostalgia in which the full resources of the words of time and place are used, almost surrealistically, to contrast the present with the past, to contrast it with the present seen in the light of past memories, and to contrast it with the past seen in the light of recollected feelings. The first verse, not easy to grasp, but again delightful to read aloud, is filled with the longing for time and place to be other than they are:

> Here it was here and now, but never
> There and now or here and then.
> Ragweed grows where a house dies
> Whose children are no longer children
> And what you see when you close your eyes
> Is here and never: never again.

Everything is always changing and the place we leave is not, once left, as we remember it, or once we return, the same as before:

> Here it was coming and going, but never
> Coming the same, or the same gone.

Our links are tenuous indeed for even "the posted photograph seems only/The twitch of a corpse". For "here", wherever "here" may be, home or some loved and remembered place important in one's life, "Here it was living and dying, but never/Lifelong dying or dead-alive". If we look back on that small intimate and re-assuring world where "all knew all", the important memory is of "Landscape and seascape at one's call", and above all, "The senses five or more than five". Because of this vividness of recollection "here means now to the opened eye", the eye that has been "opened" to the values of both immediacy and recollection, so that "both mean ever, though never again".

The shifts of time in this poem produce an atmosphere similar to that in the second half of Virginia Woolf's *To the Lighthouse*, in which what is immediate and present is made unreal by the vivid recollection of the past. This sadness, because time just remem-bered with pleasure and affection cannot be retrieved, and be-cause the present is rarely happy enough, is frequently implied in MacNeice's poetry.

In 'April Fool' MacNeice tries to find reassurance by clinging to the myths and customs which affect to explain, and to accom-

modate the changes of the seasons, the passing of the years, while
generations are born, follow the same customs however modified
and disguised, and then pass away. In 'Apple Blossom' he turns
for comfort to the other side of the coin, and to the doctrine of
Heraclitus that "the sun is new every day" and "Nothing ever is,
everything is becoming". Certainly, for a time this helps him to a
less despairing view of life, and we have a simple, charming poem,
which opens *Solstices*. Its meaning is clear:

> The first apple was the best apple
> For Adam before he heard the sentence;
> . . .
> But the first verdict seemed the worst verdict
> When Adam and Eve were expelled from Eden;
> Yet when the bitter gates clanged to
> The sky beyond was just as blue.

So we find that

> however often the sun may rise,
> A new thing dawns upon our eyes.

This is no great conclusion. No systems of metaphysics are
developed from it. But it is *something*. It is not despair. It is as
near as we get to turning sensitivity to the real world into an
article of faith:

> For the last blossom is the first blossom
> And the first blossom is the best blossom
> And when from Eden we take our way
> The morning after is the first day.

The mood does not hold fully or for long. In the next lyric,
'Invocation', the poet is once more calling upon some unspecified
power to bring back to him from afar his nursery toys, his
mother's hand, the painted joys. The longing for the lost childhood, for the lost mother, which informs his earlier poetry, is
still there. For the rest he asks first for those "so ephemeral
things" which always fascinated him, "the breeze in the heat",
"the curl of the wave", "a moon in a tree", "a phrase of the wind",

and with a return to his concern with the remorselessness of
time, he asks for the verb "To Be". Less usual for him, and with
echoes of the ethics and religion of his childhood and youth, he
asks

> And when the other faces throng
> Fetch me far a place in the mind
> Where only truthful things belong.
> . . .
> And when the last horn burns the hills
> Fetch me far one draught of grace
> To quench my thirst before it kills.

The little refrain that begins and closes the poem:

> Dolphin plunge, fountain play.
> Fetch me far and far away.

is redolent of strength and grace and coolness. In the poem grace
and coolness are there but strength is missing. Its theme is the
converse of that of 'Autobiography'. The poem is charming and
musical but its philosophy is hedonist and it is slight.

'Jigsaws' V is concerned with the negative need of mankind
for religious belief so that there may be "One taboo to break, one
sin to dare". It is in fact one more of the poems in which Mac-
Neice expresses, without resolving, the dichotomy in his nature
that results from the conflict of a religious upbringing in the
comfort and safety of home, and the loneliness of intellectual
agnosticism. From this struggle there still emerges an element of
schoolboy daring in the opening lines: "Although we say we disbelieve,/God comes in handy when we swear". The phrase "we
say" is both noticeable and revealing. Merely to say that we
disbelieve is not to confess that in our hearts we are actually
without belief. We are reminded that four years later in 'The
Blasphemies' MacNeice traced more fully the change in attitude
towards the existence of God from the basic infantile fear of
sinning against the Holy Ghost, through the "gay" blasphemy of
adolescence, through the use of God as "a mere expletive" (as

here), through mythologizing, to near-agnosticism based on a feeling that the problem of whether there is or is not a God is irrelevant to day-to-day human living. Neither the earlier nor the later poem shows any real development in MacNeice's religious thinking since he wrote some 10 or 15 years earlier, in 'The Stygian Banks', "heretics all . . . can choose what we despair of". In 1957 this has become "That God exists we cannot show,/So do not know but need not care". In 'The Stygian Banks' it was "our privilege – / . . . to recognize the insoluble/And going up with an outstretched hand salute it". In 'Jigsaws' V the conclusion is not much different: "we know/We need the unknown. The Unknown is There". The use of the capital letters to lend a false importance to the words "Unknown" and "There" has, in fact, the reverse effect and exposes the weakness of the thought. In 1961 he had reached no further in his thinking than "whether there were a God or not/The word was inadequate". Poetry that can make no more affirmation of either belief or disbelief than this watered-down agnosticism has not wings to soar.

It may well be that MacNeice's knowledge of the classical philosophies was a major factor in preventing him from finding satisfaction in the religion of his childhood. An incomplete appreciation of comparative religious thought, and an indisposition to follow the hard thinking required to achieve such an understanding, nurtured an insufficiently disciplined agnosticism. His inability either to accept or reject is well displayed in the curious, allusive, but not fully satisfactory poem 'The Other Wing'. Included in *Visitations* (1957), it was first commissioned and published (in their series of 'Ariel Poems') by Faber & Faber in 1953, when it gained little from the illustrations of Michael Ayrton, a very gifted artist, but not temperamentally akin to MacNeice. The poem opens by reminding us of the war-like dances of the Curetes as they beat their bronze shields with their swords (on Mount Ida) so that Cronos should not hear the cries of the infant Zeus who was destined to supplant him. Heaven is described as "tenterhook", presumably 'on tenterhooks' since it "cranes through the cracks of its blue enamel/To spot the usurper", a somewhat strained attempt to recreate the stretched blue beyond blue effect of the Mediterranean sky. The second verse takes us on to the time when Zeus, drowned and saved by the noise of metal on metal, is enthroned in his "talk-happy heaven", a description which reminds us neatly of the poetic longueurs that have been lavished on the all too human and all too vocal Olympians. The myth of the birth of Pallas Athene is rather facetiously described: Zeus feels "suddenly harassed, a sky-splitting headache/With nothing to cause it" – a piece of sly humour (and possibly a Freudian thought) since the cause lay in Zeus having swallowed his wife Metis to prevent her children becoming more powerful than he was himself. According to the legend, Hephaestus relieved the headache by splitting open the skull of Zeus with an axe, and Athene sprang from the wound: "out of that nothing/Hard-eyed and helmeted vaulted a goddess". She was the goddess of storm and of lightning, so "a long spear flew", and she excelled in the art of making cloth, so a shuttle also "flew like a clacking fish", a good simile that catches the shape of a shuttle, its glint as it flies across the shed, and the sound as it is beaten from one side of the warp to the other. We are then told that the journeymen artists produced their images of Athene, their 'Palladia', in stone "Or in bronze or chryselephant" (a combination of gold and ivory). The Palladia are the means of a violent transition to the present day. The same images are now to be found in a modern museum with "muted/Miles of parquet, these careful lights./This Aquarium of conditioned air". Although we are wrenched forward through time, we are only allowed a moment in this ordered world. We are told that just beyond the amphorae "lies a red/Letter or birth day, another wing . . .". Here is confusion of time and place; place now represents time and a day is a place. In this other wing (though a different time) are two pupae. One "lagged in his/Mummicose death-dress"; this adjective evokes the world of Egyptian myth and since a contrast is implicit, may perhaps refer to Osiris, the God of the Dead. The other in his swaddling clothes "lagged against life" is the son of Mary, but had no Martha (as he had later) to "tidy the stables", which reminds us both of the manger and the Augean stables. Then comes the most severe comment: this is "Poor Tom O'Bethlehem", a punning reference to the village of Christ's birth and to the mendicants who sought alms and were known as Tom o'Bedlam; and the Virgin, the ox, the ass, the halo, and the crucifixion thus become the trappings of a lunatic.

The last verse is an attempt to convey the feeling that all religions, involved as they are of necessity in the mysteries of death and life, somehow overlap endlessly in the time-scale of the universe. "The centuries unwinding the swaddling/Bands and the death-bands; the long thin pupa/Always must wait for the small round one". The God of the Dead is deaf until he hears the warm voice intoning: "I am the resurrection and the life" when "the fire kindled; and I spake with my tongue" (The Book of Common Prayer: The Burial of the Dead). There is still no solution. There is a third person in the trinity, "Condemned to another, a haunted, wing". This is surely the poet himself, unable to find a religion or philosophy that satisfactorily explains birth, death, or life itself and who therefore lives unsatisfied and haunted. "For all his fire", "Though I speak with the tongues of men and of angels and have not charity" (in the sense of Christian love) – "For all his fire poor Tom's a-cold"; and with this last quotation we are left as bleakly forlorn as Lear himself. In spite of the force of the ending and the wealth of references, this remains a contrived poem, a bespoke poem, a commissioned poem. The images, which are based on myths intended to embody resurrection and life, are used to stress the inevitability of death and are, in consequence, overwrought and over-written. The concept of the poem is not new. Religions and mythologies can no longer move us, but life is inexplicable and there is no escape from death's inevitability. MacNeice in The English Novelist says "The philosopher makes a judgment, but the poet and the novelist on their different planes make statements." The distinction might well be challenged, but here he fails on both counts. There is no judgment and there is no statement. There is only a picture of daunting lack of faith, or of equal lack of confidence in disbelief. The poem moreover is singularly lacking in the music which is a major element in most of his verse and it would seem to justify Edith Sitwell's comment, quoted by Cyril Connolly, that his verse is "either sticky in texture or disintegrated, gritty and sabulous", a spiteful criticism that has little but envy to sustain it except on occasions such as this.

It is emphatically not true of the first section of 'Visitations', the series of six poems which gives the volume its title, and deals with the various sources of poetic inspiration. The first 'Visitation' is a recollection of the 'pastoral' poetry of Horace, of the classic poetry of ancient Greece and the pantheism of yet earlier times. John Waterhouse has said that to hear MacNeice reading Latin, and more especially Greek, verse was to appreciate their music for the first time, "Setting both ears and nerves a-tingle". Again there is the insoluble problem of time. "The ghosts of pastoral", MacNeice says, mingle with the ghosts "from that dark day/Which means our own". Then this becomes doubtful. So deeply does he understand the times that were "Never so lithe in the green dingle,/Never so ripe in the grown hay", that this may be more real than 'time, now', and we are reminded of the reality of that glimpse into the ancient world we have in *Autumn Journal* when he thinks "Of the crooks, the adventurers, the opportunists".

Now he sees the Greeks "Never so young in their green fettle/ Never so glad in their gleaned light". We cannot keep them out, they come back and "Divulge their day to shame our night". Because of their company we "could boast when dying/We had not always lived alone". His first source of inspiration then is the classical literature in which he was a scholar.

The second and still musical 'Visitation' covers, by implication, what might be called the 'mystical' aspect of MacNeice's sources of inspiration; and the strange mélange of references reflects the chameleon-like quality of his mind which so often refuses to follow a thought, an emotion, to its final conclusion. Although the first verse seems to be based partly on Plotinus and his theory of essences, we are still entangled in the space-time relationship and reminded by MacNeice's "indefinable/Moment" of Eliot's "Point of intersection of the timeless/With time". If MacNeice found, or thought he found (for in the whole range of his writing that part consciously inspired by philosophical concepts is the least successful) that this was a source of poetic inspiration, we are reminded by Eliot that to apprehend it "is an occupation for the saint", and therefore beyond the range of the poet. We are more convinced by the second stanza which refers to sources of inspiration more natural to MacNeice, although he constantly and illogically attempted to equate them with the importance of essences :

> With cabbage-whites white
> And blue sky blue
> And the world made one
> Since two make two,
> This moment only
> Yet eras through
> He walks in the sun
> No longer lonely.

With butterflies and blue skies we are back to the sensual appreciations so all-important to him. Life, to him, as to Shelley, was "a dome of many coloured glass" which did indeed stain "the white radiance of Eternity" until eternity itself was obscured by the stains. The critic of *The Times Literary Supplement* came close to an understanding of this aspect of MacNeice's inspiration when he said :

It is as if, in his most personal poems, his inward world became appreciable to us only through faintly-coloured and slightly rippled glass, or as if it were lit by a sun different from ours. The result is often beautiful, always vivid, always arresting both intellectually and emotionally; but always disturbing, too.

This sensual inspiration appropriately enough includes the love poem when the world becomes "one/Since two make two" (and again we are reminded of "Two and two, necessarye coniunction" in *East Coker*). The rest of the poem is a song to the ecstasy of love songs, when the "Seeming-disdaining/Vision is captured". The poet finds "stars in the head/And the grail next door" and "All things existent/Grow suddenly dearer".

Compared with the understanding of I, and the sudden musical upsurge of II, the remaining 'Visitations' are unconvincing in their exploration of sources of the poetic urge. Parable, allegory, myth, though of constant interest to him, and the basis of his posthumously published *Clark Lectures*, fail here to mirror the spark of inspiration. 'Visitations' VI, while striking accurately enough the atmosphere in which the poet waits baffled for the "indefinable moment" is pedestrian, except for the second verse:

> So those who carry this birthright and this burden
> Regardless of all else must always listen
> On the odd chance some fact or freak or phantom
> Might tell them what they want, might burst the cordon
> Which isolates them from their inmost vision.

This is worth quoting in full because its personal message is all in the last line and a half. Here is a recognition by the poet himself of a dilemma which we have several times noted. From time to time in his poetry we have the feeling that he is about to break through to a moment when belief, or vision, and words unite – that combination of uniquely observed truth and precisely wrought expression which we recognize as poetry. Time and again his failure is by the narrowest of margins. Here is his recognition that some "cordon" isolates him from the inmost vision he is striving to explore and express.

Perhaps because they recognize by implication that all hope of bursting the cordon and achieving this inmost vision is irrevocably lost; perhaps because they catch by direct and vivid imagery Eliot's "still point of the turning world", where "the dance is,/But neither arrest nor movement", three poems, 'Hold-up', 'After the Crash', and 'Charon' reach the highest level of all MacNeice's work. Because of this total submission to the conviction that in human terms the problems of the self located on a pinpoint in eternal space, and in eternity, must remain unresolved, we are made to feel that in these, rather than in any others of his poems, he is near to breaking through. The three poems have a common subject, and a common source of imagery derived from transport, which recalls his lifelong use of images from trams and buses and cars. His feeling that train journeys and indeed all journeys involving speed, intensified moments of awareness, may owe something to popular expositions of Einstein's theory of relativity, which were nearly always illustrated by reference to an observer moving through space, and his consequent relationship to time. Dunne's *Experiment with Time* was on every bookstall in the 'thirties, and the changing concept of time-space had at least as much impact on the thinking of the mid-twentieth century man of intellect as any of the new theories of the unconscious mind. For those who could not take refuge in the mathematics and enjoy the elegance of theoretical exposition, and for those who realized vividly that here was progress only of proof but not of conception, and that in consequence we were back two thousand years to aspects of Greek thought, there could be no comfort in the new knowledge, and little new hope for the individual personality.

'Hold-up' is a nightmare of the technological age. The opening lines: "The lights were red" may puzzle future generations, when traffic control is either more sophisticated or even unnecessary. Today we know their meaning and at once and in practical terms have an uneasy conviction that if the lights "refused to change" we too should be reduced by a paralysis of the will to this sort of inert helplessness. The observation, in the poem, of communal apathy, is sharp: "Ash-ends grew longer, no one spoke". Anyone who has been in a group of strangers forced to wait by a plane delayed, or a train broken down, will recognize its exactness. Here the trivia of our age are exposed to the face of eternity and this is expressed by clever word-play that is perhaps a trifle over-indulgent. As the 'Hold-up' continued, the promise of the football pools, those weekly pipe-dreams, faded and their "bubbles" "Went flat". The so immediate, so essential, so modern "hot news froze" and the "dates", the appointments that could no longer be kept, were as little thought of as the matches that, having lit a cigarette, are shaken out and thrown away. Humanity and youth disappeared, "the girls no longer flagged/Their sex", as taxis flag their readiness for fares. Then there was silence in this one place, the silence of death which comes to the dying, but not to those around, and death itself is described in the trappings of our times; "a tall glass box/On the pavement held a corpse in pickle". The glass boxes of the G.P.O. telephones become the glass bottles on the shelf of the anatomy laboratory. There was the final inertia:

> for miles behind
> The other buses nudged and blared
> And no one dared get out. The conductress
> Was dark and lost, refused to change.

For MacNeice this is an unusually complete statement. It casts one's mind, in its completeness, back to 'Snow'. 'Snow' stopped short in face of the strange complexities of everyday events, but admitted its inability to comprehend the truth in diversity of perception: "There is more than glass between the snow and the huge roses". 'Hold-up' stops short of an explanation at the end of all effort, of all perception, but is positive in its recognition of that final paralysed moment.

The same outraged reaction to the passing of time and of life, the same grudging recognition of death, here conceived as having suddenly happened, informs 'After the Crash'. It is the only poem which tentatively explores the eternal question of what comes after life. Again the situation is in modern terms, and the poem, with its special reference to our times with their cool acceptance (taking it all in all) of death by vehicle may well become an unusually vivid contemporary document. Its real point lies in the way it conveys a sense of shocked desolation. The simplicity of the language makes an immediate impact: "When he came to" is colloquial. What he found is nightmare again, "The asphalt", that deadening, apparently final cover of the earth which, given time, plant life will overcome, was high not with grass, or flowers, or the normal weeds or trees, but "with hemlock", the herb of death, the herb that is associated through Socrates with the end of wisdom. Time has disappeared and when "he crawled to his crash/Helmet" he "found it no more/Than his wrinkled hand what it was". We are left to imagine it as become only dessicated rubble. The next verse is both satire and despair:

> Yet life seemed still going on:
> He could hear the signals bounce
> Back from the moon and the hens
> Fire themselves black in the batteries
> And the silence of small blind cats
> Debating whether to pounce.

Then comes realization that there is no final court of appeal: "he looked up and marked/The gigantic scales in the sky". Perhaps these are Pope's scales of "Poetic Justice" – "Where, in nice balance, truth with gold she weighs". Now both pans of the scales are "dead" empty, there is no judgment, no arbiter, no "well done thou good and faithful servant". Once again we are with Coleridge's Life-in-Death, where "in the dead, dead calm/It was too late to die".

So we come by way of nightmare and paralysis of the will to 'Charon', one of the finest death-wish poems in the English language. Its simplicity is apparent, not real. The expression is that of a cultured and cultivated spirit imprisoned, half by accident, half by surrender to the habits of society, in its own half-admired civilization. With progress or change, much of its impact must be lost. We are again in the remorseless grinding world of public transport. Its grime and lack of respect for human individuality are in the first three lines:

> The conductor's hands were black with money:
> Hold on to your ticket, he said, the inspector's
> Mind is black with suspicion,

There is no real hope, for all we have to guide us here, as in the realm of thought, is "a dissolving map". The mundane sights we have seen so often through the bus windows are sinister and

229

charged with uncomprehending meaning. We look at the pigeons but fail to hear their echo of St Matthew's "wars and rumours of wars". The lost dog's bark is the "cock's shrill clarion" which reminds us not only of the "lowly dead" but again of the time when a god died and a mystery was born. So time has passed; "we just jogged on" and "at each request stop", those occasional moments when choice, a severely limited choice, is permissible, we found only "a crowd of aggressively vacant/Faces", with which there was no communication. Nor was there any escape into Vaughan's eternity "like a great ring of pure and endless light", which is here reduced to a concept that "Gave itself airs in revolving lights". When the poet came to the edge of the last river, the Thames, or Acheron, it matters not which, the further shore was lost in the fog of death. If we looked at our guide, our priest, our conductor for advice, he could only say "Take the ferry/Faute de mieux." Although the journey is by bus we find Charon waiting, as we learnt to expect from our reading of the poets, "just as Virgil/And Dante had seen him". This being the end, "he looked at us coldly" because "his eyes were dead". But like our guide, our conductor, our priest, his hands too were black from the handling of fares. His greeting is the last line of the poem: "If you want to die you will have to pay for it". What is inevitable is not to be made easy.

It is too facile to see, in a poem written so soon before the poet's death, premonition when in fact there is mere coincidence. MacNeice died because he allowed a cold to develop into pleurisy and pneumonia before, too late, he sought help. It is not psychologically impossible that to insist on sharing risks with B.B.C. engineers making a pot-holing feature programme, and to neglect the consequent chill were each part of a progressive yielding to weariness and fear of growing old. Certainly this was not a conscious approach to escape from life, not a conscious seeking of death. It was maybe a yielding to the utter weariness that comes with the inability to say (with Eliot) "to my soul, be still, and wait without hope".

In the poems from the last three volumes that are concerned

with eternal questions of life and death we find some of the same virtues that informed those that concerned themselves with the other prime subject of the Romantic poet, self. This time and in some half-dozen poems we are a little closer to transcendentalism, "The feeling of the universe experienced as a presence". Behind 'April Fool', 'The Here-and-Never', and 'Invocation' there is the sense of another life which can never quite be reached because it can never quite be expressed. Beyond 'Hold-up', 'After the Crash', and 'Charon' is a veil waiting to be torn aside to reveal the ultimate secret of being, which again, because it cannot be known, cannot be expressed. Gone are the tortuous seekings after explanation that we suffered in 'Plurality' and 'The Stygian Banks'. Now there is only statement and from that a new calmness and a new acceptance. Again, the achievement is matched by the clearest and aptest imagery and sparse, monosyllabic diction, as in 'Apple Blossom':

> Yet when the bitter gates clanged to
> The sky above was just as blue.

and in 'Invocation':

> when the last horn burns the hills
> Fetch me far one draught of grace
> To quench my thirst before it kills.

The examples might be multiplied by reference to many equally clean, simple lines, but the simplicity and the finality are both caught up in the last line of 'Charon'.

V

After the deliberate experimentations of *Ten Burnt Offerings* it is tempting to say of the last three books: "Here is the MacNeice of old." Ian Hamilton felt that in *Visitations* and *Solstices* he "was able to rediscover much of his old concentration and vitality", and it is true that the subject matter may remind us of his poems of the 'thirties and 'forties. There is the same concern with childhood influences and the passing of life. 'Invocation', for example, takes one's mind back immediately to 'Autobiography'. These auto-biographical influences persist, but it is a far cry from 'Carrick-fergus' to 'Soap Suds'. Similarly if there is in 'Birmingham' or 'Sunday Morning' an element of social criticism, an appreciation of the meretricious standards of judgment in common in our modern civilization, 'In Lieu' deals with the same subject more savagely, more truly and in greater depth. If he has always been concerned, however unsuccessfully, with finding a reason for living in the face of the inevitability of old age and decay and death as in 'The Stygian Banks', in these last three books there is an acceptance, albeit tinged with foreboding, in the face of death itself. MacNeice wrote of *Solstices*:

I would say myself that I have become progressively more humble in the face of my material, and therefore less ready to slap poster paint over it. I have also perhaps found it easier to write poems of acceptance even of joy.

It is a far cry from 'The Stygian Banks':

> when our own existence is cut off
> That stroke will put a seal upon our value.

to the final verse of 'Invocation'. As well as fear, self-pity has disappeared. It was there, more than a little, in 'Prayer Before Birth'. In 'The Slow Starter' and 'Birthright' we are faced with statement of bleak, uncomplaining fact:

> He took their tip, he took his time,
> And found his time and talent gone.

and:

> I said 'To mount him means to die',
> They said 'Of course',

The "so ephemeral things" that in 'An Eclogue for Christmas' he had wished to be "somehow permanent" become permanent in

the macabre 'Hold-up', and he answers his question "Can you
not take it merely on trust that life is/The only thing worth living
and that dying/Had better be left to take care of itself in the end"
with the inevitability of 'After the Crash' and the bleak clear
vision of 'Charon'. It is true that there is, in these poems, a new
note of courage and acceptance, but there is little trace of "joy"!
"Sooner let nightmares whinny if we cannot/Retrieve our dreams
of dalliance" ('Dreams in Middle Age') "I never ordered/Jam,
God damn you, leave me alone" ('Il Piccolo Rifiuto'), "And yet,
whatever drinks are downed/Someone has got to pay for the
round" ('Yours Next'), and:

> he was merely fifty,
> No one and nowhere else, a walking
> Question but no more cheap than any
> Question or quest is cheap. The sin
> Against the Holy Ghost – What is it?

With this new fortitude goes a more concise, closely knit
prosody. Auden said:

I am confident that posterity will sustain my conviction that his later
poems show an advance upon his earlier, are more certain in their
craftsmanship, brilliant though that always was, and more moving.

They are more moving because they are more courageous. In
what does the improvement in their craftsmanship lie? The verse
is spare. The words are short. The sentence structure is concise.
We read in 'Apple Blossom':

> The first blossom was the best blossom
> For the child who never had seen an orchard;
> For the youth whom whisky had led astray
> The morning after was the first day.

and we recognize a distillation of ideas that informed 'Mutations':
"Surprises keep us living: as when the first light/Surprised our
infant eyes" and 'The Drunkard':

> Such was the absolute moment, to be displaced
> By moments; the clock takes over – time to descend
> Where Time will brief us, briefed himself to oppress

> The man who looks and finds Man human and not his friend
> And whose tongue feels around and around but cannot taste
> That hour-gone sacrament of drunkenness.

In 'Apple Blossom' emotion and observation are combined in a simple universal, and yet unique statement, well illustrating his opinion that "A sentence in prose is struck forward like a golf ball; a sentence in verse can be treated like a ball in a squash court". In the same way when we read 'All Over Again', "Nor now shall I ask for anything more of future or past/This being last and first sound sight on eyes and ears" we recognize an abiding statement of the effect of love, especially love discovered afresh. We are reminded of an earlier love poem 'Trilogy for X' which also dealt with "One kiss ingathered world":

> O my love, if only I were able
> To protract this hour of quiet after passion,
> Not ration happiness but keep this door for ever
> Closed on the world, its own world closed within it.

We know at once that the earlier poem dealt with transient and earthly rapture. The later one, dealing with an unexpected love, has wings. The conclusions of the two poems emphasize this point. Compare:

> The first train passes and the windows groan,
> Voices will hector and your voice become
> A drum in tune with theirs, which all last night
> Like sap that fingered through a hungry tree
> Asserted our one night's identity.

with:

> And each long then and there suspended on this cliff
> Shining and slicing edge that reflects the sun as if
> This one Between were All and we in love for years.

We can conclude this brief summary of the last three books with a reference to what must be the last of his original poems ('Carpe Diem', published with it, was a translation). 'Thalassa' repeats in the last verse an image from 'Explorations' written some 20 years previously. The early poem begins "The whale butting through scarps of moving marble", and continues with other images to prove that the animal world is governed by instinct but that "ours is not. For we are a unique, a conscious/ Hoping and therefore despairing creature" and that "Our end is our own to be won by our own endeavour/And held on our own terms". This is ratiocination; but the image persisted. In 'Thalassa' it becomes, in the final verse, "Butting through scarps of moving marble/The narwhal dares us to be free". Now however, with memories of the Magi, "By a high star our course is set,/Our end is life".

It is too easy to see in 'Thalassa', as others have seen in 'Charon', a premonition of death. The coincidence lies in the correlation in verse, at the last moment of creative effort granted to him, of his fear of the unknown blankness of death with the hope that life can still be made to offer more.

MacNeice in his life, we are told, and we can believe from what we know, devoted himself to the task in hand. Whatever he did for his publisher, for the B.B.C., or for the British Council, he did to the best of his ability. The melancholia that enfolded him and that his friends accepted, was perhaps part of the price he paid. With another task to perform, another programme to prepare, he wrote the clear, simple, traditional poem 'Thalassa', intensely personal for all its echoes of Tennyson's 'Ulysses':

> Run out the boat, my broken comrades;
> Let the old seaweed crack, the surge
> Burgeon oblivious of the last
> Embarkation of feckless men,
> Let every adverse force converge –
> Here we must needs embark again.
>
> Run up the sail, my heartsick comrades;
> Let each horizon tilt and lurch –
> You know the worst: your wills are fickle,
> Your values blurred, your hearts impure
> And your past life a ruined church –
> But let your poison be your cure.

Put out to sea, ignoble comrades,
Whose record shall be noble yet;
Butting through scarps of moving marble
The narwhal dares us to be free;
By a high star our course is set,
Our end is Life. Put out to sea.

CHAPTER SIX

Retrospect

MacNeice defined a poet as "an ordinary man with specialised gifts". His own gifts were an acute sensory, and especially visual, perception; colour, shape, light and shade, sound, smell, touch and taste, lend to his verse an immediacy closely connected with time and place. For him emotional recollection was bound up with where and when, as in the whole of *Autumn Journal*, in 'Birmingham' and 'Belfast'. He exploited the pathetic fallacy for all it was worth, not as a mere device, but because his experiences were bound up with actual times and places, as we see clearly in 'Solitary Travel', in Canto III of *Autumn Journal* and, above all, in 'Snow'. This external sensory perception was an integral part of the deeper emotional or intellectual feeling he was trying to express. So when he had to try even harder to convey an emotion whose validity he doubted, as in 'Flowers in the Interval', he relied on the association with places both to recall and heighten it.

One criticism of MacNeice, related to his keen sense of place and time, and repeated from reviewer to reviewer, remains to be dealt with. It is a charge that he brought upon himself, that he was more journalist than poet. In *Modern Poetry* he had said:

My own prejudice . . . is in favour of poets whose words are not too esoteric. I would have a poet able-bodied, fond of talking, a reader of the newspapers, capable of pity and laughter, informed in economics, appreciative of women, involved in personal relationships, actively interested in politics, susceptible to physical impressions.

Though this is a Romantic concept, it is likely to be an enervating one. He recognized the danger himself: "Those who take the whole modern world for canvas are liable to lapse into mere journalism." In spite of this awareness he still maintains: "It is my own opinion . . . that the normal poet includes the journalist." This offered too easy a handle to those critics who could not envisage the lesser contained in the greater, the newsman in the poet. His descriptions of the urban and suburban world, and the occasional passages, as in *Autumn Journal*, dealing with headline news, could be superficially written off as 'journalism'. The critics are rarely specific. In the descriptive pieces like 'Sunday Morning' or despatches from the front like Canto XXIII of *Autumn Journal* that can be compared to 'special articles', surely the poetic craftsmanship is sufficient to give the lie to the description of 'journalism' used in a pejorative sense. Although we can reject the jibe as not applying to most of his poetry, it remains true that because he clung to the idea that the poet contains the journalist, his subject was occasionally ephemeral and too smartly on target, as in Canto X of *Autumn Sequel*:

Daily news. And today? There is not so much to note.
Much talk in Cairo of the Suez Canal,
Much talk in Capetown of the Coloured Vote

(And Kaffirs have rallied sharply — Fal-de-lal!),
Much talk in Margate where the dextral faction
Of Labour has outplayed its left cabal,

Much talk throughout the world of action and reaction
And explanation centres and isotopes
And interzonal permits; for distraction

Much talk of football pools and Britain's hopes
On the greens of Virginia Water.

But if we criticize this we should perhaps pause for a moment
and recall Wordsworth's lines: "I've measured it from side to
side:/'Tis three feet long, and two feet wide" or "These hedge-
rows, hardly hedge-rows, little lines/Of sportive wood run wild".
In other words, it is not balanced criticism to dismiss the
minutiae of daily life as being unsuitable stuff for poetry; though
we must recognize the skill required not to fall into banality, for
all inspiration weakens at times. On the other hand there is, as
we have seen, reportage that is true poetry. It ranges from:

Man's heart expands to tinker with his car
For this is Sunday morning, Fate's great bazaar;
Regard these means as ends, concentrate on this Now,
And you may grow to music or drive beyond Hindhead anyhow,
Take corners on two wheels until you go so fast
That you can clutch a fringe or two of the windy past

to the clear-cut topical descriptions of 'Christmas Shopping':

Spending beyond their income on gifts for Christmas –
Swing doors and crowded lifts and draperied jungles –
What shall we buy for our husbands and sons
    Different from last year?
. . .
The great windows marshal their troops for assault on the
    purse
Something-and-eleven the yard, hoodwinking logic,
The eleventh hour draining the gurgling pennies
    Down the conduits
. . .
While over the street in the centrally heated public
Library dwindling figures with sloping shoulders
And hands in pockets, weighted in the boots like chessmen,
Stare at the printed

Columns of ads,

Perhaps one of the most evocative of all these descriptions taking his world for canvas, but not lapsing into journalism, is in *Autumn Journal* VII:

> They are cutting down the trees on Primrose Hill.
> The wood is white like the roast flesh of chicken,
>   Each tree falling like a closing fan;
> No more looking at the view from seats beneath the branches,
>   Everything is going to plan;
> They want the crest of this hill for anti-aircraft,
>   The guns will take the view
> And searchlights probe the heavens for bacilli
>   With narrow wands of blue.
> And the rain came on as I watched the territorials
>   Sawing and chopping and pulling on ropes like a team
> In a village tug-of-war; and I found my dog had vanished
>   And thought 'This is the end of the old régime,'
> But found the police had got her at St. John's Wood station
>   And fetched her in the rain and went for a cup
> Of coffee to an all-night shelter and heard a taxi-driver
>   Say 'It turns me up
> When I see these soldiers in lorries'—

This is a picture that combines the objective and subjective effect of momentous news and it is brilliantly continued in the next canto. In the last three books this element of reportage becomes absorbed into the more universal nature of his poetry. We can see this most clearly in the compassion and precision of 'The Suicide':

> There are the bills
> In the intray, the ash in the ashtray, the grey memoranda
>   stacked
> Against him, the serried ranks of the box-files, the packed
> Jury of his unanswered correspondence
> Nodding under the paperweight in the breeze
> From the window by which he left; and here is the cracked
> Receiver that never got mended and here is the jotter
> With his last doodle which might be his own digestive tract
> Ulcer and all

He had learnt from Eliot how to absorb into his poetry the impedimenta from the everyday life of our urban civilization. For MacNeice was an urban man. From 'Turf-Stacks' onwards, his rural landscapes were those of the visitor; his sympathetic, almost 'natural' response was to the town. Although Pound and Eliot, and to some extent Auden and Spender, preceded him in admitting urban and industrial images into poetry, it was MacNeice who had the true romantic relationship with the City. This kind of relationship is not entirely new in English poetry; Milton's "Tower'd cities please us then/And the busy hum of men", and Wordsworth's

> This City now doth, like a garment, wear
> The beauty of the morning; silent, bare,
> Ships, towers, domes, theatres, and temples lie
> Open unto the fields, and to the sky;

both express the same kind of elated reaction. MacNeice brought it up to date. The escalators of the Underground Railway, the vacuum cleaners in Lyons' Corner House, the moving advertisements of Piccadilly Circus, cars and their headlights and windscreen wipers, buses, traffic lights, telephones, all the paraphernalia of modern life were his landscape and provided his images. He belonged to the town as Wordsworth belonged to the landscape of the Lakes, and if the town failed to provide him with an equivalent to a pantheistic philosophy, it provided him with sparkling words and images fit to be used in his poetry. He loved the music of words. He had a sense of rhyme that made him free with all the variations that Hopkins and Owen and their predecessors had explored – half rhyme, bad rhyme, pararhyme, internal rhyme, assonance, alliteration, were his to command. He rarely departed from what he described in *Modern Poetry* as "the running trochees and dactyls of ordinary English speech". He had in fact what G. S. Fraser in *The Modern Writer and His World* calls "a way with words"; and Fraser points out that:

It was this disturbing, uncomfortable use of language, the supple closeness to the rhythms of intelligent speech, that poets of a later generation, like Auden and MacNeice, were to take over from Eliot and from the Pound of *Mauberley*;

but MacNeice had the defect of his virtues. He could be misled into inept punning, as in "Was he that once, the sole delight of my soul?" He could give the impression of building a whole poem to make appropriate a clever phrase of conclusion. One wonders, for example, whether 'Off the Peg' was written to accommodate the last line: "And off the peg means made to measure now"; or 'Déjà Vu' for "It does not come round in hundreds of thousands of years", or 'Birthright' for "My gift horse looked me in the mouth". There is occasionally a certain slickness in his work, but it is the obverse of his prosodic and verbal facility. He was early aware of the danger: "Any word" he says "is itself a trick to start with . . . We should not show the works, and our tricks should be suited to our subject matter." He could also be tedious; and the efficient versification of some of his agnostic sermonizing does not rescue it from banality; but he had a subtle command of rhythm from the heaviest of hymnal metric beats to the finest sense of stressed line. He had thought long about imagery and his metaphors and similes were apt, striking, illuminating, and drawn from scholarship and observation. He had resources of scholarship and deployed them with ease. With this equipment he passed rapidly through the early experimental stages in a poet's development. After 1929, except in the less successful parts of *Ten Burnt Offerings* and in *Autumn Sequel*, he progressed fairly steadily to the sparse, clear poetry of the last three books.

By 1932 he is writing 'Turf-Stacks', which we have already recognized as central to the nostalgic elements in his thought and which meets the need of the reader for reassurance that he is not alone. "For *we*" (note the plural) "For we are obsolete who like the lesser things". A year later he is describing these "lesser things" in 'Birmingham' in great swinging lines of four stresses rhymed, or half-rhymed couplets (and metrically, as we have seen, in all likelihood derived from Noyes) and the thought anticipates much of *Autumn Journal*. In the same collection, *Poems* (1935), he distils in the sonnet 'Sunday Morning', of contemporary construction (lines of irregular length syllabically, but with four stresses rhyming in couplets), something of the essence of the suburban life which he half criticized and half loved, in words sufficiently striking to be echoed by Eliot in 'The Rock'.

In 1935 he wrote 'Snow', a poem which attracted, as we saw in Chapter One, much misplaced critical attention, but which has a sharp appeal, both sensual and visual. So by way of 'The Jingles of the Morning' and the inexpressibly sad 'The Sunlight on the Garden', where the wrought craftsmanship of the poem matches perfectly the nostalgic despair, he reaches, as the threshold to *Autumn Journal*, the ironical 'Bagpipe Music' in which the music is such fun that the deep satirical undertone is in danger of being overlooked.

Here then is his poetry of the first decade. The threads that run through those of the poems that we have admired are the sharp impact of the world of the senses upon him, the inability to choose a political stance, the realization both as observer and participant of the limitations of urban life, the sadness of life passing, and the impossibility of catching the golden moment. Step by step his craftsmanship had kept pace with his subject matter and he was ready to begin the long poem which John Waterhouse told me he had suggested that MacNeice should attempt.

So we have *Autumn Journal*, Larkin's "brilliant quotidian reportage", and praised by other critics as among the best pictures of the Munich crisis, and of the immediate pre-war days. This surely is a poem which will live because we have one man, harassed by those who would wish him to accept a political view, but prevented from doing so by an intellectual honesty and natural scepticism, who sets out in diary-form the daily impact upon his senses of a civilization ill at ease and filled with foreboding. "The blue smoke rising, and the brown lace falling in the empty glass of stout" in *Autumn Journal* III is a picture that in two lines says as much as all the "false friend" sequence of *The Waste Land*. Of course there are inequalities in *Autumn Journal*. Of course we must not demand that it is more than it sets out to be. Its very modesty ensures that it revives memories of those small and intimate moments when great disaster threatens the individual; the recognition that these moments, common to us all, have an element of universal truth, makes the poem live; and if, in this instance, this truth is based on uncertainty and insecurity, its appeal is no less; as in Clough's 'Amours de Voyage', human inability to decide, to achieve, to be complete in understanding, reaches in *Autumn Journal* the stage of being a truth in itself. The prosody matches the impotent casualness of the commentary; the discipline of the rhyme and the latitude of the rhythmic stress are in constant balance.

When we consider the poetry that followed *Autumn Journal* we would do well to recall Auden's lines:

> Intellectual disgrace
> Stares from every human face,
> And the seas of pity lie
> Locked and frozen in each eye.

We must realize that it is in the atmosphere of intellectual shame that the poetry of the war had, inevitably, to be written. Mac-Neice, writing at the time, first took refuge in personal poetry. 'Meeting Point', the converse of 'The Sunlight on the Garden' (since he now "cages the minute/Within its nets of gold") turns the intensely personal into a moment of truth by the simplicity of the language, the breadth of the imagery contained within a deliberately claustrophobic moment outlined by the cunning use of a one-line refrain in each stanza. Then, rather like a child hiding his head in his mother's bosom when danger threatens, he gives us two more poems dwelling on the psychological burdens of early experience, 'Christina' and 'Autobiography', again with skilful use of refrain. When he turns from this to a subject relevant to the times, we have 'Bar-room Matins', neat, simple, ending with the apt line "Give us this day our daily news", from which it is impossible to divorce the too easy cynicism.

At this point he is in danger of dying poetically from a surfeit of craftsmanship over subject. This is not surprising, for he had 'sold himself' to the Establishment. Impressed into the service of the B.B.C. in war-time, all truth, all doubt, all feeling had to be employed in total war, and the end-product, if not confined to the personal, had to be propaganda, not art. The wonder is not that within the intellectual suffocation of these demands he could not do better, but that he could do at all well. Nor should it be surprising that from the midst of this inevitably schizophrenic situation should come such an intimately personal poem, so full of universal despair, as 'Prayer Before Birth' on the one hand, or such shrewd extrovert observation as 'The Mixer' and 'The Libertine' on the other, and so little truly 'war' poetry. What is perhaps surprising and only to be understood in the context of general relief from conscripted conformism at the end of the war, is a poem such as 'Bluebells', with its deep psychological understanding of the problems of renewal of normal life. The third stanza of this poem has a noble simplicity of language wrought into a calm certainty of rhythm, assonance and rhyme; and the other poem of the same period that compares with it in prosody is 'The Drunkard', which also has the same relationship of universal to particular and the same simplicity of expression.

Then came the difficult years. Not too long, only 1950 to 1953, and not all of the last. They were at first cerebral years, as though in *Ten Burnt Offerings* he had set himself the task of writing only intellectual scholarly poetry related to the places in which he found himself. They have, as we have seen, their felicities; though *Autumn Sequel* is but passable. True poetry returns only with *Visitations*. From then until his death, we have poems which combine the early music, the craftsmanship of the middle years, and the compulsive themes, but shorn of self-pity and introspection. Here is a fiercer MacNeice. 'April Fool' is a better poem than 'Bagpipe Music', for the avenues of thought and dream imagery that are opened to us in it are at once more coherent and more controlled. "Sooner let nightmares whinny" is a stark opening to 'Dreams in Middle Age', a poem of psychological self-knowledge. *Solstices* has, as we have seen, much good poetry set around three memorable, possibly great, poems. 'Apple Blossom' has the strong effect that comes from embodying a simple but hitherto not clearly perceived statement in the simplest of verse forms, and the most natural language. 'Hold-up' in 15 lines of four-stress unrhymed verses, sets in amber a universal experience, and 'All Over Again' we have already praised as a great poem of middle-aged love. If we turn back from any of these poems to earlier ones such as 'Sunday Morning' or perhaps more appositely, 'Hidden Ice', we cannot but be struck by the economy and force of the later poetry compared with the looseness of expression and consequent dissipation of effect of the earlier. Even 'Meeting Point' has an almost artificial and repetitive effect if it is read side by side with the control, the internal rhyme, assonance and alliteration of 'All Over Again'. When we turn to the last volume, there are more memorable poems than in any single section of his work of equal size. If the thought is embedded in a kind of nostalgic inevitability, the craftsmanship has met the theme and is spare and direct, so that the overall effect is one of earnest and slightly deprecating fatalism. 'Soap Suds', 'Déjà Vu' and 'Off the Peg', granted an element of artificiality in their construction, escape sentimentality by a straightforward, almost stark, mode of expression. 'Birthright' and 'The Habits' in stanzas of equal simplicity seem, at last, to perform the act of catharsis he had sought in his prose autobiography; while the lyric aspect comes to fruition in the determined surrender of 'Charon' and the hopeless hope of 'Thalassa'. In each of these poems the marriage of form and content, in the first group a little contrived, in the second as inevitable as in all good art, is its highest achievement.

In considering the progress of MacNeice's verse in all its aspects to its apogee in *The Burning Perch*, we have omitted that portion which explored the philosophical aspects of his thought. When we look back upon it this is not surprising. The longer works of vague philosophizing or agnostic sermonizing, such as 'Plurality' or 'The Stygian Banks', even when pleasing or interesting to read, make no deeper impact.

In *Modern Poetry* he had written: "I have already maintained that major poetry usually implies a belief", though he tries to qualify this by the view that by the poet "any belief . . . should be compromised with his own individual observation". Three years later in *The Poetry of W. B. Yeats* he came nearer to expressing in words the dichotomy which he never resolved in poetry: "The faith in the *value* of living is a mystical faith. The pleasure in bathing or dancing, in colour or shape is a mystical experience." By using the word "mystical" in both phrases, he was attempting to overcome the age-old dilemma of equating emotional apples with sensual pears. He knew, and expressed again and again in his poetry, the delights of the senses and he experienced them so fully that he could half deceive himself into believing that they were a "mystical experience" and half way to faith, or belief. A quarter of a century later, in *Varieties of Parable*, he could still say of belief: "This, as always, is a puzzler", but having recognized this, he avoids the issue which, for him, was unpalatable. He lacked, in the last analysis, the moral fibre, the capacity for intellectual achievement, or the single-mindedness, to attain belief, even in disbelief. The question of belief and poetry is one of considerable difficulty. In general terms it is surely true to say that poetry must be based on conflict and passion, and whether it is employed to support or resist belief, the conflict and passion are all-important to the poetry. MacNeice came no nearer to a passionate resolution of philosophical or religious conflict than the expression of doubt in 'Didymus', the regression of 'Prayer Before Birth', and the terrible fear that lies at the heart of 'Charon'.

We approached the poetry of MacNeice expecting to find, as he had himself indicated that we should, a poet in the Romantic tradition, and this indeed we have found. We may compare his achievements with Raymond's definition of the Romantic poet with which we began our study. His primary "form of knowledge" as displayed in his poetry, is self-centred. Every shift of ground, every alteration of emphasis is, in his verse, a contribution to the "metaphoric" or "symbolic" portrait of himself, pored over, again and again, with the nostalgic longing for the moment it embodies. His metamorphoses range from the lonely child, cursed with a lifelong Oedipus complex, the schoolboy and student, then the townsman, the deserted lover, the husband, father, academic and author. The word "enjoyment" is echoed in the use of "mystical" to cover the experiences of the senses. Only when we come to the phrase "a feeling of the universe, experienced as a presence" are we forced to pause. A feeling of the minutiae of the universe, its colour, sounds, touch and smell, was indeed an integral part of his poetry and gives it an immediacy, a sense of heightened reality, that might at first sight satisfy the requirement of this definition, but the pleasure in colour or shape is not enough. It is not "a mystical experience". "A feeling of the universe, experienced as a presence" calls for a transcendental understanding of which he was only occasionally capable, as in the last few poems.

MacNeice remained the prisoner of his childhood. He could never escape the nostalgic chains this placed upon him either as lover or thinker. That his love for his mother rested, not unusually, on so profound a sexual base that her early death was permanently crippling emotionally, he half realized, as we see from the story of the twig that he tells in *The Strings are False*. In prose that comes near to poetry, he describes the occasion:

That had been a fresh spring morning and everyone well and gay and my father was perched on a ladder clipping the arbour which was made of little trees we called poplars. The long sprays fell on the ground with light green lively leaves and I gathered some of them up to arrange in a jam-jar. But one of my twigs was too long, whenever I put it in the jar the jar fell over. My mother came up smiling, folded the twig double, put it in the jar and the jar stayed upright. And I was outraged, went off in a sulk.

In *Experiences with Images* he comments in a note:

Almost the most disastrous experience of my childhood is for ever associated in my mind with a doubled-up poplar twig – but I have never yet used this image as a symbol of evil. Were I to do so, I should certainly elucidate the reference.

The importance of this lies in the last phrase. He never brought himself to "elucidate the reference". His ambivalent attitude to this story, so that he must tell it, shows that he realized that it contained a significance which it was difficult to face. His inability to use it in his poetry constituted in a major degree a moral failure in one for whom self was a major source of interest and inspiration. A parallel and not dissociated failure lay in his inability to make the intellectual effort either to achieve faith, to deny all belief, or to systematize his agnosticism. This ethical and intellectual weakness led to a certain sentimentality in his approach to social criticism and equally made any firm political attitude impossible. So MacNeice could find neither spiritual faith, political belief, or personal love and understanding to form the basis of his poetry, but relied instead on the conflicts of indecision. In so far as it lacks a passionate attempt to cope with the conflicts that arise from doubt and indecision, the poetry of MacNeice sometimes falls short of greatness. The tragedy is that he could not escape from within himself to wider exploration.

Perhaps the last words should be allowed to rest with two admired fellow-poets, both his friends. Auden has been included in the group of 'thirties poets in what he described as the "customary journalistic linkage". Eliot was at first MacNeice's inspiration, then his publisher, and finally his friend and admirer. In his memorial address Auden said:

Louis MacNeice was clearly a poet who shared Cesare Pavese's belief that 'the only joy in life is to begin', that, from the poet's point of view, the excitement of tackling a problem, whether of technique or subject matter, which one has never attempted before, is even more important than the result. I am confident that posterity will sustain my conviction that his later poems show an advance upon his earlier, are more certain in their craftsmanship, brilliant though that always was, and more moving; but, even if I thought otherwise, I should still admire him for risking failure rather than being content to repeat himself successfully.

T. S. Eliot, speaking 'ex cathedra' (as we said at the very beginning of our study of MacNeice's poetry), had this to say in *The Times* of 5 September 1963:

There is little that I can add to the encomiums of Louis MacNeice which have already appeared in the press, except the expression of my own grief and shock. The grief one must feel at the death of a poet of genius, younger than oneself . . .

MacNeice was one of several brilliant poets who were up at Oxford at the same time, and whose names were at first always associated, but the difference between whose gifts shows more and more clearly with the lapse of time. MacNeice in particular stands apart. If the term 'poet's poet' means a poet whose virtuosity can be fully appreciated only by other poets, it may be applied to MacNeice. But if it were taken to imply that his work cannot be enjoyed by the large public of poetry readers, the term would be misleading. He had the Irishman's unfailing ear for the music of verse, and he never published a line that is not good reading.

There is, indeed, so much that is good and so much more that is satisfying. There is high craftsmanship and a developing capacity to achieve an almost classical clarity. His imagery gains its force from a precise expression of the impact of the world upon his senses. Just occasionally when this is married to deeper feelings, when for example he explores true doubt, true defiance of "God or whatever means the Good", when he faces true despair, and truly accepts the consequences of ultimate nothingness, of ultimate inability to contact other human beings, we salute the high genius of his poetry.

Bibliography

1   Works by Louis MacNeice

Poetry

Blind Fireworks, Gollancz, 1929.
Poems, Faber & Faber, 1935.
The Earth Compels, Faber & Faber, 1938.
Autumn Journal, Faber & Faber, 1939.
The Last Ditch (450 copies, 1–25 signed by author), Cuala Press, Dublin, 1940.
Selected Poems, Faber & Faber, 1940.
Plant and Phantom, Faber & Faber, 1941.
Springboard, Faber & Faber, 1944.
Holes in the Sky, Faber & Faber, 1948.
Collected Poems, 1925–1948 (includes most of the poems from the above and eight poems from *Out of the Picture* (see under *Plays*); published 1937), Faber & Faber, 1949.
Ten Burnt Offerings, Faber & Faber, 1952.

Autumn Sequel, Faber & Faber, 1954.

The Other Wing (published as an 'Ariel Poem'), Faber & Faber, 1954.

Visitations (includes 'The Other Wing'), Faber & Faber, 1957.

Eightyfive Poems (selected by author), Faber & Faber, 1959.

Solstices, Faber & Faber, 1961.

The Burning Perch, Faber & Faber, 1963.

Selected Poems (ed. W. H. Auden, with brief critical introduction), Faber paper covered editions, Faber & Faber, 1964.

'Thalassa' (possibly MacNeice's last poem) and 'Carpe Diem' (Horace Odes I, II) appeared in *The London Magazine*, Vol. 3, No. 11, Feb. 1964.

The Collected Poems of Louis MacNeice (ed. E. R. Dodds), Faber & Faber, 1966.

Prose

Roundabout Way (a novel under the pseudonym of Louis Malone), Putnam, 1932.

Letters from Iceland (with W. H. Auden, poetry and prose), Faber & Faber, 1937, (republished in Faber's paper covered editions, 1967).

I Crossed the Minch (verse and prose), Longmans, Green & Co., 1938.

Modern Poetry. A Personal Essay (criticism), Oxford University Press, 1938 (reprinted, Clarendon Press, 1968, with an introduction by Walter Allen).

Zoo, Michael Joseph, 1938.

The Poetry of W. B. Yeats, Oxford University Press, 1941 (republished in Faber's paper covered editions, 1967).

Meet the U.S. Army, Board of Education, Ministry of Information, 1943.

The Sixpence that Rolled Away (a tale for children), Faber & Faber, 1956.

Astrology (a lavishly illustrated survey), Spring Books, 1964.

The Strings are False (MSS. written at various times), Faber & Faber, 1965.

Varieties of Parable (the Clark Lectures, 1963), Cambridge University Press, 1965.

Plays (mainly for radio)

The Station Bell (produced by Birmingham University Dramatic Society, c. 1935), in manuscript.
The Agamemnon of Aeschylus (translation), Faber & Faber, 1936.
Out of the Picture (verse-drama: eight poems included in *Collected Poems, 1925–48*), Faber & Faber, 1937.
Christopher Columbus (radio drama), Faber & Faber, 1944.
The Dark Tower (and other radio scripts), produced by B.B.C. in 1946, published by Faber & Faber, 1947.
Goethe's Faust (translation), Faber & Faber, 1951.
The Dark Tower, Faber's paper covered editions, 1964.
The Mad Islands and *The Administrator*, Faber & Faber, 1964.
One for the Grave, Faber & Faber, 1969.
Persons from Porlock and Other Plays for Radio, introduction by W. H. Auden, B.B.C. Publications, 1969.

Literary Articles (a selected list)

'Poetry', *The Arts Today*, an anthology, ed. Geoffrey Grigson, John Lane, The Bodley Head, 1935.
'Sir Thomas Malory', *English Novelists*, ed. D. Verschoyle, Chatto & Windus, 1936.
'Subject in Modern Poetry', *Essays and Studies, XXII*, Oxford University Press, 1936.
'Keats', *Fifteen Poets*, Clarendon Press, 1941.
'Eliot and the Adolescent', *T. S. Eliot*, a symposium edited by March and Tambimutti, Editions Poetry, London, 1948.
'Poetry, the Public and the Critic', *New Statesman*, 8 October 1949.
'Experiences with Images', *Orpheus, A Symposium of the Arts*, Vol. 2, ed. John Lehmann, published by John Lehmann, 1949.
'Dylan Thomas. Memories and Appreciations',* *A Casebook of Dylan Thomas*, ed. J. M. Brinnin, 1960.

* The only library copy in this country is now reported to be missing.

11 Biographical and critical studies of Louis MacNeice (a selected list)

C. Day-Lewis, *A Hope for Poetry*, Basil Blackwell, Oxford, 1934.

John Peale Bishop, 'The Hamlet of Louis MacNeice', *The Nation*, 11 May 1940 (reprinted in *Collected Essays*).

J. Southworth, *Sowing the Spring*, Oxford, 1940 (contains a chapter on MacNeice's early poetry).

F. Scarfe, *Auden and After*, Routledge, 1942.

R. L. Cook, 'Louis MacNeice: an appreciation', *Poetry Review*, vol. 38 no. 3 (1947), pp. 161–70.

D. S. Savage, 'The Poet's Perspectives', in *Modern British Writing*, ed. D. Val Baker, Vanguard, New York, 1947.

'A Poet of our Time', *Times Literary Supplement*, 28 October 1949 (a long review of *Collected Poems 1925–48*).

R. C. Cragg, 'Snow, a philosophical poem: a study in critical procedure', *Essays in Criticism*, (vol. 3 no. 4 1953).

(1) M. A. M. Roberts and (2) R. C. Cragg, Notes on 'Snow', *Essays in Criticism*, vol. 4 no. 2 (1954).

D. J. Enright, 'Criticism for Criticism's sake', *Essays in Criticism*, vol. 4 no. 3 (1954).

Literature for Man's Sake, Kinkyusha Press, Tokyo, 1955.

A. Thwaite, *Essays on Contemporary English Poetry*, Kinkyusha Press, Tokyo, 1957 (contains a section on MacNeice's poetry).

Marie Barroff, 'What a Poem is: for instance "Snow"', *Essays in Criticism*, vol. 8 no. 4 (1958).

G. S. Fraser, 'Evasive Honesty: The Poetry of Louis MacNeice' in *Vision and Rhetoric*, Faber & Faber, 1959.

Thomas Blackburn, *The Price of an Eye*, Longmans, Green, 1961, pp. 188–9.

Conrad Aiken, 'Louis MacNeice', in *Reviewer's A.B.C.*, W. H. Allen, 1961.

Cyril Connolly, 'Louis MacNeice', in *Previous Convictions*, Hamish Hamilton, 1963.

Ian Hamilton, 'Louis MacNeice', *London Magazine*, vol. 3 no. 8 (1963).

Babette Deutsch, 'Wars and Rumours of Wars', in *Poetry in our Time*, Anchor Books, 1963.

John Betjeman, 'Louis MacNeice and Bernard Spencer', *London Magazine*, vol. 3 no. 9 (1963).

Richard Elman, 'The Legacy of Louis MacNeice', *New Republic*, vol. 149 no. 17 (26 Oct. 1963).

W. H. Auden, 'Louis MacNeice', *Encounter*, vol. 21 no. 5 (November 1963).

W. H. Auden, *Louis MacNeice: a Memorial Address*, privately printed, 1963.

Allen Curnow, 'Louis MacNeice', *Landfall*, no. 69 (March 1964).

S. Wall, 'Louis MacNeice and the Line of Least Resistance', *The Review*, 11–12 (1964).

John Press, *Louis MacNeice: Writers and their Work No. 187*, Longmans, Green (for the British Council), 1965.

V. S. Pritchett, 'Bog Asphodel', *New Statesman*, no. 70 (3 Dec. 1965).

W. H. Auden, 'The Cave of Making', in *About the House* (In Memoriam Louis MacNeice), Faber & Faber, 1966.

John Wain, 'MacNeice as Critic', *Encounter*, vol. 23 no. 5 (November 1966).

III   Other reading

Cyril Connolly, *Enemies of Promise*, Routledge, 1938; revised edition Macmillan, New York, 1948.

Stephen Spender, *Life and the Poet*, Secker & Warburg, 1942.

Stephen Spender, *Poetry since 1939*, Longmans, Green (for the British Council), 1946.

C. Day-Lewis, *The Poetic Image* (Clark Lectures), 1946.

Malcolm Muggeridge, *The Thirties*, Collins, 1940; new edition 1967.

Richard Hoggart, *Auden: An Introductory Essay*, Chatto & Windus, 1951.

C. Dyment, *Day-Lewis: Writers and their Work*, No. 62, Longmans, Green (for the British Council and the National Book League), 1955.

Richard Hoggart, *W. H. Auden: Writers and their Work*, No. 93, Longmans, Green (for the British Council and the National Book League), 1957.

Julian Symons, *The Thirties*, Cresset Press, 1960.

C. Day-Lewis, *The Buried Day*, Chatto & Windus, 1960.

Ian Hamilton, 'Poetry of the Forties', *London Magazine*, vol. 4 (1964):
Part I in no. 1, p. 81; Part II in no. 3, p. 67; Part III in no. 5,
p. 75; Part IV in no. 10, p. 83.

G. S. Fraser, *The Modern Writer and His World*, revised edition, André
Deutsch, and Penguin Books, 1964: new edition with epilogue
1970.

Index of poems discussed

Figures in square brackets indicate page numbers in *The Collected Poems of Louis MacNeice*, edited E.R. Dodds, Faber Faber, 1966, except where shown otherwise.